T0254949

Lecture Notes in Computer Science 13634

Founding Editors

Gerhard Goos
Karlsruhe Institute of Technology, Karlsruhe, Germany

Juris Hartmanis
Cornell University, Ithaca, NY, USA

Editorial Board Members

Elisa Bertino
Purdue University, West Lafayette, IN, USA

Wen Gao
Peking University, Beijing, China

Bernhard Steffen
TU Dortmund University, Dortmund, Germany

Moti Yung
Columbia University, New York, NY, USA

More information about this series at https://link.springer.com/bookseries/558

Pari Delir Haghighi · Ismail Khalil ·
Gabriele Kotsis (Eds.)

Advances in Mobile Computing and Multimedia Intelligence

20th International Conference, MoMM 2022
Virtual Event, November 28–30, 2022
Proceedings

Springer

Editors
Pari Delir Haghighi
Monash University
Melbourne, VIC, Australia

Ismail Khalil
Johannes Kepler University Linz
Linz, Austria

Gabriele Kotsis
Johannes Kepler University Linz
Linz, Austria

ISSN 0302-9743 ISSN 1611-3349 (electronic)
Lecture Notes in Computer Science
ISBN 978-3-031-20435-7 ISBN 978-3-031-20436-4 (eBook)
https://doi.org/10.1007/978-3-031-20436-4

© The Editor(s) (if applicable) and The Author(s), under exclusive license
to Springer Nature Switzerland AG 2022
This work is subject to copyright. All rights are reserved by the Publisher, whether the whole or part of the material is concerned, specifically the rights of translation, reprinting, reuse of illustrations, recitation, broadcasting, reproduction on microfilms or in any other physical way, and transmission or information storage and retrieval, electronic adaptation, computer software, or by similar or dissimilar methodology now known or hereafter developed.
The use of general descriptive names, registered names, trademarks, service marks, etc. in this publication does not imply, even in the absence of a specific statement, that such names are exempt from the relevant protective laws and regulations and therefore free for general use.
The publisher, the authors, and the editors are safe to assume that the advice and information in this book are believed to be true and accurate at the date of publication. Neither the publisher nor the authors or the editors give a warranty, expressed or implied, with respect to the material contained herein or for any errors or omissions that may have been made. The publisher remains neutral with regard to jurisdictional claims in published maps and institutional affiliations.

This Springer imprint is published by the registered company Springer Nature Switzerland AG
The registered company address is: Gewerbestrasse 11, 6330 Cham, Switzerland

Preface

This volume includes the papers presented at the 20th International Conference on Advances in Mobile Computing and Multimedia Intelligence (MoMM 2022), which was organized in conjunction with 24th International Conference on Information Integration and Web Intelligence. Due to safety concerns as well as other restrictions preventing travel and gatherings, it was decided to organize MoMM 2022 as a virtual conference.

MoMM is one of the leading international conferences that brings together a wide range of cutting-edge research works from across the continents. The submitted papers are evaluated based on their originality, clarity, relevance, contribution, and impact. This year, the accepted papers are published by Springer in their Lecture Notes in Computer Science (LNCS) series. LNCS volumes are indexed in the Conference Proceedings Citation Index (CPCI), part of Clarivate Analytics' Web of Science; Scopus; EI Engineering Index; Google Scholar; DBLP; etc.

MoMM 2022 attracted 34 papers, from which the Program Committee selected eight regular papers and eight short papers, yielding an acceptance rate of 23% in both categories. Each paper was reviewed by at least three reviewers and in some cases up to four.

The dominant research focus of submitted papers was artificial intelligence and machine learning. The accepted papers present advances and innovations in an array of areas such as online teaching, activity and movement detection, greenhouse gas emission, smart irrigation, network security, and video delivery.

This year, we had three distinguished keynote speakers, Antonio Liotta from the Free University of Bozen-Bolzano, Italy, Janika Leoste from Tallinn University of Technology, Estonia, and Robert Wrembel from Poznan University of Technology, Poland. We also had our second World ABC (Artificial Intelligence and Big Data Convergence) Forum with world-renowned speakers, which was hosted by Won Kim from Gachon University, South Korea.

We would like to express our sincere gratitude to the MoMM 2022 participants, dedicated authors, Program Committee members, the keynote speakers, session chairs, Organizing and Steering Committee members, and student volunteers for their continuous and generous support and commitment that made this event a success.

We are looking forward to seeing this conference grow further over time and expecting more researchers, scientists, and scholars to join this global platform to share and discuss their ideas, findings, and experiences.

November 2022   Pari Delir Haghighi

Organization

Program Committee Chair

Pari Delir Haghighi   Monash University, Australia

Steering Committee

Gabriele Kotsis	Johannes Kepler University Linz, Austria
Ismail Khalil	Johannes Kepler University Linz, Austria
Dirk Draheim	Tallinn University of Technology, Estonia
Syopiansyah Jaya Putra	Universitas Islam Negeri, Indonesia

Program Committee

Amin Beheshti	Macquarie University, Australia
Paolo Bellavista	University of Bologna, Italy
Agustinus Borgy-Waluyo	Monash University, Australia
Svetlana Boudko	Norsk Regnesentral (Norwegian Computing Center), Norway
Carlos Calafate	Universitat Politècnica de València, Spain
Ping-Tsai Chung	Long Island University, USA
Luca Davoli	University of Parma, Italy
Abdur Forkan	Swinburne University of Technology, Australia
Panayotis Fouliras	University of Macedonia, Greece
Yusuke Gotoh	Okayama University, Japan
Charles Gouin-Vallerand	Université de Sherbrooke, Canada
Sami Habib	Kuwait University, Kuwait
Clemens Holzmann	University of Applied Sciences Upper Austria, Austria
Tzung-Pei Hong	National University of Kaohsiung, Taiwan
Prem Jayaraman	Swinburne University of Technology, Australia
Wen-Yang Lin	National University of Kaohsiung, Taiwan
Antonio Liotta	Free University of Bozen-Bolzano, Italy
Rene Mayrhofer	Johannes Kepler University of Linz, Austria
Tommi Mikkonen	University of Helsinki, Finland
Andrze Romanowski	Technical University of Lodz, Poland
Andreas Schrader	University of Lübeck, Germany
Wolfgang Schreiner	Johannes Kepler University of Linz, Austria

Sougata Sen	BITS-Pilani, India
Tsutomu Terada	Kobe University, Japan
Klaus Turowski	Otto-von-Guericke-University Magdeburg, Germany
Hong Va-Leong	Hong Kong Polytechnic University, Hong Kong
You-Chiun Wang	National Sun Yat-sen University, Taiwan
Ali Yavari	Swinburne University of Technology, Australia
Fernando Zacarias-Flores	Universidad Autonoma de Puebla, Mexico
Yuxin Zhang	Monash University, Australia

External Reviewers

Przemysław Kucharski	Lodz University of Technology, Poland
Matthias Pohl	Otto von Guericke University Magdeburg, Germany
Abhijith Remesh	Otto von Guericke University Magdeburg, Germany
Mikołaj P. Woźniak	University of Oldenburg, Germany

Organizers

Embedded Machine Learning for Data Quality Enhancement in Smart Systems (Abstracts of Keynote Talk)

Antonio Liotta

Faculty of Computer Science, Free University of Bozen-Bolzano, Italy

Abstract. The Internet of Things, the idea that the physical world around us can be digitized, monitored and controlled, is fascinating as it complex. IoT is a mix of smart and dumb 'things', a digital ecosystem that keeps growing in size and complexity, generating a vast variety of incomplete, unstructured data. IoT is emerging as one of the biggest big-data problems at hand but is unlike any other data science projects. It is a complex spatio-temporal problem, whereby data sources are heterogeneous, unreliable, unreliably connected, and often hard to correlate. So how can we make sense of IoT data? How can we avoid turning it into an unpredictable mess? And which hurdles do we need to overcome when it comes to smart systems?

In this talk, I explore the missed potential of Cloud-based smart systems, whereby the sensed data is transferred pretty much un-processed to the Cloud. I argue that to make significant insights from IoT data, we need to initiate intelligent processes at the micro-edge (at the sensor nodes). By means of recent pilot studies, I illustrate the value of shallow learning and other lightweight learning methods, which may be employed to improve data quality and address communication and energy bottlenecks in typical smart systems. I advocate an extensive use of embedded machine learning to perform a range of data analysis tasks at the very edge of the IoT, employing intelligent processes for tasks such as data cleaning, missing-data management, compression, anomaly detection, and for self-tuning the data collection itself. All-in-all, this talk is about smart methods to enhance data quality in smart systems.

Contents

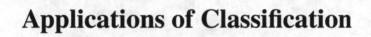

Applications of Classification

Classification and Impact
of Call-to-Actions in Push-Notifications

Sam Walsh, Kieran Fraser[✉], and Owen Conlan

ADAPT Centre, Trinity College Dublin, Dublin, Ireland
{walshs56,kfraser,owen.conlan}@tcd.ie

Abstract. Push-notifications are a constant presence in our lives today
due to the growing ubiquity of devices and services with push-technology
enabled. Each push-notification is created with a purpose driven by the
spawning device or application, however this purpose is not always clear
to the users receiving the notifications. This paper explores the text
content of push-notifications and the subsequent Call-to-actions (CTAs)
associated with them. Using an existing notification data set annotated
with CTAs, we present the results of a number of classifiers capable of
inferring 11 distinct CTA categories within push-notifications. By subsequently applying the CTA classifier to two existing user-studies on
push-notification engagement in-the-wild, the impact of CTAs on push-
notification receptivity was quantified and the implications for marketers
creating and subscribers receiving them was analysed.

Keywords: Push-notification · Call-to-action · Text classification ·
Marketing · Human-computer interaction

1 Introduction

Smartphone devices today are ubiquitous. It is estimated that over two thirds
of the world's population own at least one device [10]. One of the core features attributed to smartphone devices are their ability to grab their owner's
attention and make them aware of information. This usually occurs through the
notification mechanism first created in Blackberry's Research in Motion (RIM)
Lab [18]. First used solely for email alerts, notifications have grown to support a wide range of use-cases and communication channels. In addition, as
the phenomenon of the Internet-of-Things grows, more and more devices support push-technology, which in turn is increasing the noise they create[1] The net
result of this is a distracted world [12,13,24]. Technology giants have moved to
improve the notification ecosystem in recent years, with both Apple and Google
implementing tools to combat the subsequent information overload. However,
the effectiveness of these systems at helping users better cope with disruptive
technology is still debated [19].

---

[1] 10 billion notification messages sent every day via a single push-platform: https://
onesignal.com/blog/insights-from-118-billion-push-notifications-sent-through-
onesignal/.

© The Author(s), under exclusive license to Springer Nature Switzerland AG 2022
P. Delir Haghighi et al. (Eds.): MoMM 2022, LNCS 13634, pp. 3–17, 2022.
https://doi.org/10.1007/978-3-031-20436-4_1

The research community has in recent years therefore explored methods to improve the process of publishing [7], delivering [15,20] and managing [5,14,23] notifications as well as providing notification subscribers with a better means of understanding important facets of notifications as they arrive. One such facet recently explored was the Call-to-action of a push-notification [4]. Brands and marketing teams creating push-notification campaigns do so with an intent to encourage particular actions from their users (the subscribers receiving the notifications they push). For example, a common marketing CTA is for "purchasing". Notifications are sent with the sole purpose of encouraging subscribers to make a "purchase" thus, the text copy and features (time of delivery, LED lights, vibration pattern) of the notification are optimized by the creators to maximize the likelihood that subscribers will carry out this action.

To our knowledge, no work has yet explored the relationship between CTAs found in push-notifications and the receptivity of those push-notifications in-the-wild (i.e. whether users' opened or dismissed the notifications containing a CTA). This paper bridges this gap in literature by presenting a CTA classifier which can be applied to both mobile and web push-notifications for extracting 11 distinct CTA types and applies it to two push-notification user-studies in which the receptivity to notifications was recorded. Finally, through a quantitative analysis, conclusions on the impact of CTAs on notification receptivity are drawn out and the implications for both marketers and subscribers highlighted to inform future work in the domain of Notification Management.

This paper is structured as follows: Sect. 2 discusses existing literature pertaining to notification management, Sect. 3 outlines the methodology undertaken for creating and evaluating CTAs in push-notifications, Sect. 4 describes the creation and performance of the proposed CTA classifier, Sect. 5 analyses the relationship between CTAs and notification receptivity in-the-wild and finally Sect. 6 summarizes the contributions of the work discussed.

2   Background

It is estimated that users receive over 65 notifications a day, with the majority of these coming from instant messenger and email apps [21]. In certain applications, push notification technology can provide real value and is a benefit across multiple domains, but this can also lead to issues. Primarily, notifications can be disruptive and compete for a user's attention rather than provide a tangible benefit [6]. Dr. Larry Rosen, a psychology researcher, claims that one of the big issues surrounding apps and notifications today is that app designers are now enlisting behavioural scientists to aid them when designing their apps and notifications [9]. Therefore the app ecosystem has become a competitive landscape. Attention is a finite resource that is fiercely sought by pushers of notifications [7]. Many apps are competing against each other for the attention of the user and subsequently this results in the user experiencing an overload due to the torrent of information being pushed at them.

The U.S. Small Business Administration defines a Call-to-action as "an instruction to a user in order to encourage them to take some kind of action" [1]. Examples could include encouraging a user to *purchase* a product or *discover* more about a certain news item, *watch* a video online or *claim* a reward. Figure 1 gives an example of a notification that encourages a subscriber to open a notification to *watch* a football match.

Fig. 1. Illustration of a notification with a "watch" call-to-action.

Notifications have also been found to be interruptive and distracting. Previous research has claimed that receiving a notification can now have the same interruptive impact as that of receiving a call or message [17]. This is important to note as, whilst receiving ≈61 notifications a day, a lot of time is lost tending to notifications and this in turn leads some users to modify their overall behaviour and receptivity toward notifications.

Notifications often arrive on a user's device instantly, meaning an obligation is placed on the user to perform an instantaneous action. Pielot et al. [21] found that notifications from emails and social networks could often evoke negative emotional responses as users felt as if these notifications kept them from doing something else or put them under pressure to respond. Consequently, users would then feel overwhelmed, stressed, interrupted and annoyed. In this work, we add to the analysis by Pielot et al. by providing additional granularity with respect to the actions that may be pressuring users upon receiving notifications and their subsequent receptivity to them. This includes actions which span beyond social notifications, such as "make a purchase", "download an asset", "watch a video", all of which could have time-sensitive language associated with them to encourage faster reactions from users.

A common thread seen throughout notification literature is that busier people recognize notifications as more disruptive. This is best espoused by Mehrotra et al. [16] who found that notifications are perceived to be most disruptive when users are in the middle of, or just about to complete, a task and least disruptive at the beginning of a task. The more disruptive a notification is perceived to be, the less chance there is that the notification will be accepted. A CTA could be a useful feature for determining the disruptiveness of a notification as, depending on the action that is being encouraged, the notification may distract the user for seconds or hours. An example would be a notification encouraging a user to "watch" a live video on *TikTok*, which if accepted could lead the user to waste hours scrolling through the social platform. Therefore, notifications with this particular CTA may perform worse for users who perceive this disruption as very large - useful information for both marketers and notification subscribers to be aware of.

It is clear that the disruption caused by notifications is a cause for concern, yet switching them off totally is not an option for many who may depend on notifications for work, keeping in touch with family members or emergencies. Disruptive notifications sent at inopportune times can negatively affect the users cognitive, emotional and productive state [11]. This should also cause concern for the pushers of notifications whose messages may cause users to unsubscribe from their apps. Details regarding the CTAs present in notifications at certain points of time could also provide value to marketers and subscribers. No analysis currently exists within literature which describes the days and times in which CTA types are delivered through push-notifications. For instance, CTAs which encourage a user to "discover" some new content may perform better in days where they are idle and free as opposed to busy. Indeed, certain CTA types pushed at times in which they are out-of-context may be a contributing factor to users unsubscribing from brands and apps. Section 5 discusses the relationship between notification delivery and inferred CTAs.

Research has also explored how to maximise metrics such as Click Through Rate (CTR). For example, Wohllebe et al. [25] discovered the use of text titles within a push-notification was found to have a positive impact on interaction rates, specifically for mobile shopping apps. Gavilan et al. [8] subsequently found that in news media, the use of vivid wording - defined as "concrete words that tell a news story and identify/focus the central theme of the news, or which include written commands" - in push notifications tend to increase users' CTRs. One interesting point to note is that both Wohllebe et al. and Gavilan et al. found the use of images within notifications secondary such that users primarily based their decision on the text and title and gave little consideration to the imagery used. Building further on these findings, this work attempts to shed further light on the relationship between CTRs and text by extracting CTAs from notification text content using state-of-the-art Natural Language Processing (NLP) techniques.

Whilst the research discussed in this section has shone light upon many issues that notification subscribers face when attempting to manage their notifications, as of yet, none have explored the advantages of utilizing the semantic information of notification Call-to-actions to further understand subscriber receptivity. The following sections of this paper seek to address this gap.

3   Methodology

Call-to-actions, and the influence they have on subscriber acceptance of notifications, is an area yet unexplored by the research community and has the potential to improve the transparency of pushed notifications as well as provide greater understanding of receptivity in different contexts.

In this work, a data-driven approach was adopted to explore the relationship between CTAs, notification text and subscriber receptivity. In order to achieve this, three main resources were sourced/created to carry out this research:

– **User Notification Data** - data set(s) containing notifications pushed at users in-the-wild, including both the notification content and subsequent user action (open/dismiss) taken.

– **CTA classifier** - as CTAs are not currently supported as a feature in any mechanism collecting push-notification data today (or in any existing notification data sets), a model had to be trained for inferring CTAs given a notification entity.
– **Annotated Notification Data** - in order to train a CTA classifier, a data set of notifications labeled with their corresponding CTA was required. The user notification data could not be used for annotation due to ethical constraints and the personal/sensitive text data contained within the notifications.

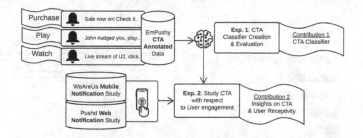

Fig. 2. Process of experimentation.

From the outset of this work, two experiments were proposed. The first experiment was to create a CTA classifier, specifically using notification text content, and evaluate its performance at predicting CTA labels. The second experiment, building on the work of the first, utilized the classifier to label notification data collected in-the-wild from users to facilitate an analysis between CTAs, user receptivity and other notification or contextual features of interest. The logical process is illustrated in Fig. 2. It also must be noted that an important goal of this work was to minimize the use of private and sensitive data, which notifications notoriously contain an abundance of. The CTA classifiers proposed in Experiment 1 were designed such that raw text data need not necessarily be exposed in order to complete CTA predictions. Additionally, the user data shared in Experiment 2 was both anonymized and shared in numerical format such that the notification text could not be decoded and read.

4   Call-to-Action Classification

This section outlines the creation of a number of CTA multi-class classification models tasked with extracting 11 distinct CTA labels from push-notifications.

4.1   Annotated CTA Data

EmPushy[2], a push-notification intelligence platform, provided notification data sourced over a period of 463 days from their social listening tool and annotated with CTA labels using the *Appen*[3] annotation platform which contains a

---

[2] Push-notification intelligence platform: https://www.empushy.com.
[3] Crowdsource annotation platform: https://appen.com/.

diverse and global crowd of annotators. The ontology for the Annotation of Push-Notifications (APN), proposed by Estevez et al. [4] defines CTAs with respect to push-notifications and was used in this work for identifying 11 distinct types of CTA types[4]. In total, 9,461 notification instances were shared, of which 6,907 instances were found to have a clear primary CTA label as determined by annotator agreement. None of these instances were spawned from instant messaging applications or contained sensitive user information. The notifications were generated by 432 apps across 36 Google Play Store categories[5]. Figure 3 illustrates the distribution of CTAs and app categories within the annotated data set.

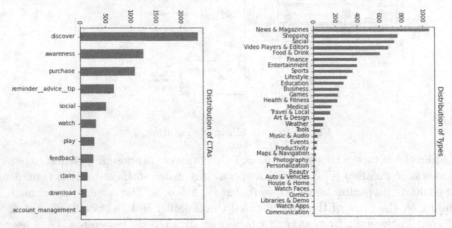

(a) Distribution of CTAs in annotated notification data set.

(b) Distribution of *app type* in annotated notification data set.

Fig. 3. Distribution of CTAs and app categories within the annotated data set

4.2 Data Augmentation

As illustrated in Fig. 3, the notification data set annotated with CTA labels was imbalanced. The most frequent CTA found within the data set, "Discover", had 2,331 instances whilst the least frequent CTA, "Account Management", had just 91 instances. In order to combat this limitation, data augmentation techniques were considered for facilitating the addition of further instances of minority classes, which would, in theory, help classifiers better generalize and prevent over-fitting.

Considering the feature types in the annotated data set, two approaches of data augmentation were adopted and applied:

1. **SMOTE**: the Synthetic Minority Oversampling Technique [2] was used to generate synthetic samples of encoded categorical and numerical features.

---

[4] CTA category definitions: https://protect.oeg.fi.upm.es/apn/apn.html#x5-cta.

[5] App categories: https://shorturl.at/xyAFI.

2. **Synonym Swapping**: this data perturbation technique [22] was performed on the text of notifications in order to generate additional instances of text which differed subtly (certain words swapped for their synonym value) but could retain the same CTA as the original instance and be used to increase the quantity of minority classes.

4.3 Implementation

Three variations of multi-class classification models were designed and evaluated in this work and are defined as follows:

- **Feature Model**: this classification model used categorical and numerical features of the notification to predict the CTA. The set of categorical features were: {notification category, app category}. The set of numeric features were: {clarity, agreement}. The "clarity" feature in this case, described how clear the Call-to-action was in the text of the notification and was represented by averaged answers to a 5-point Likert scale. The "agreement" feature, described the confidence with which the annotators agreed on the CTA label and therefore is an alternative representation of "clarity". The "notification category" feature is a value set by the marketer or app pushing the notification and the "app category" feature is the assigned category as per the Google Play Store. The combined categorical and numerical features were combined and used to fit a Random Forest classifier for predicting CTA categories.
- **Text Model**: this was a pre-trained Transformer model, BERT ("bert-base-uncased") [3], fine-tuned on just the text of notifications. The problem was defined as a sequence classification task with each word of the notification encoded and fed in sequence to the model for predicting the CTA label. This model decoupled the dependence of prediction on any notification context features which could be difficult to attain due to user permission and privacy constraints.
- **FeatureText Model**: the final model combined the "app type" feature and text together as a single string, using the special separator token "[SEP]" to distinguish between features. This was to add additional context to the text of the notification as it was previously shown that notification text differs significantly between app types [4].

4.4 Evaluation

For evaluation, 15% of the annotated notification data set was held-back for testing. The remaining 85% was used for training and validation. Stratified sampling was used to maintain real class distributions. Each model was trained and evaluated using non-augmented and augmented data sets. Data augmentation only occurred after the held-back test set was removed (i.e. on the remaining 85%) to best reflect real-world application, therefore no augmented data was included in the test set. In the augmented data scenarios, all classes were balanced using the

SMOTE or *Synonym Swapping* techniques, therefore the augmented data set comprised 21,791 instances compared with the original set of 5,871 notification instances used for training and validation. 1,037 instances were used for testing.

Table 1. *Feature classifier* performance predicting 11 distinct CTA labels using *original* annotated data.

Label	Prec	Rec	F1
Discover	0.00	0.00	0.00
Purchase	0.44	0.34	0.38
Play	0.00	0.00	0.00
Awareness	0.38	0.77	0.51
Feedback	0.00	0.00	0.00
Reminder/advice/tip	0.00	0.00	0.00
Watch	0.23	0.08	0.12
Account mangmt.	0.54	0.48	0.51
Social	0.01	0.03	0.06
Claim	0.24	0.07	0.10
Download	0.00	0.00	0.00
Macro avg	0.26	0.16	0.15

Table 2. *Feature classifier* performance predicting CTA labels using *augmented* annotated data.

Label	Prec	Rec	F1
Discover	0.00	0.00	0.00
Purchase	0.38	0.42	0.04
Play	0.04	0.11	0.06
Awareness	0.54	0.23	0.32
Feedback	0.00	0.00	0.00
Reminder/advice/tip	0.02	0.03	0.02
Watch	0.15	0.23	0.18
Account mangmt.	0.48	0.58	0.53
Social	0.23	0.15	0.19
Claim	0.19	0.31	0.24
Download	0.15	0.27	0.19
Macro avg	0.20	0.21	0.19

Table 3. *Text classifier* performance predicting 11 distinct CTA labels using *original* annotated data.

Label	Prec	Rec	F1
Discover	0.48	0.73	0.58
Purchase	0.65	0.71	0.68
Play	0.50	0.44	0.47
Awareness	0.48	0.44	0.46
Feedback	0.60	0.08	0.15
Reminder/advice/tip	0.42	0.22	0.29
Watch	0.46	0.36	0.41
Account mangmt.	0.00	0.00	0.00
Social	0.62	0.21	0.32
Claim	0.01	0.16	0.27
Download	0.57	0.27	0.36
Macro avg	0.53	0.33	0.36

Table 4. *Text classifier* performance predicting 11 distinct CTA labels using *augmented* annotated data.

Label	Prec	Rec	F1
Discover	0.49	0.61	0.55
Purchase	0.74	0.65	0.70
Play	0.74	0.74	0.74
Awareness	0.50	0.47	0.48
Feedback	0.61	0.61	0.61
Reminder/advice/tip	0.55	0.24	0.34
Watch	0.47	0.59	0.53
Account mangmt.	0.62	0.57	0.59
Social	0.50	0.36	0.42
Claim	0.71	0.79	0.75
Download	0.52	0.87	0.65
Macro avg	0.59	0.59	0.58

Table 1 shows the precision, recall and F1-score achieved by the *Feature* model when trained using the original, non-augmented data set. Results illustrate that the model performs poorly across all classes, with "Account Management" alone achieving an F1-score higher than 0.5. Table 2 illustrates the same metrics but when trained using the augmented, balanced data. The macro average F1-score increases, albeit marginally, therefore whilst the proposed data augmentation technique may provide value, it can be concluded that using the features described in the *Feature* model alone, are not sufficient for predicting CTAs of notifications.

Tables 3 and 4 illustrate the metrics achieved for the *Text* model when trained upon non-augmented and augmented data respectively. Once again, the augmented and balanced data set outperforms the original annotated data in all cases except for the "Discover" CTA class. The macro average F1-score is also much improved, with the model trained on augmented data achieving 0.58, illustrating that the use of notification text represented through BERT encoding is preferable over standalone features and random forest.

Finally, Tables 5 and 6 illustrate the results achieved by the *FeatureText* model when trained upon non-augmented and augmented data respectively. Similarly, the augmented data outperforms the original imbalanced data, achieving 0.6 macro F1-score, illustrating that the "App Type" and text features perform well when combined and can be quite indicative of notification CTA.

Table 5. *FeatureText classifier* performance predicting 11 distinct CTA labels using *original* annotated data.

Label	Prec	Rec	F1
Discover	0.51	0.64	0.57
Purchase	0.71	0.67	0.69
Play	0.45	0.44	0.44
Awareness	0.46	0.49	0.48
Feedback	0.33	0.06	0.10
Reminder/advice/tip	0.34	0.34	0.34
Watch	0.33	0.39	0.36
Account mangmt.	0.00	0.00	0.00
Social	0.50	0.24	0.32
Claim	0.71	0.26	0.38
Download	0.40	0.40	0.40
Macro avg	0.43	0.36	0.37

Table 6. *FeatureText classifier* performance predicting 11 distinct CTA labels using *augmented* annotated data.

Label	Prec	Rec	F1
Discover	0.54	0.62	0.58
Purchase	0.74	0.68	0.71
Play	0.83	0.74	0.78
Awareness	0.53	0.42	0.47
Feedback	0.54	0.58	0.56
Reminder/advice/tip	0.47	0.41	0.44
Watch	0.46	0.61	0.52
Account mangmt.	0.67	0.57	0.62
Social	0.50	0.37	0.43
Claim	0.55	0.95	0.69
Download	0.67	0.93	0.78
Macro avg	0.59	0.63	0.60

The results of each model are consolidated in Fig. 4 in which the *FeatureText* model is shown to clearly outperform all others in the majority of CTA classes. Significantly, Fig. 4b also highlights the improvement the use of augmented data has on each model, strengthening the case for using the proposed augmentation techniques, *SMOTE* and *Synonym Swapping*, for this and potentially other push-notification classification tasks.

5   Impact of Call-to-Actions In-the-Wild

The previous section described the creation and evaluation of a classifier capable of predicting CTAs for notifications given the notification text and other features. This section builds upon this work and provides further insight by applying the classifiers to two past user notification-engagement studies and analysing significant relationships between notification receptivity and CTAs.

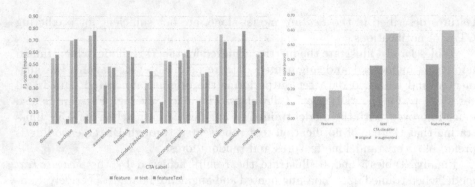

(a) CTA Classifier Performance per CTA label   (b) Original vs Augmented data

Fig. 4. Comparing classifier performance across CTA labels and data sources.

5.1   Web Push-Notification Evaluation

The *Pushd* study was designed by Fraser et al. [6] to study web push-notification engagement in-the-wild. The data set includes 12,081 notifications collected from 91 users and were pushed from 1,733 different domains. News websites such as *rte.ie* and *independent.ie* were the most heavily featured with 548 and 502 notifications pushed from these domains respectively. The key features of this data set are the notification text and the user action features. The "text" feature facilitates the *Text* classifier (described in the previous section) to infer a CTA for the notification and the "action" feature (which is a binary features describing whether the notification was "opened" or "dismissed" by the user) facilitates an analysis of the receptivity to web notifications by differing users. 85.6% (10,342) of notifications in the *Pushd* data set were dismissed by users while 14.4% (1,739) were opened.

Figure 5a illustrates the distribution of CTAs inferred when the *Text* and *FeatureText* classifiers were applied to the web push-notifications. From the results, interesting conclusions can be drawn. All classifier variants predicted the majority of CTAs to be of type "Discover". As previously mentioned, this could be attributed to the large portion of "News" type domains having pushed notifications (such as *rte.ie* and *independent.ie*) and these types of notification are encouraging subscribers to "discover" content and stories within their website domain. Additionally, the "Awareness" CTA was found to have a high frequency across all classifiers. This too is logical, as "News" type websites generally push statements alerting subscribers to new statuses such as football match alerts. It should be noted that the CTA "Claim" receives very few predictions for any notification in any of the classifier variants. Therefore it suggests web push-notifications, in the case of this data set, saw very few "Claim" notifications pushed and indicates a potential missed opportunity for marketers to re-engage subscribers.

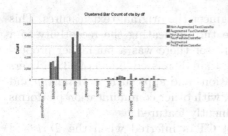
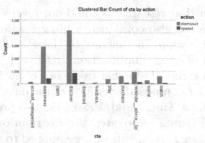

(a) Inferred distribution of CTAs in web push-notifications.

(b) Distribution of user actions (web push) over inferred CTAs

Fig. 5. Web push-notification CTA and user action distributions

Figure 5b shows the proportion of opened notifications per CTA type inferred. "Discover" and "Claim" CTAs had the highest number of opened notifications, but also had the largest number of dismissed notifications, indicating the apps/marketers implementing these CTAs were doing so poorly. A Friedman test was run to determine if there were a differences in CTR for different CTA categories. All tests rejected the null hypothesis. Therefore, for all classifiers, CTRs were statistically significantly different for different CTA categories. Figure 6 illustrates the two-way analysis of CTR variance by ranks in CTA categories.

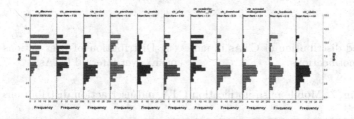

Fig. 6. Related-Samples Friedman's Two-Way Analysis of CTR Variance by Ranks in CTA categories of *Web* push-notifications.

5.2   Mobile Push-Notification Evaluation

The WeAreUs data set was collected via an in-situ study [7] of mobile notifications in-the-wild. It features 11,773 notifications collected from 13 users with over 79 applications logged as pushing notifications. Unlike the web push-notification data set, the WeAreUs data set contained push-notifications from messaging and other direct communication apps which could contain Personally Identifiable Information (PII) and were used much more ubiquitously by users than web-push notifications. The data set shared had PII redacted and the text encoded such that researchers could not reverse-engineer the original text features. This data set also contained a binary action feature indicating the receptivity to a notification. In contrast to the *Pushd* data set there was a far higher proportion of opened notifications, 6,088 (51.7%), than dismissed, 5,685 (48.3%). Users also received a higher frequency of notifications and apps such as *WhatApp* and *Gmail* comprised over 53% of the data set, with other communication platforms such as *Tinder* and *Messenger* also prominently featured.

Figure 7 illustrates the distribution of CTAs inferred when the *Text* and *FeatureText* classifiers were applied to the mobile push-notifications. In contrast to the web notification data set, the classifiers predicted a richer variety and quantity of CTAs for the mobile data set. As the mobile data set includes a wider array of "App Types", in particular social messaging applications, this is not surprising. The training data set also closer resembles the WeAreUs data set as both were gathered from mobile devices as opposed to the web. In particular "Account Management" and "Download" CTAs were found to be more prevalent predictions in the WeAreUs data set.

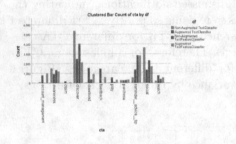 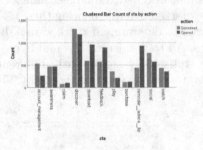

(a) Inferred distribution of CTAs in mo-   (b) Distribution of user actions (mobile
bile push-notifications.   push) over inferred CTAs

Fig. 7. Mobile push-notification CTA and user action distributions

Figure 7b shows the proportion of opened notifications per CTA type inferred in the mobile data set. Interestingly users were least receptive to "Discover", "Account Management", "Play", "Social" and "Watch" CTA notifications as each had more dismissals than they had positive *open* actions. Users were as equally receptive as non-receptive to "Purchase" and "Awareness" notifications. "Claim", "Download", "Feedback" and "Reminder" CTAs performed best, which could indicate that when users are likely to receive something within a notification (such as an asset to download or a loyalty coupon to claim), they are more likely to be receptive and open the notification.

A Friedman test was once again run for all classifier variants to determine if there was a difference in CTRs for different CTA categories. For this data set, the *Text* classifier trained using augmented data retained the null hypothesis. All other classifiers rejected the null hypothesis, indicating the user CTRs were statistically significantly different for different CTA categories. This suggests that

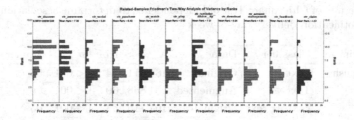

Fig. 8. Related-samples Friedman's two-way analysis of CTR variance by ranks in CTA categories of *Mobile* push-notifications

marketers should pay close attention to the type of CTA they include their notifications in order to maximize receptivity and engagement with them. Figure 8 illustrates the two-way analysis of CTR variance by ranks in CTA categories of push-notifications in the WeAreUs mobile data set.

In addition to user receptivity to push-notification CTAs, an analysis of two additional notification and context features was carried out. The first was to identify if a relationship existed between the topic of a notification and the CTA present. Table 7 illustrates the results of Goodman and Kruskal's Lambda test which was performed to determine whether the CTA of a notification could be better predicted by knowledge of the notification text topic. It was found that this was indeed the case, and as such, indicates that marketers should be aware of CTAs that match particular topics when crafting the notifications they intend to push to maximize engagement. This also provides evidence that the notification topic should be included when attempting to predict the intent of a notification as it could facilitate better transparency for subscribers attempting to prioritize their time.

Table 7. Results of Goodman and Kruskal's Lambda to determine relationship between topic and the CTA inferred by FeatureText classifier.

Experiment	Data	λ	p
Web push	Original	0.178	<0.001
	Augmented	0.056	<0.001
Mobile push	Original	0.086	<.05
	Augmented	0.116	<.05

Table 8 then illustrates the results of a chi-square test of independence which was conducted to measure the association between the day-of-week a notification was delivered to a user and the inferred CTA of it. This was carried out to identify whether trends existed in-the-wild in which apps pushed certain CTAs an particular days in order to, potentially, maximize engagement. A statistically significant relationship was found between the day of delivery and CTA of a notification.

Table 8. Results of Chi-Square Test of Independence to determine association between CTA and notification delivery day-of-week

Experiment	Classifier	Data	λ^2	DoF	p	Cramer's V
Web push	Text	Original	184.911	54	<.001	.05
	Text	Augmented	204.868	60	<.001	.06
	FeatureText	Original	164.715	54	<.001	.05
	FeatureText	Augmented	264.729	60	<.001	.06
Mobile push	Text	Original	257.651	48	<.001	.06
	Text	Augmented	332.329	60	<.001	.07
	FeatureText	Original	269.288	60	<.001	.06
	FeatureText	Augmented	540.321	60	<.001	.09

6 Conclusions

This work explored Call-to-actions with respect to push-notifications. A rigorous examination of existing literature indicated a lack of knowledge on the association between CTAs, push-notifications and user receptivity and thus motivated the work. A number of CTA classification models were proposed, evaluated and applied to past user studies of push-notification engagement in-the-wild. Results indicate that pre-trained transformer based models, such as BERT, have capacity and show promise at predicting CTAs within notification text content and a subsequent analysis of CTAs in-the-wild indicate a number of significant associations between user receptivity and context.

Acknowledgements. This research has been supported by Science Foundation Ireland under Grant Agreement No. 13/RC/2106_P2 at the ADAPT SFI Research Centre at Trinity College Dublin.

References

1. Campbell, A.: What is a call to action and why do you need one on your website (2018). https://www.sba.gov/blog/what-call-action-why-do-you-need-one-your-website
2. Chawla, N.V., Bowyer, K.W., Hall, L.O., Kegelmeyer, W.P.: SMOTE: synthetic minority over-sampling technique. J. Artif. Intell. Res. **16**, 321–357 (2002)
3. Devlin, J., Chang, M.W., Lee, K., Toutanova, K.: BERT: pre-training of deep bidirectional transformers for language understanding. arXiv preprint arXiv:1810.04805 (2018)
4. Esteves, B., Fraser, K., Kulkarni, S., Conlan, O., Rodríguez-Doncel, V.: Extracting and understanding call-to-actions of push-notifications. In: International Conference on Applications of Natural Language to Information Systems (2022)
5. Exler, A., et al.: UbiTtention 2019: 4th International Workshop on Smart & Ambient Notification and Attention Management, UbiComp/ISWC 2019 Adjunct, pp. 1054–1057 (2019)

6. Fraser, K.: ETHOS push: an approach toward empathetic orchestration of scrutable push. In: Ph.D. thesis. University of Dublin, Trinity College (2021)
7. Fraser, K., Conlan, O.: Enticing notification text & the impact on engagement. In: UbiComp-ISWC 2020 (2020)
8. Gavilan, D., Fernández-Lores, S., Martinez-Navarro, G.: Vividness of news push notifications. Technol. Forecast. Soc. Chang. **161**, 120281 (2020)
9. Goode, L.: A brief history of smartphone notifications (2019). https://www.wired.com/story/history-of-notifications/
10. Kemp, S.: Digital 2022: Global overview report (2022). https://datareportal.com/reports/digital-2022-global-overview-report
11. Kushlev, K., Proulx, J., Dunn, E.W.: "Silence your phones" smartphone notifications increase inattention and hyperactivity symptoms. In: Proceedings of the 2016 CHI Conference on Human Factors in Computing Systems, pp. 1011–1020 (2016)
12. Mark, G., Iqbal, S., Czerwinski, M.: How blocking distractions affects workplace focus and productivity, pp. 928–934 (2017)
13. Mark, G., Iqbal, S., Czerwinski, M., Johns, P.: Focused, aroused, but so distractible: temporal perspectives on multitasking and communications. In: 18th Conference on Computer Supported Cooperative Work & Social Computing. ACM (2015)
14. Mehrotra, A., Hendley, R., Musolesi, M.: Prefminer: mining user's preferences for intelligent mobile notification management. In: Proceedings of the 2016 ACM International Joint Conference on Pervasive and Ubiquitous Computing (2016)
15. Mehrotra, A., Hendley, R., Musolesi, M.: NotifyMeHere: intelligent notification delivery in multi-device environments. In: Proceedings of the 2019 Conference on Human Information Interaction and Retrieval, pp. 103–111 (2019)
16. Mehrotra, A., Pejovic, V., Vermeulen, J., Hendley, R., Musolesi, M.: My phone and me: understanding people's receptivity to mobile notifications. In: Proceedings of the 2016 CHI Conference on Human Factors in Computing Systems (2016)
17. Meyer, R.: Phone notifications are very distracting (2015). https://www.theatlantic.com/technology/archive/2015/07/push-notifications-versus-phone-calls/398081/
18. Middleton, C., Cukier, W.: Is mobile email functional or dysfunctional? Two perspectives on mobile email usage. Eur. J. Inf. Syst. **15**, 252–260 (2006)
19. Pardes, A.: Google and the rise of 'digital well-being' (2018). https://www.wired.com/story/google-and-the-rise-of-digital-wellbeing/
20. Pielot, M., Cardoso, B., Katevas, K., Serrà, J., Matic, A., Oliver, N.: Beyond interruptibility: predicting opportune moments to engage mobile phone users. ACM Interact. Mobile Wearable Ubiquit. Technol. **1**, 1–25 (2017)
21. Pielot, M., Church, K., De Oliveira, R.: An in-situ study of mobile phone notifications. In: Proceedings of the 16th International Conference on Human-Computer Interaction with Mobile Devices & Services, pp. 233–242 (2014)
22. Shorten, C., Khoshgoftaar, T.M., Furht, B.: Text data augmentation for deep learning. J. Big Data **8**(1), 1–34 (2021)
23. Sutton, R., Fraser, K., Conlan, O.: A reinforcement learning and synthetic data approach to mobile notification management. In: Proceedings of the 17th International Conference on Advances in Mobile Computing & Multimedia (2019)
24. Thornton, B., Faires, A., Robbins, M., Rollins, E.: The mere presence of a cell phone may be distracting: implications for attention and task performance. Soc. Psychol. **45**(6), 479 (2014)
25. Wohllebe, A., Adler, M.R., Podruzsik, S.: Influence of design elements of mobile push notifications on mobile app user interactions. Int. J. Interact. Mobile Technol. **15**(15), 35–46 (2021)

An Intelligent ML-Based IDS Framework for DDoS Detection in the SDN Environment

Ameni Chetouane[1]([✉])[ID], Kamel Karoui[1,2][ID], and Ghayth Nemri[2]

[1] RIADI Laboratory, ENSI, University of Manouba, Manouba, Tunisia
chetouaneameni@gmail.com
[2] National Institute of Applied Sciences and Technologies, University of Carthage, Carthage, Tunisia
kamel.karoui@insat.rnu.tn

Abstract. Software Defined Networking (SDN) is a new approach that has the potential to revolutionize the way we run network infrastructure. In order to provide a network with attack countermeasures, an Intrusion Detection System (IDS) must be integrated into the SDN architecture. In this paper, we focus on IDS based on Machine Learning (ML) methods. The most problematic step in IDS evaluation is determining the appropriate dataset. Therefore, we propose a method that allows us to select the most appropriate dataset. In addition, the selection of an ML intrusion detection method related to an SDN architecture rather than another is another issue of this paper. We propose to integrate the severity of attacks into the standard metrics to differentiate between the quality of the results of ML methods. The severity of attacks will be computed using an adequate weighting of undetected intrusions (FN and FP) obtained in the testing phase.

Keywords: Software Defined Networking (SDN) · Network security · Security attacks · DDoS · Intrusion Detection System (IDS) · Machine Learning (ML)

1 Introduction

Software Defined Networking (SDN) is a new network design that is dynamic and adaptable, making it ideal for today's high-bandwidth, dynamic applications. This architecture allows separating the control plane from the data plane, which makes the system easier to use for network administrators, as management changes can be made more easily through network programming [1]. Because the control and data layers are separated, new attack opportunities arise, and the SDN can become the target of various attacks such as Distributed Denial of Service (DDoS) [2]. They have become a serious threat to network infrastructure and have the potential to cause significant damage to information and communication technology infrastructure [3]. Therefore, in order to provide a network with attack countermeasures, an Intrusion Detection System (IDS) must

© The Author(s), under exclusive license to Springer Nature Switzerland AG 2022
P. Delir Haghighi et al. (Eds.): MoMM 2022, LNCS 13634, pp. 18–31, 2022.
https://doi.org/10.1007/978-3-031-20436-4_2

be integrated into the SDN architecture [4]. In recent years, Machine Learning (ML)-based intrusion detection systems have become increasingly popular, especially for detecting DDoS attacks in the SDN environment [5]. The most challenging part of the IDS evaluation is finding the appropriate dataset. Researchers use both datasets to test and train ML algorithms for DDoS attack detection. Several public datasets have been used, such as KDD Cup 1999 and NSL-KDD [6,7]. However, the authors do not take into account the quality of the datasets before using them to train an ML intrusion detection model. Furthermore, these datasets are not specific to the SDN environment and are not updated. The second problem with IDSs is the selection of the ML intrusion detection method. The used metrics in all the presented research methods to evaluate a prediction model's results (such as accuracy, precision, and recall) and then choose between different models based on their results do not consider the danger of the predicted intrusions.

In this paper, we present an intelligent IDS framework based on ML for DDoS attack detection in the SDN environment. The presented system includes two main steps, such as the data acquisition and the selection of an ML method. The contributions in this paper include:

- The improvement of the data acquisition step by selecting the most appropriate dataset using a multi-level test. This is an important step, knowing that the results obtained by one model or another largely depend on the quality of the dataset used for training the model. We proposed two metrics to help us choose which dataset is the most compliant with our needs.
- The selection of the ML model by the integration of the severity of attacks into the standard metrics to differentiate between the quality of the results of ML methods. We evaluated the performance of ML models using a multi-level evaluation and chose the model that best suits our needs and our dataset.
- The application of our proposed method in a case study of three types of DDoS attacks. We first selected the most appropriate dataset. Then, we used the proposed metrics to evaluate the performance of Machine Learning (ML) approaches using the selected dataset and select the most important method for DDoS detection.

The remainder of the paper is organised as follows. In Sect. 2, we present the related works. The proposed method is described in Sect. 3. Section 4 presents the case study. Finally, in Sect. 5, we conclude our research.

2   Related Works

DDoS attacks are one of the most serious risks in SDN [8]. The goal is to deplete network resources, resulting in network system unavailability. Several ML methods for detecting DDoS assaults in the SDN have been tried and tested. There are some review papers that present ML approaches for detecting DDoS attacks in SDN [9–12]. In [4], the authors presented a Network Intrusion Detection System (NIDS) using Machine Learning (ML) methods to detect malicious behavior in the SDN controller. Various ML approaches, such as Decision Tree, Random Forest, and XGBoost, were employed to demonstrate the detection of an attack. The NSL-KDD dataset is used to train and test these methods. A multi-class classification task is performed, which involves detecting an attack and classifying the type of attack (DDoS, PROBE, R2L, and U2R) using only five features, with a 95% accuracy. Moreover, the authors used the NSL-KDD dataset which is not relevant to the SDN environment, and which is not updated. Nadeem et al. [13], used various ML methods such as SVM, KNN, NB, RF and DT to detect DDoS in SDN. They employed a variety of feature selection strategies to identify the best features for training and testing machine learning models. The best features are chosen based on the machine learning algorithms' classification accuracy and the SDN controller's performance. A comparison of feature selection and machine learning classifiers was performed to detect SDN attacks. The 5experimental results reveal that utilizing the Recursive Feature Elimination (RFE) method, the Random Forest (RF) classifier trains the most accurate model with 99.97% accuracy. In [5], the authors evaluated the application of several ML algorithms for Intrusion Detection Systems (IDS) in SDN. The majority of real-world datasets in this domain lack sufficient intrusion samples and are out of date. To cope with it, the authors used the traffic flow generator to produce a dataset. For traffic classification, the authors compared the performances of Support Vector Machine (SVM), Naive-Bayes, Decision Tree, and Logistic Regression. The best results were obtained using SVM. In [14], the authors compared and analyzed four ML techniques for detecting DDoS assaults in SDN: multilayer perceptron, SVM, DT, and RF. Three forms of DDoS attacks are proposed to be detected using these algorithms: flow table, bandwidth, and controller attacks. The results show that the DT surpasses all other algorithms since it takes the least amount of time to process. The maximum accuracy is achieved using RF, but it takes a long time to process.

3   Proposed Method

In this section, we present the proposed intelligent DDoS attack detection framework in the SDN environment. The presented system includes two main steps in which improvements have been introduced with respect to the works presented earlier (see Sect. 2): the data acquisition and the selection of the most adaptable ML method for DDoS detection. Several preprocessing techniques, such as data preprocessing, feature selection, and other techniques, are used to train the different ML models. Various advanced machine learning techniques, such as Decision Tree (DT), Random Forest (RF), Naive Bayes (NB), Support Vector Machine (SVM), and K Nearest Neighbors (KNN) were used. These methods are commonly used for DDoS detection in SDNs and perform well with high accuracy [15]. We introduce our new DDoS intrusion detection system, which will be used to select the most adaptable dataset and the most suitable ML model based on the severity of the attacks. The proposed framework is illustrated in Fig. 1.

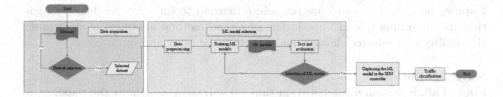

Fig. 1. The DDoS attack detection framework.

After selecting the most adaptable ML method, we will deploy the prediction model on an SDN controller. The architecture of our SDN environment is presented in Fig. 2.

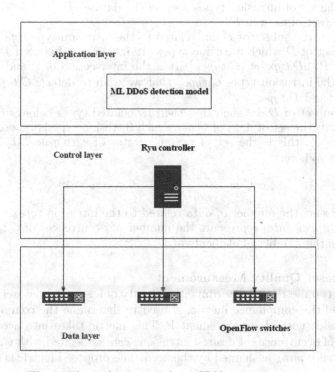

Fig. 2. The architecture of our SDN environnement.

3.1 Data Acquisition

The prediction results of a ML model greatly depend on the quality of the dataset used to train and test the model. Finding a dataset that increases the performance of a ML model becomes a crucial step. In addition, the data acquisition or collection stage is considered an important step in the life cycle of a machine learning project. Therefore, we propose a method to improve the data acquisition step (see blue box in Fig. 1). The proposed method allows us to determine the quality of a selected dataset and to select the most appropriate one.

3.1.1 Notation

First of all, let's define the notation that we will use throughout the paper.

- $P = \{p_i\}$: this set of intrusion types is chosen by the institution's network security specialists based on several criteria, such as for example, intrusion dangerousness and statistics.
- $Pim = \{pim_l\}$ such that $p_l \in P$: a scale of importance pim_l should be established by the security specialist according to the dangerousness of the intrusion for the institution.
- D : the selected dataset.
- $D.type$: the set of intrusion types used in the dataset D.
- $D.dat$: the set of data in D.
- $D.type_i.dat$: the subset of $D.dat$ related to the intrusion type $type_i$.
- C : a subset of D which intrusion types are in common between P and D.
- $C.type = P \cap D.type = \{C.type_k\}$: It is the intersection of P and $D.type$, it includes the intrusion types $C.type_k$ that we wish to detect. $C.type_k$ belong to both P and $D.type$.
- $C.dat$: a subset of $D.dat$ such that their associated types belongs to P.
- $C.type_k.dat$: the set of data of $C.dat$ which intrusion type is $type_k$.
- $Cw = \{cw_k\}$: this is the set of presence rates of each rule $C.type_k$ in the dataset D. Where:

$$cw_k = \frac{|C.type_k.dat|}{|D|} \quad 0 \leq cw_k \leq 1 \tag{1}$$

- cw_k represents the number of data related to the intrusion $type_k$ in $C.dat$.
- Where $|C.type_k.data|$ represents the number of occurrences of $C.type_k$ in D and $|D|$ is the number of elements of D.

3.1.2 Dataset Quality Measurement

We propose two metrics to determine the quality of a selected dataset. The first metric, called the compliance metric, is used to determine the compliance of a selected dataset with the requirement P. This metric takes into account both the number of occurrences of desired intrusions cw_k associated with $C.type_k$ and their importance pim_k as defined by the need. The proposed metric is calculated as follows:

$$Comp(D, P) = \frac{\sum_{k=1}^{|C|}(pim_k + cw_k)}{4 * \sum_{i=1}^{|P|} pim_i} \quad 0 \leq Comp(D, P) \leq 1 \tag{2}$$

We also propose another metric called usefulness to determine the representativeness of the selected dataset $C.type$ with respect to the whole seeked intrusion types P. It is computed as follows:

$$Usefulness(D, P) = \frac{|C.type|}{|P|} \quad 0 \leq Usefulness(D, P) \leq 1 \tag{3}$$

- $|C.type|$ represents the number of elements of $C.type$ and $|P|$ represents the number of elements of P.

3.1.3 Choice Between Two Datasets

To choose one dataset over another, we can use an approach based on the following two tests:

- **Quality test:** To say that a Dataset D_i has a satisfactory quality, we need to define two thresholds, $SComp$ and $SUseful$ from which we can decide if the quality is good or not, i.e. if :

$$Comp(D_i, P) \geq SComp \quad and \quad Usefulness(D_i, P) \geq SUseful$$

- **Test of the most adapted dataset to the needs:** Let there be two datasets D_i and D_j, we will say that D_i is more adapted to our needs than D_j if:

$$Comp(D_i, P) \geq Comp(D_j, P) \quad and \quad Usefulness(D_i, P) \geq Usefulness(D_j, P)$$

3.2 Selection of ML Method

In this section, we present the proposed method to select the most adaptable Machine Learning (ML) method for DDoS detection using the severity of attacks (see pink box in Fig. 1). The standard metrics used to evaluate the performance of ML methods can give similar results and are also commonly used in binary classification. Besides, these metrics do not determine the severity and the impact of attacks on the performance of these different models. In order to evaluate the considered ML methods, we propose a new approach to compute the standard metrics, namely precision, recall, accuracy, and F1-score by weighting FN (False Negative) and FP (False Positive) using the severity of attacks. We propose a multi-level evaluation using the modified metrics in the first step and the two gravity coefficients (FN_{coeff} and FP_{coeff}) in the second step. We consider FP and FN to be the most serious and dangerous cases that we have to address. FN occurs when traffic is identified as acceptable when it is an attack. This is the most dangerous situation because the security professional has no idea that an attack has taken place. This can have dangerous consequences. For example, if a system is successfully penetrated, the attacker may encrypt all data and refuse to release it unless a high ransom is paid [16]. On the other hand, FP occurs when normal traffic is identified as an attack. These false alerts increase the noise for already overburdened security teams and can include unorganized network traffic [17]. In addition, FP can cause a legitimate flow to be stopped until it is verified. This takes time and can have a significant financial impact [18]. Therefore, to calculate our modified metric, we first classify the types of DDoS based on their impact on the SDN environment, and then calculate the weighted FN and the weighted FP.

3.2.1   Notation

Since the performance of the ML model depends closely on the quality of the dataset used for the training, we propose to use a notation where the model is represented in an association with the dataset used to train it.

- $D_i.M_k$: it's the ML model M_k (KNN or SVM or DT or RF or NB) obtained by training and testing on the dataset $Di.dat$.
- $D_i.M_k.E_j$: is the evaluation E_j (FP or accuracy or precision or FN...) of a model M_k trained on the dataset D_i.

3.2.2   Proposed Metrics

In order to evaluate the performance of the different ML methods, we propose a multi-level evaluation.

- First step: We compare the different methods using our proposed modified metrics. $D_i.M_k.FN_w$ and $D_i.M_k.FP_w$ are calculated as follows:

$$D_i.M_k.FN_w = \sum_{i=1}^{|D_i.M_k.FN|} D_i.M_k.FN_i * pim_i \qquad (4)$$

$$D_i.M_k.FP_w = \sum_{i=1}^{|D_i.M_k.FP|} D_i.M_k.FP_i * pim_i \qquad (5)$$

The importance pim_i as it is defined in Sect. 3 (see Sect. 3.1.1) takes on a value depending on the type of DDoS attack and its impact on the SDN. The standard metrics will then be calculated as follows:

$$D_i.M_k.Accuracy_w = \frac{D_i.M_k.TP + D_i.M_k.TN}{D_i.M_k.TP + D_i.M_k.FP_w + D_i.M_k.TN + D_i.M_k.FN_w} \qquad (6)$$

$$D_i.M_k.Precision_w = \frac{D_i.M_k.TP}{D_i.M_k.TP + D_i.M_k.FP_w} \qquad (7)$$

$$D_i.M_k.Recall_w = \frac{D_i.M_k.TP}{D_i.M_k.TP + D_i.M_k.FN_w} \qquad (8)$$

$$D_i.M_k.F1-score_w = 2 * \frac{D_i.M_k.Precision_w * D_i.M_k.Recall_w}{D_i.M_k.Precision_w + D_i.M_k.Recall_w} \qquad (9)$$

- Where $D_i.M_k.TP$ (True Positive) is the successful identification of an attack.
- $D_i.M_k.TN$ (True Negative) represents the correct classification of normal traffic.
- $D_i.M_k.Accuracy_w$ denotes the ratio of correct predictions to all predictions made using $D_i.M_k.FN_w$ and $D_i.M_k.FP_w$.
- $D_i.M_k.Precision_w$ represents the ratio of correctly identified DDoS attack traffic entries to the total number of predicted DDoS attack traffic entries using $D_i.M_k.FN_w$ and $D_i.M_k.FP_w$.

- $D_i.M_k.Recall_w$ is the ratio of correctly identified DDoS attack traffic entries and the total number of DDoS attack traffic entries that are actually appearing using $D_i.M_k.FN_w$ and $D_i.M_k.FP_w$.
- $D_i.M_k.F1 - Score_w$ is an overall performance measure balancing $D_i.M_k.Precision_w$ and $D_i.M_k.Recall_w$ by calculating the harmonic mean of both values.

- Second step: If we cannot choose the ML model in the first step, we can use two other metrics: the gravity coefficient $D_1.M_k.FN$, and the gravity coefficient $D_1.M_k.FP$.

$$D_i.M_k.FN_{coeff} = \frac{D_1.M_k.FN_w}{D_1.M_k.FN} \qquad (10)$$

$$D_i.M_k.FP_{coeff} = \frac{D_1.M_k.FP_w}{D_1.M_k.FP} \qquad (11)$$

The method that produces the lowest values for the $D_i.M_k.FN_{coeff}$ and $D_i.M_k.FP_{coeff}$ is regarded as the best.

Once the machine model has been selected, it is deployed in the SDN architecture controller as shown in Fig. 2.

4 Case Study

In this section, we apply the different methods presented in the previous sections to a case study to detect DDoS in the SDN environment.

4.1 Dataset Selection

In this section, we select the most adaptable dataset used for the assessment of the different Machine Learning (ML) methods. We will apply the proposed method to evaluate and compare two different datasets. Then, we select the dataset that meets our needs. In particular, we aim to include three important types of DDoS attacks: ICMP, UDP, and TCP, that have a dangerous impact on SDN [19]. We select two datasets: the "DDoS attack SDN" [20] and the "SDN-DDOS-TCP-SYN" [21].

The characteristics of the used datasets are presented in Table 1.

Table 1. Characteristics of the used datasets.

Dataset D_i	Number of samples $|D_i.dat|$	Number of features	Types of attacks D_i.type
DDOS attack SDN [20]	104345	23	TCP syn
			UDP flood
			ICMP flood
SDN-DDOS-TCP-SYN [21]	1047500	28	TCP syn

4.1.1   Dataset Quality Measurement

Let's call D_1 the dataset "DDoS attack SDN" and D_2 the dataset "SDN-DDOS-TCP-SYN". We try to determine the quality of each dataset and select the most adaptable to our needs.

– **Processing of D_1:** In the first step, we define a group of sets:
– $D_1.type = \{ICMP, TCP, UDP\}$: It presents the intrusions types in the selected dataset "D_1".
– $P = \{ICMP, UDP, TCP\}$: It presents the intrusions types that we aim to detect.
  We give a weight pim_l (see Sect. 3.1.1) to each type of DDoS attack. The weight pim_l is chosen according to the importance of this type and its impact on the SDN environment. The flood attacks (ICMP and UDP) are the most important DDoS attacks in the SDN environment because they saturate and consume the bandwidth of the network infrastructure [22]. The ICMP attacks have the most dangerous impact on the SDN environment, and the UDP attacks have proven to be a real threat in SDN [23]. Therefore, we give the following weights for each type of DDoS:
– $Pim = \{(10, 5, 1)\}$
  Where the value of 10 is given to ICMP, 5 to UDP and 1 to TCP.
  Then, we define the types of intrusions that belong to P and $D_1.type$.
– $C.type = P \cap D1.type = \{ICMP, UDP, TCP\}$
  We calculate also the presence rates of each rule (ICMP, UDP, TCP) in the dataset D_1. Then, we calculate the value of the two proposed metrics: the conformity metric and the usefulness metric (see equation (2) and (3)).
– **Processing of D_2:** In the second step, we determine the quality of the second dataset D_2 ("SDN-DDOS-TCP-SYN ").
  We define a group of sets:
– $D_2.type = \{TCP\}$: It represents the intrusion type of the selected dataset.
– $P = \{ICMP, UDP, TCP\}$: It represents the intrusion types we want to detect. We give a weight for each type of DDoS attack:
– $Pim = \{(10, 5, 1)\}$
  We define the types of intrusions that belong to P and $D_2.type$.
– $C.type = P \cap D2.type = \{TCP\}$
  We calculate also the presence rates of each rule (TCP) in the dataset D_2. Then, we calculate the value of the two proposed metrics: the conformity metric and the usefulness metric. The results of the different metrics for the two datasets are presented in Table 2.

Table 2. The different metric results for the datasets.

Dataset	Presence rates of each rule in D			Comp(D, P)	Usefulness(D, P)
	Cw_{ICMP}	Cw_{UDP}	Cw_{TCP}		
D_1	0.13	0.16	0.09	0.68	1
D_2	0	0	0.10	0.04	0.33

4.1.2 Choice of the Dataset

To select the most adaptable dataset, we use multi-level test. For example, we suppose that $SComp = 0{,}5$ and $SUseful = 1$.

- **Quality test:** We can see from Table 2, that $Comp(D_1, P) > SComp$ and $Usefulness(D_1, P) = SUseful$.
  However, Table 2 shows that $Comp(D_2, P) < SComp$ and $Usefulness(D_2, P) < SUseful$. Therefore, We can say that D_1 has a satisfactory quality.
- **Test of the most adapted dataset to the needs:** Table 2 shows that $Comp(D_1, P) > Comp(D_2, P)$ and $Usefulness(D_2, P) > Usefulness(D_1, P)$. Therefore, we can say that D_1 is more adaptable to our requirements P than D_2 and we chose this dataset.

4.2 Choice of ML Model

For the assessment of the different machine learning methods, we used the "DDoS attack SDN" dataset noted D_1. In this section, we present the different results for ML algorithms such as $D_1.SVM$, $D_1.KNN$, $D1.DT$, $D_1.NB$, and $D_1.RF$. The ICMP attacks have the most dangerous impact on the SDN environment [8,24]. Therefore, we used the weights presented in Pim (see Sect. 4.1) such as follows (TCP = 1, UDP = 5, ICMP = 10). As presented before, we propose a multi-level evaluation for the different ML methods.

- First Step: We first compare the results using the modified metrics. In Table 3, we present the results given by the selected methods using the modified metrics.

Table 3. Comparison of ML classifiers using modified metrics.

Classifier	D1.Mk.Accuracy$_w$ (%)	D1.Mk.Recall$_w$ (%)	D1.Mk.Precision$_w$ (%)	D1.Mk.F1-score$_w$ (%)
D1.SVM	89	85	85	85
D1.KNN	57	44	50	44
D1.DT	99	99	99	99
D1.NB	24	17	19	17
D1.RF	99	99	99	99

As can be seen in Table 3 $D_1.DT$ and $D_1.RF$ outperform the other methods in the different metrics. They give a value of 99% which is considered a good classification index. This can be explained by the fact that these two methods have a low number of $D_1.M_k.FN_w$ and $D_1.M_k.FP_w$. We can note that these methods can classify the four classes correctly. $D_1.SVM$ method gives the second best results for the different metrics. It gives a value of 89% for the $D_1.SVM.Accuracy_w$ metric and a value of 85% for the other metrics. This method has a large number of $D_1.SVM.FN_w$ and $D_1.SVM.FP_w$ with significant impact. The $D_1.KNN$ method allows to have the third best results. It has an

$D_1.KNN.Accuracy_w$ of 57%, 50% for the $D_1.KNN.Precision_w$ metric, and 44% for the $D_1.KNN.F1-score_w$ metric. However, it gives a low $D_1.KNN.Recall_w$ of 44 %. This could be explained by the fact that this method gives an important number of $D_1.KNN.FP_w$. The $D_1.NB$ method has the following results: it has a $D_1.NB.Recall_w$ of 17%, a $D_1.NB.Precision_w$ of 19%, an $D_1.NB.F1-score_w$ of 17%, and it gives a low $D_1.NB.Accuracy_w$ of 24%. This method gives a high number of $D_1.NB.FP_w$ and $D_1.NB.FN_w$.

As shown in Table 3, we cannot choose between the $D1.RF$ and $D_1.DT$ methods because they have similar results, which can be explained by the fact that these methods give a low number of $D_1.M_k.FN_w$ and $D_1.M_k.FP_w$. We can also note that we cannot select the method that gets the lowest number of $D_1.M_k.FN$ and $D_1.M_k.FP$ because the impact value of each attack (TCP = 1, UDP = 5, ICMP = 10) is important. In our case, the $D_1.DT$ method gives a low number of $D_1.M_k.FP$ and $D_1.M_k.FN$ compared to the $D_1.RF$ method. However, when we calculate $D_i.M_k.FN_w$ and $D_1.M_k.FP_w$, the $D_1.RF$ method gives better results than the $D_1.DT$ method. It has a low number of $D_1.RF.FN_w$ and $D_1.RF.FN_w$. In this example, we can see the importance of our modified metrics and the integration of attack severity in the evaluation of ML methods.

- Second Step: Therefore, to more clearly explain the multi-level evaluation, we used two other metrics: the $D_1.M_k.FN$ gravity coefficient and the $D_1.M_k.FP$ gravity coefficient. We present the results of these coefficients in Fig. 3.

We can note from Fig. 3 that the $D_1.RF$ method outperforms the other methods in the two metrics. It gives the lowest $D_1.M_k.FN$ gravity coefficient and the lowest $D_1.M_k.FP$ gravity coefficient. The $D_1.DT$ method has the second best results for the two metrics. In contrast, the $D_1.NB$ method has the highest value for both metrics. Therefore, according to the different results given by the modified metrics and the $D_1.M_k.FN_coeff$ and $D_1.M_k.FP_coeff$, we can say that the $D_1.RF$ method outperforms the others for the different metrics.

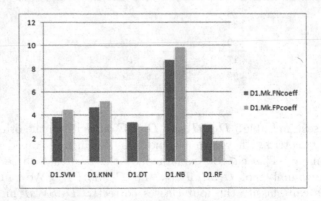

Fig. 3. The results given by the different methods for $D_1.M_k.FN_coeff$ and $D_1.M_k.FP_coeff$.

Therefore, we can deploy the $D_1.RF$ method in our SDN architecture as shown in Fig. 1.

We can note that the severity of attacks plays an important role in the performance evaluation of ML methods. It is not enough to say that one method is better than another if it has a lower number of $D_1.M_k.FP$ and $D_1.M_k.FN$. On the other hand, the number of $D_1.M_k.FN_w$ and $D_1.M_k.FP_w$ especially for the class with the highest impact value, decreases the performance of different methods, such as $D_1.NB$, which gives better results using the standard metrics.

5 Conclusion

In this paper, we present an intelligent IDS for DDoS detection framework in the SDN environment. The presented IDS framework includes different parts, such as data preprocessing and traffic classification. As a case study, we focused on TCP, UDP, and ICMP, which are considered the most dangerous attacks for the SDN environment. The two main steps in our IDS framework are the data acquisition step, which allows us to select the most adaptable dataset. Furthermore, we propose a method to determine the effectiveness of a selected dataset through multi-level test using two new metrics, called the conformity metric and the usefulness metric. The second important step is the selection of an ML intrusion detection method. We present a method to select the most appropriate ML method based on the severity of attacks using a multi-level evaluation. We use different ML methods and evaluate their performance using the proposed metrics, where we propose to integrate the severity of attacks into these metrics to differentiate the quality of the results of these ML methods. The severity of attacks will be calculated using an appropriate weighting of undetected intrusions (FN and FP) obtained in the testing phase. We conclude that the $D_1.RF$ method performs better than the other methods. In future work, we will use and evaluate Deep Learning (DL) methods for DDoS detection in the SDN environment.

References

1. Kreutz, D., Ramos, F.M.V., Verissimo, P.E., Rothenberg, C.E., Azodolmolky, S., Uhlig, S.: Software-defined networking: a comprehensive survey. Proc. IEEE **103**(1), 14–76 (2014)
2. Kreutz, D., Ramos, F.M.V., Verissimo, P.: Towards secure and dependable software-defined networks. In: Proceedings of the Second ACM SIGCOMM Workshop on Hot Topics in Software Defined Networking, pp. 55–60 (2013)
3. Sachdeva, M., Singh, G., Kumar, K., Singh, K.: Measuring impact of DDOS attacks on web services (2010)
4. Alzahrani, A.O., Alenazi, M.J.F.: Designing a network intrusion detection system based on machine learning for software defined networks. Future Internet **13**(5), 111 (2021)
5. Ahmad, A., Harjula, E., Ylianttila, M., Ahmad, I.: Evaluation of machine learning techniques for security in SDN. In: 2020 IEEE Globecom Workshops (GC Wkshps), pp. 1–6. IEEE (2020)

6. Dong, S., Sarem, M.: DDoS attack detection method based on improved KNN with the degree of DDoS attack in software-defined networks. IEEE Access **8**, 5039–5048 (2019)

7. Sudar, K.M., Beulah, M., Deepalakshmi, P., Nagaraj, P., Chinnasamy, P.: Detection of distributed denial of service attacks in SDN using machine learning techniques. In: 2021 International Conference on Computer Communication and Informatics (ICCCI), pp. 1–5. IEEE (2021)

8. Lubna Fayez Eliyan and Roberto Di Pietro: DoS and DDoS attacks in software defined networks: a survey of existing solutions and research challenges. Futur. Gener. Comput. Syst. **122**, 149–171 (2021)

9. Chetouane, A., Karoui, K.: A survey of machine learning methods for DDoS threats detection against SDN. In: Jemili, I., Mosbah, M. (eds.) DiCES-N 2022. CCIS, vol. 1564, pp. 99–127. Springer, Cham (2022). https://doi.org/10.1007/978-3-030-99004-6_6

10. Gupta, s., Grover, D.: A comprehensive review on detection of DDoS attacks using ml in SDN environment. In: 2021 International Conference on Artificial Intelligence and Smart Systems (ICAIS), pp. 1158–1163. IEEE (2021)

11. Aljuhani, A.: Machine learning approaches for combating distributed denial of service attacks in modern networking environments. IEEE Access **9**, 42236–42264 (2021)

12. Sultana, N., Chilamkurti, N., Peng, W., Alhadad, R.: Survey on SDN based network intrusion detection system using machine learning approaches. Peer-to-Peer Network. Appl. **12**(2), 493–501 (2019)

13. Nadeem, M.W., Goh, H.G., Ponnusamy, V., Aun, Y.: DDoS detection in SDN using machine learning techniques

14. Santos, R., Souza, D., Santo, W., Ribeiro, A., Moreno, E.: Machine learning algorithms to detect DDoS attacks in SDN. Concurr. Comput. Pract. Exper. **32**(16), e5402 (2020)

15. Aslam, M., et al.: Adaptive machine learning based distributed denial-of-services attacks detection and mitigation system for SDN-enabled iot. Sensors **22**(7), 2697 (2022)

16. Zimba, A.: Malware-free intrusion: a novel approach to ransomware infection vectors. Int. J. Comput. Sci. Inf. Secur. **15**(2), 317 (2017)

17. Pietraszek, T.: Using adaptive alert classification to reduce false positives in intrusion detection. In: Jonsson, E., Valdes, A., Almgren, M. (eds.) RAID 2004. LNCS, vol. 3224, pp. 102–124. Springer, Heidelberg (2004). https://doi.org/10.1007/978-3-540-30143-1_6

18. Latah, M., Toker, L.: Minimizing false positive rate for dos attack detection: a hybrid SDN-based approach. ICT Express **6**(2), 125–127 (2020)

19. Sen, S., Gupta, K.D., Manjurul Ahsan, M.: Leveraging machine learning approach to setup software-defined network (SDN) controller rules during DDoS attack. In: Uddin, M.S., Bansal, J.C. (eds.) Proceedings of International Joint Conference on Computational Intelligence. AIS, pp. 49–60. Springer, Singapore (2020). https://doi.org/10.1007/978-981-13-7564-4_5

20. Mukhopadhyay, N.A.D., Singal, G.: DDoS attack SDN dataset (2020)

21. Shivam, K.S.G., Karan, S.: SDN-DDoS-TCP-SYN dataset (2021)

22. Sakthivel, E., Anitha, R., Arunachalam, S., Hindumathy, M.: Detracting TCP-Syn flooding attacks in software defined networking environment. In: Hemanth, D.J., Kumar, V.D.A., Malathi, S., Castillo, O., Patrut, B. (eds.) COMET 2019. LNDECT, vol. 35, pp. 888–898. Springer, Cham (2020). https://doi.org/10.1007/978-3-030-32150-5_89

23. Wei, H.-C., Tung, Y.-H., Yu, C.-M.: Counteracting UDP flooding attacks in SDN. In: 2016 IEEE NetSoft Conference and Workshops (NetSoft), pp. 367–371. IEEE (2016)
24. Karoui, K.: Risk analysis linked to network attacks. In: Cyber-Vigilance and Digital Trust: Cyber Security in the Era of Cloud Computing and IoT, pp. 105–140 (2019)

Effects on Separated Learning of Acquiring Physical Movement Skills Classified by Level of Difficulty

Shuhei Tsuchida[✉][iD], Tsutomu Terada[iD], and Masahiko Tsukamoto[iD]

Kobe University, 1-1, Rokkodai-cho, Nada-ku, Kobe, Japan
t.sway.tmpp@gmail.com

Abstract. Several supportive methods have been proposed to assist learners by moving their bodies while receiving information by means of visual, auditory, and tactile information presentation. Previous research proposed a learning method called "separated learning," which divides the learning process into two phases: one concentrates on receiving information presentation without moving the body, whereas the other involves moving the body. This study developed a system to provide informative presentations on learning dance steps. The system was evaluated to determine whether it can be applied to learning dance steps and whether the level of difficulty affects separated learning. Experiments showed that there was no significant difference between the effects of learning the dance step without moving the body and the ones of while involving body movement.

Keywords: Training · Learning method · Dance · Physical movement skill · Information presentation

1 Introduction

Several previous studies claimed that providing information presentation such as visual, tactile, or auditory information presentation in real-time helps people learn physical movement skills, such as skipping, throwing a ball [5], and playing music [3]. In conventional learning, researchers created support systems under the premise that learning physical movement skills while moving a body is effective. However, the movement tasks referred to in these studies often adopt simple tasks such as skipping and tapping. However, for more complicated tasks, the expected benefit from the information presentation is not obtained. Todorov et al. [6] developed a support system for learning difficult multijoint movements by minimizing information presentation. Still, it was not sufficient for transfer to complicated real-world tasks. We should consider a method of providing information presentations that should be adapted to various complicated tasks.

Therefore, we assumed that moving the body and receiving information presentation simultaneously when learning the skills can exhaust our brain's working

© The Author(s), under exclusive license to Springer Nature Switzerland AG 2022
P. Delir Haghighi et al. (Eds.): MoMM 2022, LNCS 13634, pp. 32–37, 2022.
https://doi.org/10.1007/978-3-031-20436-4_3

memory. Working memory is a function that deals with other processing tasks in parallel, while temporarily storing the information required for various changing purposes. Complicated body movements consume considerable working memory, leaving no room for information presentation. There are several papers on information presentation and working memory. Buszard et al. [2] reported that when they provided children with five explicit instructions that were specific to the technique of shooting a basketball, higher working memory capacity children displayed consistent improvements, whereas lower working memory capacity children demonstrated the opposite effect.

To address the aforementioned problem, our previous research proposed a separated learning [4], which separates the learning phase. This method of information presentation is not provided while the learners are performing complicated movement tasks. The learners first receive the presentation of performance information (they are given and internalize information), and they practice the received information, so this is a two-part learning process. The previous research [4] applied this separated learning to support learners to master percussion skills. The percussion skills involve fingertip-only movements with complex rhythms. Learners who practiced percussion skills after internalizing information about the skills mastered the skills approximately five minutes faster than those who were provided informative presentation. Learners must be attentive to various aspects when performing complicated movement tasks and have difficulty doing this simultaneously, which leads to a decrease in the effect of information presentation while performing complicated movement tasks. Therefore, separated learning can be more suitable for helping learners master complicated skills than conventional simultaneous learning.

However, separated learning is not robust for all task levels of learning movements, so we must investigate at which difficulty threshold separated learning must be applied for obtaining optimal results. For example, for simple movement tasks such as skipping, the working memory can deal with both moving the body and receiving information presentation simultaneously. Therefore, conventional simultaneous learning which provides information presentation in real-time is suited to these tasks. Moreover, when addressing complicated tasks, such as dance steps involving whole-body movements, the learners lack working memory, which deals with moving the body and receiving information presentation simultaneously, so separated learning should be applied.

Therefore, this study verifies the above hypothesis, which primarily focuses on mastering dance steps and investigates the effects of separated learning on learning dance steps as classified by levels of difficulty. We aim to clarify the movements and difficulty levels that affect working memory consumption. This study clarifies what the most consuming factor is the working memory, which helps us understand which of the learning procedures must be practices by learners who want to master the skills. It will help teachers support learners practice according to individual competencies and conditions.

A user study prepared four dance steps corresponding to four levels of difficulty. Participants were required to learn these four dance steps with separated and conventional learning that provides real-time information presentation.

Participants received auditory information presentation via a musical piece, visual information presentation via a reference video displayed on the laptop (where a dancer shows the correct steps), and tactile information presentation via multiple vibration motors.

2 Implementation

We implemented a system for information presentation that can be applied to separated learning that involves learning dance steps. Our proposed system constitutes vibration information presentation devices with four vibration motors for tactile information presentation, the main module for controlling the vibration information presentation devices, a PC for video and audio output, and a timing editing application for vibration information presentation.

A disk-shaped vibration motor (FM34F) was used for the vibration motor, and a MacBook Pro (13-inch, 2019, Four Thunderbolt 3 ports) as the PC. The main module is controlled via ZigBee by the PC. The PC sends instruction information to the main module in synchronization with the rhythm of the musical piece in the video, the vibration motor connected to the main module vibrates, and the LED flashes in conjunction with the vibration. A strap and rubber band fix the vibration information presentation device and the main module to the learner's body. The PVC wires connecting the main module to the vibration information presentation device are wired so that they do not interfere with the learner's dance steps.

An application was implemented using openFrameworks v0.11.0. We conducted the operation check on macOS Catalina. The application allows users to control the video and edit the timing of the vibration information presentation. The musical piece included in the video uses *mBR0* with an 80 BPM tempo, from AIST Dance Database [7].

3 Experiment

We experimented to clarify the effects of separated learning on learning whole-body dance steps classified according to the levels of difficulty. The participants were 12 university students in their 20s (9 men and 3 women). The dance experience was at a beginner's level, and these participants had taken part in group dance performances at school events or in physical education classes in junior and senior high school. The experiment was conducted in a university dance studio that had a $43m^2$ wooden floor.

Participants wore the vibration information presentation device. The four dance steps were designed by the first author, with over 10 years of street-dance experience, to make each dance step progressively more difficult to learn. Specifically, the dance steps were designed concerning the combinations of left and right steps.

We assumed that the learners would have more difficulty learning dance steps with more variations in footstep combinations. Furthermore, we also asked a dancer with over five years of street-dance experience to observe the four dance steps and confirm that they were graded by increasing difficulty. We filmed the first author dancing four steps. The video was cut to approximately 12 s and 16 counts at 80 BPM.

3.1 Learning Method

In the experiment, while receiving auditory information by sound, visual information presentation by video, and tactile information presentation by vibration, participants learn the dance steps by the following two methods:

Conventional learning. Learners learn the dance steps by dancing while receiving information.

Separated learning. Learners first receive information presentation and then dance.

Participants learn the dance steps in each phase and with each learning method. The participants received three types of information presentation: auditory information presentation by an audio output from the PC's built-in speaker, visual information presentation by a reference video in which the dancer performs dance steps on the PC's display, and tactile information presentation by vibration information presentation devices that vibrate in sync with the music. During the *learn phase*, the video of the dance step was repeatedly played. The participants, who cannot stop the video, constantly received information presentation based on the dance step.

In the *learn phase* of conventional learning, participants receive information presentation while performing the dance steps.

In the *test phase*, the evaluators check the dance step that the participants learned in the *learn phase*. In order to judge whether the participant performs the dance steps correctly and continuously, evaluator A, who has more than 5 years of street-dance experience, and evaluator B, who has more than 10 years of street-dance experience, respectively judged. Finally, whether the dance steps were performed correctly was judged by the agreement of the two evaluators.

3.2 Learning Cost

In our experiments, we regarded the *learn phase* and the *test phase* as one set of learning costs, and we defined it as the minimum unit of learning costs. For example, if the participant conducts the *learn phase* three times, and they performs the dance step correctly in the third *test phase*, the learning cost is three sets.

3.3 Experimental Conditions

All participants learned the four dance steps (*Step1*~*Step4*) in the same order because the four dance steps were designed to be progressively more difficult.

Furthermore, the more difficult dance step was designed based on the movements of the easier dance step. We assumed that if the participant once learned the more difficult dance step, it would take less time to learn the easier dance steps. All participants learned the dance steps twice, once in conventional learning and once in separate learning. For example, a participant applied conventional learning to *Step* 1 and 2 and separated learning to *Step* 3 and 4. We conducted these six combinations of conventional learning and separated learning in two sessions for 12 participants.

4   Results

4.1   Effects of Separated Learning for Learning the Dance Steps

To examine the effects of separated learning to learn the dance steps involving whole-body movements, we analyzed the learning costs of each learning method.

The learning cost for conventional learning was $M = 3.0$, $SD = 1.8$, and that for separated learning was $M = 2.8$, $SD = 1.7$. We conducted a significance test using a T-test according to the two learning methods, and we found no significant differences ($p > .05$). This implies that there is no difference in the time taken to learn dance steps between practicing without moving under the condition of receiving information presentation and practicing while moving the body under the condition of receiving information presentation from the system.

One reason for the no significant difference is the insufficient information presentation. As the learning tapping skills in the previous study [4] were limited to fingertip movements, there was a limitation on the information presented on the sequence and timing of striking. However, to learn the dance steps, the system must provide an information presentation that considers three-dimensional whole-body movements. The information presented through the vibration of the timing of the movement might be insufficient for learning the dance steps.

In the post-experiment interviews, all participants reported that they found conventional learning easier than separated learning. The lack of information presented may have led to this trend. However, experiments showed no significant differences between the learning methods. While the participants may have felt that it was more efficient to practice the dance steps while in motion, this method is not always more efficient. Thus, we plan to investigate methods of information presentation that enable learners to grasp and understand clear three-dimensional whole-body movements. We aim to propose more effective separated learning.

In the interview, one of the participants commented *"In the second half, I learned how to remember the movements, so I proceeded smoothly"*. This comment was translated by Google translate. In separated learning, learners imagine their own motions in the *learn phase*. However, compared to the index finger tapping movements that were adopted in the previous study [4], dance steps required whole-body movements, making it difficult for the participants to perceive their movements if they had minimal dance experience. Bertram et al. [1] showed that video information presentation may hinder beginners' learning, so there is room for improvement with visual information presentation. However, this experiment could not confirm that the effects of separated learning changed according to the difficulty levels of learning. This warrants further investigation.

5 Summary

This study developed a system to provide information presentation for learning dance steps involving whole-body movements. We examined whether separated learning is effective in learning dance steps. Experiments showed that there was no significant difference in the effect of learning dance steps between receiving information presentation while moving the body and that without moving the body when performing dance steps. Based on the experimental findings, the proposed system can be improved to apply separated learning.

Acknowledgements. This work was supported by JST, CREST Grant Number JPMJCR18A3, Japan.

References

1. Bertram, C.P., Marteniuk, R.G., Guadagnoli, M.A.: On the use and misuse of video analysis. Int. J. Sports Sci. Coaching **2-suppl**(1), 37–46 (2007)
2. Buszard, T., et al.: Working memory capacity limits motor learning when implementing multiple instructions. J. Front. Psychol. **8**, 1350 (2017)
3. Holland, S., Bouwer, A.J., Dalgelish, M., Hurtig, T.M.: Feeling the beat where it counts: Fostering multi-limb rhythm skills with the haptic drum kit. In: Proceedings of the 4th International Conference on Tangible, embedded, and embodied interaction, TEI 2010, pp. 21–28 (2010)
4. Kanke, H., Terada, T., Tsukamoto, M.: A percussion learning system by rhythm internalization using haptic indication. In: Proceedings of the 12th International Conference on Advances in Computer Entertainment Technology. ACE 2015 (2015)
5. Kimura, T., Mochida, T., Ijiri, T., Kashino, M.: Real-time sonification of motor coordination to support motor skill learning in sports. In: Proceedings of the 2nd International Conference on Sports Sciences Research and Technology Support, icSPORTS 2014 (2010)
6. Todorov, E., Shadmehr, R., Bizzi, E.: Augmented feedback presented in a virtual environment accelerates learning of a difficult motor task. J. Mot. Behav. **29**(2), 147–158 (1997)
7. Tsuchida, S., Fukayama, S., Hamasaki, M., Goto, M.: AIST dance video database: multi-genre, multi-dancer, and multi-camera database for dance information processing. In: Proceedings of the 20th International Society for Music Information Retrieval Conference, ISMIR 2019, pp. 501–510 (2019)

Now, Later, Never: A Study of Urgency in Mobile Push-Notifications

Beatriz Esteves[1]([✉])(iD), Kieran Fraser[2](iD), Shridhar Kulkarni[2](iD),
Owen Conlan[2](iD), and Víctor Rodríguez-Doncel[1](iD)

[1] Ontology Engineering Group, Universidad Politécnica de Madrid, Madrid, Spain
beatriz.gesteves@upm.es
[2] ADAPT Centre, Trinity College Dublin, Dublin, Ireland

Abstract. Push-notifications, by design, attempt to grab the attention of subscribers and impart new or valuable information in a particular context. These nudges are commonly initiated by marketing teams and subsequent delivery interruptions tend to conflict with subscriber priorities and activities. In this work, we present a definition of urgency applied to notifications. We describe its value in an ontology for push-notification annotation and also evaluate a variety of classification models tasked with distinguishing urgency levels in notification text. The best model achieved an F1-score of 0.89. The proposed models have the potential to benefit subscribers by helping them better prioritize incoming notifications and also aid marketers in creating time-relevant campaigns.

Keywords: Push-notification · Urgency · Semantic web · Multi-label text classification · Marketing

1 Introduction

Push-notifications were first used as a mechanism for alerting email users they had received a new message [12], with the intention of saving users' time and effort repeatedly checking for new emails. Almost 20 years later, non-urgent notifications are still pushed and delivered at the discretion of apps and marketing teams, with little regard for subscribers. The situation today is much more difficult to manage as notifications are spawned from sources beyond the original desktop email client to include mobile devices and other IoT devices.

Research in the area of intelligent Notification Management has explored the relationship between notifications and user attendance in order to help subscribers prioritize their time with respect to incoming nudges. These methods for improving notification delivery depend on clear notification features which express the intent and value of a notification in a given moment. Few notification features exist to explicitly express the time-sensitivity or the period of time for which a notification remains relevant which could be used by the subscriber to better prioritize notification attendance and could also be leveraged by the publishing app to update or remove notifications which have expired and may

© The Author(s), under exclusive license to Springer Nature Switzerland AG 2022
P. Delir Haghighi et al. (Eds.): MoMM 2022, LNCS 13634, pp. 38–44, 2022.
https://doi.org/10.1007/978-3-031-20436-4_4

contain inaccuracies or misleading information due to the time lapse between delivery and action. In this work we define a novel feature which expresses the urgency and period of relevancy for mobile notifications and evaluate a range of classification models on their ability to predict the urgency of a notification using minimal input features.

2   Background

In their work examining the prioritization of emails by subscribers, Cox et al. [5] discuss the importance of urgency as a feature indicative of email response. The authors also highlight how urgency is but one contributing factor for deciding how to prioritize incoming emails, others including the time to respond, message importance and text ambiguity. This aligns with research by Zhu et al. [16] who proposed the "mere urgency effect"[1].

Fraser et al. [7] studied the impact of this "information-gap" within push-notifications and emphasized the potential negative impact it could have if consistently used as a dark pattern by marketers for enticing engagement.

Quantifying urgency within communication channels has been explored by Kalman et al. [8] in their evaluation of "chronemic urgency of digital communication media". The authors were able to identify specific traits for media channels associated with spawning messages of high chronemic urgency - which is the urgency perceived by the message receiver. Texting and calling channels were found to have the highest associated urgency and response time. Mehrotra et al. [11] and Acosta et al. [1] opted for a binary indicator to select whether the content of a notification was urgent or not and Aranda et al. [3] used a taxonomy of four different types of notifications that also considers their enjoyability.

Whilst research to date has attempted to indicate a level of urgency within messages pushed at subscribers, few have yet attempted to extract it autonomously from push-notification text and, currently, none include predictions for the period of time which the content remains relevant. This work attempts to bridge this identified gap by defining a standard set of urgency labels for push-notifications and evaluating a range of multi-label classification models on an urgency prediction task. In this context, the usage of a Semantic Web[2] ontology seems perfectly aligned with the goals of this work, as it provides the foundation for it to be easily reused and extended by other researchers and connected with other ontologies. Although there are already some ontologies that model temporal aspects[3], no works were found to model the time urgency of text pieces.

---

[1] "people will be more likely to perform an unimportant task over an important task (...) when the unimportant task is merely characterized by *spurious* urgency".

[2] For a complete definition see https://www.w3.org/standards/semanticweb/.

[3] Time ontology: https://www.w3.org/TR/owl-time/.

3   Methodology

3.1   Mobile Push-Notification Dataset

A push-notification social listening tool, developed by EmPushy[4], was used to collect a variety of features from notifications pushed in real-time over a period of 550 d. The social listening tool was subscribed to apps sourced from 37 categories of the Google Play Store providing a wide net to be cast for notifications associated with differing types and levels of urgency and relevancy. The social listening tool was deployed within the geographical region of Ireland and was run 24/7 to ensure maximal capture of pushed notifications. Whilst 673 apps were subscribed to during this period, only 525 (78%) were found to push notifications, indicating that a large portion of apps did not exploit the use of push-notifications for driving engagement and communicating with their subscribers. A visual representation of the components of a common mobile push-notification is available at https://empushy.github.io/momm22/#push.

3.2   Annotating Urgency with APN

As discussed in Sect. 2, at the time of writing, no standard feature exists which describe the urgency of a push-notification paired with an assumed period of relevancy. This work proposes a taxonomy to address this gap – APN[5], first introduced to categorize the call-to-action of notifications [6], classifies urgency through a taxonomy of eight categories. Using such a vocabulary provides the opportunity to improve the transparency and explainability of models developed with the identified urgency labels, beyond the other advantages already mentioned in Sect. 2. A diagram with the different urgency categories defined by APN and their definitions can be found at https://w3id.org/apn/#x4-urgency. Moreover, examples of APN-annotated push-notifications are available in the ontology documentation at https://w3id.org/apn/#x9-2-urgency-cta.

3.3   Crowdsourced Annotation

As described previously, the notifications were collected using EmPushy's social listening tool. As some apps tended to push more notifications than others, a balancing script was created to ensure that notifications selected for annotation were evenly distributed amongst app categories and individual apps within those app categories. In addition, to ensure a high level of diversity, the text of the notification content was combined and converted to a sentence embedding [13] then ranked using cosine similarity to include only the least similar notifications in the final data set for annotation.

For annotation, the Appen Platform[6] was used as it provided a global workforce and self-service tool set for creating and managing the annotation task at

---

[4] https://www.empushy.com.
[5] Online documentation for APN is available at https://w3id.org/apn/.
[6] Crowdsource annotation platform: https://appen.com/.

scale. More information on the implemented process for annotation, including an illustration, is available at https://empushy.github.io/momm22/#annotation.

4   Understanding Urgency in Mobile Push-Notifications

525 applications pushed notifications during the 550 day period EmPushy's social-listening tool was running. The subsequent 120,990 notifications logged were collected across 36 unique app categories[7]. A number of text features were extracted from the notifications to better model their text content. Python packages were used to engineer a number of text features which were shown to be statistically significantly different across varying app category types[8]. Naturally, from this we can conclude that marketers crafting the text content for campaigns do so differently depending on the type of app and audience they are targeting. This is important, as it suggests urgency could be represented in different ways within notification text content across differing domains and as such, should be included in any input to algorithms seeking to extract urgency autonomously.

5   Evaluating Urgency Classification

This paper thus far has discussed labeling push-notifications with associated urgency using a human crowd of annotators armed with a novel push-notification taxonomy. Whilst human-in-the-loop inference is helpful for understanding the relationships between context, notification features and urgency labels, it is not feasible for *every pushed notification* to be manually classified. Machine Learning (ML) has the potential to facilitate autonomous categorization to an associated urgency category and provide enhanced clarity for those creating campaigns and transparency for the subscribers.

5.1   Experiment 1 - Baseline

Related research has shown that ML has worked well at predicting the likelihood of a subscriber replying to an email [14], a notification being accepted based on its text content features [10] or at extracting the urgency level of emails to help prioritize work-place tasks [2]. In this work, we considered four algorithms for the task of classifying urgency in notifications: Naive Bayes, Random Forest, AdaBoost and XGBoost[9]. The problem was framed as a multi-label classification task as the labels are not mutually exclusive, e.g., a notification may be categorized as both relevant for "weeks" and "season duration".

The annotated data was split into train (80%) and test (20%) sets and two problem transformation approaches were applied for facilitating multi-label classification, the **Classifier Chains** and the **Binary Relevance** algorithms. The

---

[7] App push statistics available at https://empushy.github.io/momm22/#app-stats.

[8] More information available at https://empushy.github.io/momm22/#test-stats.

[9] References available at https://empushy.github.io/momm22/#algorithms.

final output was the union of predictions made by each individual classifier. As a baseline experiment, only notification text and type features were used.

The performance of each algorithm is illustrated in the Figure available at https://empushy.github.io/momm22/#baseline. Even though the classifier-chain performed better than binary relevance in the AdaBoost and XGBoost cases, overall there was little discrepancy between the two approaches. In all cases, the F1-score did not surpass 0.35, which indicated relatively poor classification performance, albeit on a new and challenging task. The results of this experiment however did provide a baseline on which to evaluate future approaches.

5.2   Experiment 2 - Data Augmentation

One hypothesis for the poor results of experiment 1 was that the quantity of data was insufficient for the task at hand. Shorten et al. [15] suggested that "synonym swapping" could strengthen the decision boundary and enable a classification model to better distinguish between target labels. Therefore, this approach was implemented to augment the text within the annotated notification data set with additional instances varying only by a few number of key words "swapped out" for synonyms. In total, 29,938 additional instances were created. In addition, a neural augmentation technique was also used to further increase the quantity of data available for training. Beddiar et al. [4] paired this technique with paraphrasing and found it helped to expand the quantity of data to 20 times the original size. In total, 13,124 additional instances were created using this technique.

Overall, applying data augmentation increased the quantity of annotated notification data by a factor of ≈ 4.28, from 13,124 to 56,186 instances. Once the data augmentation step was completed, the same experimentation process was executed to train and evaluate the four models presented in the previous section. The performance of each algorithm is illustrated at https://empushy.github.io/momm22/#augmentation. The increased performance is stark compared to the baseline – the F1-score of all models increased significantly, with Random Forest being most improved from an initial score of 0.3 to 0.7.

5.3   Experiment 3 - Time Expressions

To further improve the performance of the classifier, it was hypothesized that time-related information contained within the notification could be extracted and used as an additional feature. There have been numerous research challenge tasks addressing temporal processing over the past number of years. Utilizing this body of work, time expressions were extracted from the annotated notification text and added as an additional feature to our models.[10]

Of the 13,124 notifications annotated with urgency labels, 5,020 (38%) were found to contain time-expression features (as defined in the *SCATE* schema [9]).

---

[10] See a complete list of used works at https://empushy.github.io/momm22/#time.

Of the 63 time-expression labels, just 24 appeared in notification text. A table with the 10 most frequent time-expressions and a figure illustrating the performance of each algorithm are available at https://empushy.github.io/momm22/# time. Once again, all algorithms improved in performance. The F1-score of XGBoost in particular saw a $\approx 14\%$ improvement (from 0.69 to 0.79) indicating that time-expression data is indicative of notification urgency and provides utility to algorithms tasked with predicting it using notification text content.

5.4 Experiment 4 - Delivery Date

Due to the success of extracting time-expression information and its subsequent positive impact on urgency prediction, the final experiment hypothesized that notification delivery time would also improve the algorithms ability at predicting the urgency and relevance of a notification.

The performance of each algorithm, with the addition of the delivery time as an input feature, is illustrated at https://empushy.github.io/momm22/# delivery. Once again, all algorithms show improved performance with the additional information made available. There is little difference between problem transformation approaches, but binary relevance slightly improves performance in two cases. XGBoost once again was the top performing algorithm achieving a final F1-score of 0.89 (a $\approx 12\%$ increase over experiment 3).

6 Conclusions

This work explored the importance of timeliness in the delivery of notifications for both subscribers to receive relevant content on time and for marketers to create time-relevant campaigns. No research had been done so far to create a clear categorization for these services to use. APN's urgency taxonomy fills this gap by providing terms to specify the urgency and relevancy period of notifications.

In addition, four experiments were performed and evaluated to build a set of classification models capable of predicting notifications' urgency. XGBoost was the top performing algorithm, with a final F1-score of 0.89. As future work, different modes of notification services should be studied and evaluation based on direct user feedback should be performed.

Acknowledgements. This research has been supported by the EU's Horizon 2020 research and innovation programme under the Marie Skłodowska-Curie grant agreement No 813497 as well as with the financial support of Enterprise Ireland, the ERDF under Ireland's ESIF Programme 2014–2020 and SFI under Grant Agreement No 13/RC/2106_P2 at the ADAPT Centre at Trinity College.

References

1. Acosta, M.E., Palaoag, T.D.: Characterization of disaster related tweets according to its urgency: a pattern recognition. In: ICCAI'19, pp. 30–37 (2019)

2. Alshehri, Y.A.: Tasks' classification based on their urgency and importance. In: ICCDA'20, pp. 183–189 (2020)
3. Aranda, J., Ali-Hasan, N., Baig, S.: I'm just trying to survive. In: MobileHCI'16, pp. 564–574 (2016)
4. Beddiar, D.R., Jahan, M.S., Oussalah, M.: Data expansion using back translation and paraphrasing for hate speech detection. OSNEM **24**, 100153 (2021)
5. Cox, A., Bird, J., Brumby, D., Cecchinato, M., Gould, S.: Prioritizing unread e-mails: people send urgent responses before important or short ones. HCI **36**(5-6), 511–534 (2020)
6. Esteves, B., Fraser, K., Kulkarni, S., Conlan, O., Rodríguez-Doncel, V.: Extracting and understanding CTAs of push-notifications. In: NLDB'22, pp. 147–159 (2022)
7. Fraser, K., Conlan, O.: Enticing Notification Text & the Impact on Engagement, pp. 444–449. UbiComp-ISWC '20 (2020)
8. Kalman, Y.M., Ballard, D.I., Aguilar, A.M.: Chronemic urgency in everyday digital communication. Time Soc. **30**(2), 153–175 (2021)
9. Laparra, E., Xu, D., Bethard, S.: From characters to time intervals: new paradigms for evaluation and neural parsing of time normalization. TACL **6**, 343–356 (2018)
10. Mehrotra, A., Musolesi, M., Hendley, R., Pejovic, V.: Designing content-driven intelligent notification mechanisms. In: UbiComp'15, pp. 813–824 (2015)
11. Mehrotra, A., Pejovic, V., Vermeulen, J., Hendley, R., Musolesi, M.: My phone and me. In: CHI'16, pp. 1021–1032 (2016)
12. Middleton, C.A., Cukier, W.: Is mobile email functional or dysfunctional? Two perspectives on mobile email usage. EJIS **15**(3), 252–260 (2006)
13. Reimers, N., Gurevych, I.: Sentence-BERT: Sentence Embeddings using Siamese BERT-Networks. In: EMNLP'19, pp. 3973–3983 (2019)
14. Sappelli, M., Verberne, S., Kraaij, W.: Combining textual and non-textual features for e-mail importance estimation (2013)
15. Shorten, C., Khoshgoftaar, T.M., Furht, B.: Text data augmentation for deep learning. J. Big Data **8**(1), 1–34 (2021)
16. Zhu, M., Yang, Y., Hsee, C.K.: The mere urgency effect. J. Consum. Res. **45**(3), 673–690 (2018)

Image and Video Processing

Efficient Subjective Video Quality Assessment Based on Active Learning and Clustering

Xiaochen Liu[1] , Wei Song[1(✉)] , Wenbo Zhang[1] , Mario Di Mauro[2] ,
and Antonio Liotta[3]

[1] Shanghai Ocean University, Shanghai 201306, China
wsong@shou.edu.cn
[2] Università degli Studi di Salerno, 84084 Fisciano, Italy
[3] Faculty of Computer Science, Free University of Bozen-Bolzano, 39100 Bolzano, Italy

Abstract. Subjective video quality assessment (SVQA) is essential in order to produce a sufficient benchmark dataset, which is especially important for extreme environments such as underwater videos. However, SVQA has always been plagued by its disadvantages, such as high cost and time-consuming. In this paper, we propose an effective SVQA method based on active learning and clustering (AL-SVQA). Our method initializes dual regression models for video quality prediction with a few quality-known videos. During the quality assessment process with active learning and clustering results, a batch of videos are iteratively selected by a sampling strategy and their quality is scored by a subject. The scored videos are then used to continually update the prediction models until meeting the stop criteria. When the active learning stops, the prediction models will annotate the video scores instead of humans while maintaining good performance. In this way, AL-SVQA can reduce about 40% of human the workload for subjective quality assessment. Evaluation experiments were conducted with an underwater video database.

Keywords: Subjective video quality assessment · Active learning · Save human workload · Clustering

1 Introduction

Video services are widely spread and popularized via massive propagation of the internet service networks and mobile devices. With the exploitation of ocean and underwater detection increasing, how to define high-quality deep-sea video is an urgent problem to be solved. The goal of video quality assessment (VQA) is to obtain objective, accurate and reliable video quality scores. Subjective VQA is the most accurate method because it is led and participated by human beings [1]. Besides, subjective VQA is the foundation of video technology, such as objective VQA models, video encoding and decoding algorithms. However, its fatal disadvantages are time-consuming and high labor cost, which limits the size of subjective VQA. For some special scenarios, such as medical imaging [2] and underwater video applications [3], video quality assessments are the

© The Author(s), under exclusive license to Springer Nature Switzerland AG 2022
P. Delir Haghighi et al. (Eds.): MoMM 2022, LNCS 13634, pp. 47–56, 2022.
https://doi.org/10.1007/978-3-031-20436-4_5

first step for its applications. But it is more complicated and more costly compared to normal subjective VQA because the assessments need experts to give their professional opinion scores.

Currently, some typical subjective VQA studies have produced widely-used datasets for general proposes, such as LIVE dataset [4], LIVE-VQC dataset [5] and KoNViD-1k dataset [6]. When producing LIVE dataset, each video was assessed by 38 human subjects in a single stimulus study with hidden reference removal. Hosu et al. [6] adopted a more flexible method, Crowdsourcing, when make KoNViD-1k dataset. There are about 1000 videos in all and each video is assessed about 240 times. Similarly, Sinno and Bovik [5] also used crowdsourcing to create LIVE-VQC database that has 585 videos in all, and in the process of subjective VQA, the number of the testers is finally up to 4776. Different from the subjective VQA on terrestrial natural videos, Moreno-Roldn et al. [7] and Song et al. [8] focused on underwater VQA. Their studies both applied the ACR method to obtain the subjective opinion scores that are captured in poor imaging environment of underwater videos. And they both recruited some experts, who have underwater imaging experience, to assess the QoE of underwater videos, but this undoubtedly adds additional cost.

To reduce the disadvantages of high time and labor costs, Menkovski and Liotta [9] presented an adaptive approach based on psychometric methods and Maximum Likelihood Difference Scaling (MLDS), which could save the cost by improving the model's learning rate. In his study, about 60% of the manual workload in subjective video assessment could be reduced. Active learning [10] is a competitive approach to human annotation tasks. Chang et al. [11] applied active learning to multidimensional QoE crowdsourced video QoE modelling, showing a better model performance. They conducted a field experiment on double stimulus SVQA, the results show that combining maximin and MMIG sampling strategy reduces the number of samples required in the subjective pair comparison VQA. However, they also point out that active learning may fail in subjective VQA tasks. Ling et al. [12] proposed a novel active sampling framework to reach a better trade-off between discriminability and efficiency for subjective pair comparison VQA. In their work, the results of ACR method are fully exploited for initialization, and then they aggregate the underlying ground truth quality by using the variance. Finally, human workload could be saved by distinguishing uncertain or similar pairs with active sampled pairs comparisons.

In this paper, we design an active learning based subjective VQA framework (AL-SVQA), which combines subjective and objective information based on clustering results to iteratively select videos for annotation, and trains a dual regression model until the stop criterion is met. In this way, subjective VQA can be stopped early while still meets the acceptable goal of a full-time subjective study. With the results of simulation experiments on underwater video dataset, AL-SVQA can save about 40% of the human workload.

The rest of the paper is organized as follows. Section 2 provides the details of the proposed AL-SVQA. Section 3 introduces the experimental dataset and settings used in this paper, followed by the comparative experimental results in Sect. 4. Finally, our work is summarized in Sect. 5.

2 Efficient Subjective VQA Based on Active Learning

2.1 Overview of AL-SVQA

The overview of our AL-SVQA framework of is shown in Fig. 1. It comprises three parts, namely pre-training stage, active learning stage and SVQA Completion stage. In a subjective VQA study, given a video pool $S = \{s_1, s_2, s_3, \ldots, s_n\}$, $s_i \in S$ represents a video needed to be annotated by annotators. And $\overrightarrow{s_i} = \{f_1, f_2, f_3, \ldots, f_o\}$ represents the video features of s_i. In the pre-training stage, a set of l ($l \ll n$) videos is randomly selected to form an initial labeled dataset L, and the rest of the videos in S are considered as initial unlabeled dataset U. That is, $S = L \cup U, L \cap U = \varnothing$. Next, videos in L are annotated by annotators, and the features of labeled videos in L are used to pre-train dual regression models (composed of regression model 1 and 2).

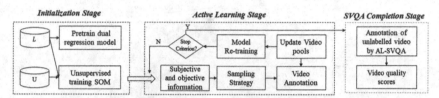

Fig. 1. Overview of AL-based subjective VQA framework.

Active learning stage is an iterative process. In each iteration, it samples a group of videos in H by a sampling strategy, and lets the annotator give the quality scores of the videos. After labelling, L and U will be updated, and the dual regression models will also be retrained with the features of all labelled videos. The process of active learning will stop when the stop criteria is met. Finally, when active learning stops, the SVQA Completion stage will predict the quality scores of unlabelled videos, and use the average score of dual regression model as the final quality labels.

2.2 Clustering Based Sampling Strategy

Many studies related to active learning have suggested that a cluster-based sampling strategy can improve the performance of model training [13, 14]. To test the effect of different sampling strategies in subjective VQA using active learning, we adopt three sampling strategies, two are based on self-organizing map (SOM) [15] clustering results and one is random sampling strategy.

- *Clustering Random Sampling strategy (CR-S):* First, we use SOM to cluster the unlabelled video in U, then we randomly select 10 different clusters and pick one sample in each cluster for annotators to label.
- *Clustering Uncertainty Sampling strategy (CU-S):* We first use SOM to cluster the unlabelled video in U. Then, we calculate the variance of video quality scores (objective scores) in each cluster. The higher the variance of the cluster, the greater the uncertainty of the cluster samples. Next, we select the top 10 clusters with the largest variance values, and randomly select one sample from each cluster.

- ***Random sampling strategy:*** Randomly pick 10 samples from U. sampling strategy is the most representative method in passive sampling strategy.

The architecture of SOM is shown in Fig. 2. Each input of SOM is vectors of $\vec{s_i}$. Each node of the 2D output layer is a vector of the same dimension as $\vec{s_i}$ whose parameters are randomly initialized when building the SOM. For clustering, the input layer of SOM accepts the samples' feature vectors $\vec{s_i}$, and the nodes of the output layer are the clusters in which the samples are grouped. When training, SOM will compute the Euclidean distance between the $\vec{s_i}$ and each output layer node. And, the output layer node with the shortest distance to $\vec{s_i}$ is regarded as the winner node. Then, SOM will update the neighboring nodes' parameters by gradient descent of the best winner. The SOM training process will iterate until it converges.

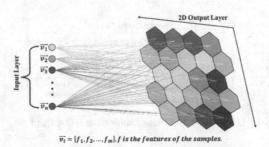

$\vec{v_i} = [f_1, f_2, \ldots, f_m], f \text{ is the features of the samples.}$

Fig. 2. Details of SOM.

By input $\vec{s_i}$ to SOM we obtain the cluster $k_j, k_j \in K, K = \{k_1, k_2, \ldots, k_a\}$, where a is the number of the output layer nodes. When two or more samples belong to the same cluster k_i, it means that these samples have a high degree of similarity.

2.3 Dual Regression Models for Video Quality Prediction

In order to obtain objective video quality information, we adopt dual regression models based on the idea of query by committee. The two models are the random forest (RF) regression model and the gradient boosting regression (GBR) model, both of which are ensemble learning models due to their effectiveness for QoE modelling [11]. But RF uses the technique of bagging and GBR uses boosting, giving them different capabilities for prediction.

The dual regression models are trained with feature vectors of videos and their corresponding quality labels. The video features we used include: (i) Two common features of image quality: contrast and colorfulness [16, 17], as defined in Eq. (1) and (2), respectively. (ii) Three video encoding parameters: bitrate, frame rate (fps) and resolution. (iii) 10 statistical features selected from Brisque [18], which has been proved that its results have a great correlation with human visual system for both underwater videos [8] and terrestrial videos. (iv) Three motion features selected from Vbliinds (a non-reference objective VQA model) [19], which contains one global motion feature and two video DCT features. (v) Four features related to spatial and temporal information of videos [20], which are the mean and variance of SI and TI of all video frames. The equations for calculating SI and TI are shown in (3) and (4).

$$Contrast = \sum_\delta \delta(i,j)^2 P_\delta(i,j) \tag{1}$$

$$Colorfulness = (\sigma_\alpha^2 + \sigma_\beta^2) + 0.3\sqrt{\mu_\alpha^2 + \mu_\beta^2} \tag{2}$$

where $\delta(i,j) = |i - j|$ is the difference of adjacent pixels in gray-scale space, $P_\delta(i,j)$ is the pixel distribution probability of $\delta(i,j)$. In (2), $\alpha = R - G$, and $\beta = 0.5 \times (R+G) - B$, where R, G and B is the channel of RGB color space, and σ represents variance and μ represents mean values along the two opponent color axes.

$$SI_t = std^{space}[Sobel(f_t)] \tag{3}$$

$$TI_t = std^{space}[M_t], M_t = f_t - f_{t-1} \tag{4}$$

where $Sobel()$ is a 3×3 Sobel filtering operator, f_t is the t-th video frame, std^{space} is the pixel standard deviation for video frame. M_t represents the difference between pixels at the same position between two frames.

2.4 Stop Criterion

The stop criteria process is run for every round of active learning, except in the pretraining stage. The basic idea is to stop annotating when more samples cannot bring big variations to the objective model performance that is related to the labelled videos.

Algorithm1: Stop Criterion

Input:
    $CT=0$; $T=0.1$; $k=10$; $m=4$;
    Number of current round: r
    Predicted quality scores: P_r; Subjective quality labels: S_r;
Function:
    Calculation of MSE: $MSE()$;
    Calculation of variance: $Variance()$;
1   While ($U \neq \emptyset$) do:
2     $e_r = MSE(P_r, S_r)$;
3   If $r \geq k$:
4       $ev_r = Variance(e_{r-k-1}, ..., e_{r-2}, e_{r-1})$;
5   If $ev_r < T$:
6   CT++;
7   else:
8         $CT=0$;
9   If $CT > m$:
10   Stop active learning;
11 End

The process is described in Algorithm 1. First of all, we initiate a set of parameters: a counter $CT = 0$, a threshold T, a minimum number of rounds to be run before stop k, and a constant of stop condition m, $m < k$. In each round, the dual regression models are re-trained by all the labeled data, and then they are used to predicting the quality scores of the samples labeled in the previous rounds of active learning. Then, calculate the mean square error (MSE) between the prediction scores and the real subjective quality scores, e_r, where r represents the number of the round and starts from 1. If the round number r is greater than k, calculate the variance of the mean square error of the previous k rounds, ev_r. If the variance is less than the threshold T, the counter CT increases 1; otherwise, the counter CT sets to 0. When CT reaches m, the active learning VQA process stops. This criterion ensures the model is converged and the predicted errors are consistent.

2.5 Automatic Labelling

Once the active learning stops, we will obtain two objective regression models that have been trained with the labelled video information. Then, the dual models will be used to predict the quality scores of unlabelled videos and their average quality scores will be taken as the final outputs instead of human annotations.

3 Experiments

To demonstrate the performance of our method, we developed a test-bed with Python and simulated the learning process with the results of a subjective study on an underwater video dataset [8]. The details of the experiments are described as below.

3.1 Dataset

The underwater video dataset proposed in [8], was produced by 25 original deep-sea videos. Considering the impact of bitrate and frame rate on the quality score, the 25 video sequences are encoded with the parameter combinations of bitrates (96 kbps–500 kbps) and frame rate (5–25 fps). In the end, underwater video dataset has a total number of 250 videos. Originally, the subjective scores of video quality were 1–5. In this work, for the convenience of model training, we converted the scores linearly to be 1–100.

3.2 Experimental Settings

In our experiments, we used triangle neighborhood function for the SOM model and trained it with the learning rate 0.1 and 2000 iterations.

In the AL stage, we set the capacity of H to 10, which means 10 samples are selected every iteration. We set the stop threshold $T = 0.1$ and the terminate condition $m = 4$, which means when the change of quality prediction performance is small for four-times consecutive rounds, the process stops.

Pearson Linear Correlation Coefficient (PLCC) and Mean Absolute Error (MAE) are used to evaluate the effectiveness of the proposed method. To ensure reliability and simulate multiple subjective quality assessment processes, all the experiments were run 10 times, and the method performance is obtained by the mean of the 10 experiments.

4 Experimental Results

4.1 Performance of AL-SVQA

Because each iteration in AL-SVQA annotates 10 samples, in the worst scenario, it will take 25 rounds to complete all the videos' quality annotation for the underwater video dataset, which has a total of 250 videos. In fact, our experimental results demonstrate that AL-SVQA with the CU-S strategy can reduce 108 videos to be annotated on average, indicating 43.2% of workload saving. Figure 3 illustrates the results of AL-SVQA with CU-S in the 10 experiments, where the blue parts represent the numbers of videos being annotated and the orange parts represent the savings.

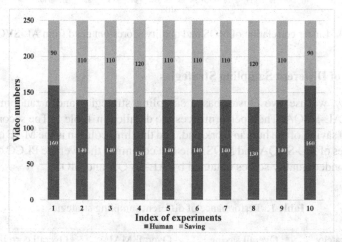

Fig. 3. Annotated video number.

When the AL-SVQA stops, we obtain the dual regression models that can be used to predict the quality scores of unlabelled videos. To evaluate the effect of the early-stop of AL-SVQA, we calculated the correlation between the quality scores by AL-VQA and the true MOS for the unlabelled videos. The PLCC reaches 0.7, indicating a statistically strong correlation. Besides, to evaluate the overall performance of AL-SVQA, the entire video quality results by AL-SVQA (composed of about 60% of subjective annotations and 40% of objective predictions) are compared with the ground truth MOS. The PLCC is finally up to 0.97, and the MAE is about 3.03 ± 0.31. Figure 4 shows that these two types of scores have a strong linear relationship ($R^2 = 0.9077$). Thus, the results show that active learning can effectively reduce the manual workload of subjective VQA.

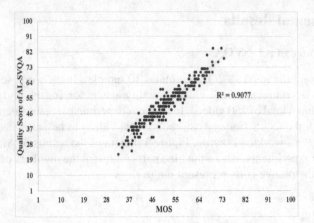

Fig. 4. Linear correlation of MOS and quality scores obtained from AL-SVQA.

4.2 Effect of Different Sampling Strategies

IN our study, we use two cluster-based sampling strategies and a random sampling strategy for AL-SVQA. Their performances are detailed in Table 1. The second column is the overall saving of the human workload, and the third column is the MAE of all video quality scores of AL-SVQA and MOS. The last column is the average PLCC correlation between all video quality scores obtained by AL-SVQA and MOS.

Table 1. Performance of different sampling strategies.

Sampling strategy	Overall saving	Overall MAE	Overall correlation
CR-S	34% ± 16%	2.95 ± 0.76	**0.92** ± 0.04
CU-S	**43.2%** ± **4%**	3.07 ± **0.31**	0.91 ± **0.02**
Random	40.8% ± 14%	**2.73** ± 0.55	**0.92** ± 0.03

The three sampling strategies can achieve similar high correlation, but the overall saving and MAE are different. Among them, CU-S saves the most human workload, 43.2%, and random strategy achieves the lowest MAE, 2.73. However, the variances of overall saving and overall MAE of random strategy are high, which indicates the random strategy is not stable. Figure 5 show the stop round of active learning with different sampling strategies in the 10 simulation experiments, where the total round is 25. From Fig. 5, we can see the CU-S (in red) is the most stable one, which stops at 13–16 round. The random strategy (in yellow) can stop very early at the round of 11 or very late at the round of 23. The worst sampling strategy is the CR-S, which is the least stable and has the least saving. Both the CR-S and CU-S are based on SOM clustering, which consider the diversity of video samples in different clusters, but the difference is the CU-S also take into account the uncertainty of video quality within a cluster.

To conclude, the CU-S sampling strategy is able to select more valuable videos for annotation by considering both diversity and uncertainty. Incorporating the CU-S sampling strategy with active learning process, it is beneficial for reducing above 40% of the human workload or time costing in SVQA, while keeping a relatively high consistency with the results of a full-time SVQA.

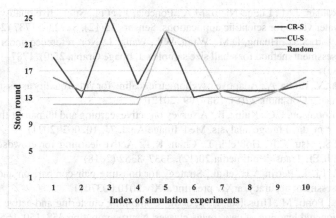

Fig. 5. Stop round of active learning in 10 simulation experiments.

5 Conclusion

In this paper, to investigate whether active learning can help subjective VQA save costs, we proposed an AL-SVQA framework, which combines subjective and objective information based on clustering results iteratively selects videos to be annotated. The process of active learning will be automatically terminated by stop criterion, and replace the rest of human annotation task by the objective models.

Experiments on a database of underwater video show that AL-SVQA can save about 40% of the human workload with a clustering-based uncertainty sampling strategy. However, our work is not limited to the SVQA for underwater videos, and can be improved by designing more competitive active learning sampling strategies. Meanwhile, we also need to verify the effectiveness in field subjective VQA in the future.

References

1. ITU-T, Recommendation P.913. https://www.itu.int/rec/T-REC-P.913-202106-I/en. Accessed 13 June 2021
2. Smailagic, A., Costa, P., Gaudio, A., et al.: O-MedAL: Online active deep learning for medical image analysis. Wiley Interdiscip. Rev. Data Min. Knowl. Disc. **10**(4), e1353 (2020)
3. Hou, G., Li, Y., Yang, H., et al.: UID2021: an underwater image dataset for evaluation of no-reference quality assessment metrics. arXiv preprint arXiv:2204.08813 (2022)

4. Seshadrinathan, K., Soundararajan, R., Bovik, A.C., Cormack, L.K.: Study of subjective and objective quality assessment of video. IEEE Trans. Image Process. **19**(6), 1427–1441 (2010)
5. Sinno, Z., Bovik, A.C.: Large-scale study of perceptual video quality. IEEE Trans. Image Process. **28**(2), 612–627 (2019)
6. Hosu, V., et al.: The Konstanz natural video database (KoNViD-1k). In: 9th International Conference on Quality of Multimedia Experience (QoMEX), Erfurt, Germany, pp.1–6. IEEE (2017)
7. Moreno-Roldán, J.M., Luque-Nieto, M.Á., Poncela, J., et al.: Subjective quality assessment of underwater video for scientific applications. Sensors **15**(12), 31723–31737 (2015)
8. Song, W., Liu, S.M., Huang, D.M., Wang, W.J., Wang, J.: Non-reference underwater video quality assessment method for small size samples. J. Image Graph. **25**(9), 1787–1799 (2020). (in Chinese)
9. Menkovski, V., Liotta, A.: Adaptive psychometric scaling for video quality assessment. Signal Process. Image Commun. **27**(8), 788–799 (2012)
10. Budd, S., Robinson, E.C., Kainz, B.: A survey on active learning and human-in-the-loop deep learning for medical image analysis. Med. Image Anal. **71**, 102062 (2021)
11. Chang, H.S., Hsu, C.F., Hoßfeld, T., Chen, K.T.: Active learning for crowdsourced QoE modeling. IEEE Trans. Multimedia **20**(12), 3337–3352 (2018)
12. Ling, S.Y., Li, J., Perrin A.F., et al.: Strategy for boosting pair comparison and improving quality assessment accuracy. arXiv preprint arXiv:2010.00370v1
13. Coletta, L., Ponti, M., Hruschka, E.R., et al.: Combining clustering and active learning for the detection and learning of new image classes. Neurocomputing **358**, 150–165 (2019)
14. Yan, X.Y., Nazmi, S., Gebru, B., et al.: A clustering-based active learning method to query informative and representative samples. Appl. Intell. **52**, 13250–13267 (2022). https://doi.org/10.1007/s10489-021-03139-y
15. Drakopoulos, G., Giannoukou, I., Mylonas, P., et al.: Self-organizing maps for cultural content delivery. Neural Comput. Appl. **34**, 19547–19564 (2022). https://doi.org/10.1007/s00521-022-07376-1
16. Yang, M., Sowmya, A.: An underwater color image quality evaluation metric. IEEE Trans. Image Process. **24**(12), 6062–6071 (2015)
17. Panetta, K., Gao, C., Agaian, S.: Human-visual-system-inspired underwater image quality measures. IEEE J. Oceanic Eng. **41**(3), 541–551 (2016)
18. Mittal, A., Moorthy, A., Bovik, A.: No-reference image quality assessment in the spatial domain. IEEE Trans. Image Process. **21**(12), 4695–4708 (2012)
19. Saad, M.A., Bovik, A.C., Charrier, C.: Blind prediction of natural video quality. IEEE Trans. Image Process. **23**(3), 1352–1365 (2014)
20. Robitza, W., Ramachandra Rao, R., Göring S., Raake, A.: Impact of spatial and temporal information on video quality and compressibility. In: 13th International Conference on Quality of Multimedia Experience (QoMEX), Montreal, QC, Canada, pp. 65–68. IEEE (2021)

Curvable Image Markers: Toward Trackable Markers for Every Surface

Zackary P. T. Sin(✉), Peter H. F. Ng, and Hong Va Leong

The Hong Kong Polytechnic University, Hong Kong, China
`{csptsin,cshfng,cshleong}@comp.polyu.edu.hk`

Abstract. Augmented reality (AR) possesses great potential for productivity, entertainment and communication, inclusive the mobile context. Although the strength of AR is the blending of physical and virtual environments, current mobile applications seem to focus only on overlaying the virtual part upon the physical one. It is argued that an important direction to explore is how to enhance the interaction in AR such that physical elements can act upon the virtual ones. ArUco is a popular choice in academia for tracking due to its relatively cheap processing cost and requiring only RGB input, making it also suitable for mobile devices. A fiducial marker like ArUco, however, is flat. To move towards enabling it for uneven surfaces, this paper proposed adapting the markers for curved surfaces to be suitable on bandages for warping around objects for tracking. It also presents an image marker making use of neighborhood features to improve its appeal for AR purposes.

Keywords: Curvable fiducial marker · Image marker

1 Introduction

Augmented Reality (AR) is an interaction methodology that augments the real world with computer-generated signals. By injecting virtual elements into the real world, it is possible to enrich the environment for productivity, entertainment and communication etc. There is much potential for this growing technology within the mobile context, but most mobile applications apparently only focus on one particular modality. Virtual objects are overlaid on reality while the user utilizes a virtual controller for interaction (e.g. phone). We believe that AR means that the reality is augmented in such a way that the virtual world and the reality become entwined. One of the major appeals of a digital environment is that people can play in it and see what happens. Therefore, it is believed that more investigation should be made regarding how to enable interaction in AR applications.

It seems that currently, there are three common modals to interact in AR. The first way, again, is to use a controller. Controllers, of course, are the most common way to interact in a digital interactive environment. However, in some cases, it may not be the most ideal mode to use for AR interaction as it is neither part of the physical environment which we try to blend with, nor part of the visual augmentation that blends with the former.

© The Author(s), under exclusive license to Springer Nature Switzerland AG 2022
P. Delir Haghighi et al. (Eds.): MoMM 2022, LNCS 13634, pp. 57–70, 2022.
https://doi.org/10.1007/978-3-031-20436-4_6

The second interactive method is hand tracking. Recently, great strides have been made in improving models for tracking the users' hands and great performance is already shown on commercial VR devices such as Oculus Quest. A problem with hand-driven interaction, however, is that current models seem to require significant processing power and depth input in order to function. Although this will work well for high-performance processing and specialized VR devices, the same may not hold true for typical mobile devices like phones and tablets. The third way to interact is via a trackable object that can blend with the physical environment. For example, if one is to play in an AR shooting game, a toy gun can be tracked for aiming.

In the human-computer interaction community, there is great interest in turning everyday objects that blend with the environment into interactable agents. There has been an attempt to convert everyday objects into additional, auxiliary and instant tabletop controllers by sticking markers on them [1]. There are many instances where there is no obvious flat surface for marker placement. As such, there are also bandage-based approaches where markers are populated on the bandage instead. This type of bandage with markers has been shown to be usable for everyday objects [2]. A similar bandage has also been shown to be applicable to a simple AR play session when wrapped around a stuffed toy [3]. It is also shown in [4] that printed paper makers can be used for a variety of tangible interfaces. It should be noted that the tracking of an object can be achieved with commercial corner-feature-based tracking methods (e.g. Vuforia) and mainstream 6D object pose estimation models based on machine learning. Most of these approaches, however, will limit the tracking to rigid objects which cannot cater to articulation and interaction like a collection of fiducial markers as discussed.

A standing issue with fiducial markers, however, is that it is assumed to be flat. It seems that existing fiducial marker algorithms can only handle markers on flat surfaces well as they rely on quad detection and perspective quad transformation. This inherent design limits current markers to relatively flat surfaces. This is not ideal as there are many uneven surfaces in more realistic environment. On the other hand, a smoothed (uneven) surface object is easier to grab for interactive purposes. Hence, there is a need for a marker that can be placed on uneven surfaces that are not flat.

In this paper, we discuss a method for registering a curved marker and correctly processing its captured image for identification. Curve modeling and content adjustment are involved. We limit our experiments by wrapping the markers around soft objects like stuffed toys via bandages, similar to [3]. To provide more visually pleasant markers that would be more attractive in AR, we proposed image markers, allowing fiducial markers to use colored content for identification. To reduce the computational cost and allow for error resilience when matching markers, we introduced the concept of neighborhood of distribution. This method converts the colored content into a grid with each cell acting as its own neighborhood. Then, the color distribution of RGB channels is computed as features. On the same time, we also compute the center of gravity as the mean for a spatial distribution as a feature.

In summary, the contributions of this paper are:

- A curvature-informed algorithm that can detect fiducial markers on curved surface more accurately.

- An image marker that utilizes neighborhoods of color and spatial distributions for identification, allowing greater visual flexibility and better appearance for markers.
- A quantitative evaluation which shows that the proposed method is able to track better on curved surfaces.

2 Related Work

The use of fiducial markers is a popular choice for academia in human-computer interaction and robotics. They are robust trackers that can be detected well under varying distances and environments. Specifications include ArUco [5], AprilTag [6] and ARToolKit [7]. Generally, their tracking works as a two-step process. The detection phase starts by extracting contours, which will be processed to discover quads. Each quad is treated as a candidate marker after a perspective transformation. In identification phase, a candidate is checked for indeed a marker. In ArUco, the content of the quad is converted into a grid of bits. A hamming distance check is applied to find the nearest and acceptable marker in a dictionary. Although current fiducial markers normally work well, they do not work well on curved surfaces, which interfere with the quad detection and content extraction. To the best of our knowledge, image marker is the first kind of fiducial markers using image content for identification. The most related one is ChromaTag [8] which uses color for content to improve false positive rejection, but not for visual purposes.

There are commercial solutions that help us track a target, such as ARFoundation, Vuforia and Wikitude, named after what they are tracking, i.e., image/object/cylinder targets. They track their targets via keypoint matching with corner features such as FAST [9]. Image target tracks an image and uses it as an anchoring point to apply augmented content. Object target tracks a 3D object for augmentation. Cylinder target is the closest to our work. By providing a cylinder's diameter, height and texture, an AR engine can track cylinder objects, like a can of soda or a water bottle. They seem to be meant for objects of relatively tall cylindrical shape, not tracking parts of an object. To the best of our abilities, we tested cylinder targets for tracking the limbs and body of the stuffed toy but it does not seem to work. Since the commercial solution is black-boxed, we cannot say with any certainty regarding this problem. It seems that if the bandage's diameter exceeds its height to a certain degree, the tracking may fail. When designing the bandages, we need to keep it short so that key locations can be wrapped for tracking.

There is a growing number of machine learning models that can perform pose estimation for 3D objects. Those models are usually referred to as 6D object pose estimation models. Objects can be tracked using only RGB input [10] and object pose can be tracked without temporal information [11, 12]. There are hand-object models that can simultaneously estimate hand and object pose [13, 14]. There are also methods to infuse depth and color information [15]. They have accomplished impressive result, but can only track the entire 3D object, ignoring movement of the parts. However, the work in [16] is able to track the articulation for a category of objects, but it requires RGBD input which may not be available for a broad range of mobile devices.

3 Methodology

In this section, we present our method for improving the tracking effectiveness when a fiducial marker is placed upon a curved surface. The proposed method involves curved candidate detection (Sect. 3.1), curve modeling (Sect. 3.2) and curved marker identification (Sect. 3.3). Finally, an image marker tracked via a neighborhood of feature is presented (Sect. 3.4).

3.1 Detecting Curved Candidates

The process of detecting marker candidates starts with thresholding. A fiducial marker highlights itself with a wide black border, and markers are assumed to be quad-like classically (Fig. 1a). Similar to [5], we adopt a multi-layer adaptive thresholding, by automatically calculating a threshold value for every block of fixed size, making it more robust to lighting conditions. In this paper, block sizes of 3, 8, 13, 18, 23, and 28 are used, being a superset of those adopted in ArUco implementation on OpenCV. This helps to deal with the curvature nature of the bandage, which creates more variation to the border width in pixels.

After thresholding, we extract the contours of the marker. Suzuki's algorithm [17] finds contours by moving along the boundaries of the thresholded regions. The extracted contours are returned as collections of boundary points, to be interpreted as polygons. Douglas-Peucker algorithm [18] is adopted to filter for important points in a set forming a polygon in an iterative manner. Given a curve filled with points, the algorithm begins with the starting and ending point, forming a line segment. Given this line segment, the algorithm looks for the furthest point among the set from the line segment. Its distance to the line is checked against a parameter ε. If it is larger than ε, then the point is retained, being a vertex of the polygon, splitting the line segment into two. If it is smaller than ε, the point is removed. If the contour approximates an n-sided polygon to a specific degree, then the algorithm should be able to keep n points. We choose $\varepsilon = 0.015$, instead of $\varepsilon = 0.03$ from the default setting of OpenCV's ArUco implementation to detect more precise polygons.

From an n-sided polygon, we need to detect a curved marker. Our observation is that a curved square marker's shape, when viewing at an angle away from the exact front, resembles a concave hexagon. This implies that they are usually detected as a 6-sided polygon as shown in Fig. 1b. The original ArUco algorithm only considers 4-sided convex polygons and curved markers will be dropped. In our approach, we include 6-sided polygons as candidate markers. A curved marker when viewed in the front is similar to its non-curved counterpart, albeit being compressed in one dimension. When the viewing angle to the marker is only slightly away from the front, it may be registered as a pentagon. It is from these observations that we include 4, 5 and 6-sided polygons as candidate markers. We discuss the algorithms to handle the curved markers next.

(a)   *(b)*

Fig. 1. *(a)* Using a quad and *(b)* a 5/6-sided polygon to approximate the curved marker. A concave hexagon can approximate a curved marker much better compared to a quad. The proposed algorithm aims to handle curved markers via processing 4/5/6-sided polygons.

3.2 Curve Extraction and Modeling

We need to extract the edges of the polygon belonging to the curve. For a curved marker, there are a pair of curves and a pair of straight lines. To detect the pair of curves, we first need to "pair" the edges (finding edges with the most similar direction). Consider the ordered vertices, $V = \{\vec{v_1}, \vec{v_2}, \ldots, \vec{v_n}\}$. They form the edges $E = \{\vec{e_1}, \vec{e_2}, \ldots, \vec{e_n}\}$, where $\vec{e}_i = \vec{v}_{(i+1)\,mod\,n+1} - \vec{v}_i$. The normalized vector of $\vec{e}_i$ is $\hat{e}_i$. A pair for an edge is $r_i = \{\vec{e}_i, \vec{e}_k\}$, where $k = \max_{j}(|\hat{e}_i \cdot \hat{e}_j|)$, $i \neq j$ and $j \in \{1, 2, \ldots, n\}$. We need to consider edges pointing at opposite directions since the vertices come from an anti-clockwise polygon. Given edge pairs, we now check for the curves. Assuming that the edges within a curve are more similar to each other directionally than the edges from the straight-line pair, we search for two edge pairs that are most similar to each other in direction. Note that edges within a pair r_i should have similar directions. Ignoring the edge order within the pairs, we pick three pairs. The average edge direction for a pair is $\check{r}_i = \frac{(\hat{e}_i - \hat{e}_k)}{2}$. The indexes of the two edges pairs forming the curve pair is $\arg\max_{i,j} |\check{r}_i \cdot \check{r}_j|$. The aforementioned steps are illustrated in Fig. 2.

The edges of the polygon belonging to curves are now known and can be modeled. We used Lagrange polynomials to model the curves. It takes several points $\vec{p_{\varsigma_i}} = (x_{\varsigma_i}, y_{\varsigma_i})$ as functions ℓ_j to construct a curve that fits all those points. As shown below, points are used to construct Lagrange basis polynomials ℓ_j, which are then used within the interpolation polynomial in the Lagrange form L,

$$\ell_j(x) = \prod_{\substack{i \\ i \neq j}}^{N_J} \frac{x - x_i}{x_j - x_i}, \quad L(x) = \sum_j^{N_J} y_j \ell_j(x), \tag{1}$$

where N_J is the number of data points for the Lagrange polynomial. It may be tempting to directly use points from the contour. However, doing so will not result in a curve that approximates the contour well since Lagrange polynomial assumes that no points share the same x_ς such that $x_{\varsigma_i} \neq x_{\varsigma_j} \wedge i \neq j$, while the points $\vec{p_{f_i}} = (x_{f_i}, y_{f_i})$ from the contour

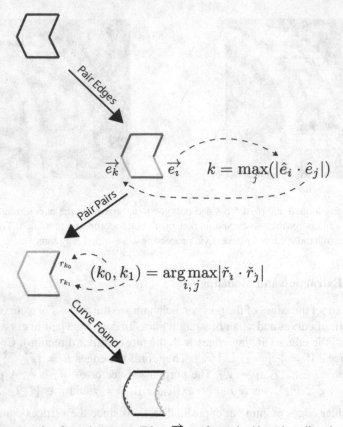

Fig. 2. Edge extraction from the curves. Edges $\vec{e}$ are first paired based on directional similarity. After they are paired, the pairs r_i are again paired with directional similarity. Finally, the paired pairs approximate the curves.

lies in image space $\mathfrak{f}$, invalidating the unique x-value assumption. To remedy this, the x-axis of the polynomial can be viewed as a temporal dimension. Given the starting $\vec{p_{\mathfrak{f}_1}}$ and ending point $\vec{p_{\mathfrak{f}_K}}$ of the curve, the temporal dimension can be viewed as time step t describing how far $L(t) \cdot P_{\mathsf{Ç} \to \mathfrak{f}} + \vec{p_{\mathfrak{f}_1}}$ is along the curve from $\vec{p_{\mathfrak{f}_1}}$ to $\vec{p_{\mathfrak{f}_K}}$, where $P_{\mathsf{Ç} \to \mathfrak{f}}$ is a projection matrix that translates a point sampled from L in curve space $\mathsf{Ç}$ to space $\mathfrak{f}$. Therefore, the x-axis aligns with

$$(i'_x, i'_y) = \hat{e}_{\mathfrak{f}_{(K,1)}}, \tag{2}$$

where $\vec{e}_{\mathfrak{f}_{(K,1)}} = \vec{p_{\mathfrak{f}_K}} - \vec{p_{\mathfrak{f}_1}}$. It is also the $i' = [i'_x \; i'_y]^T$ basis of $\mathsf{Ç}$ in $\mathfrak{f}$. j' basis is orthogonal to i', therefore $j' = [-i'_y \; i'_x]^T$. This leads us to the two transformations for changing of basis between $\mathsf{Ç}$ and $\mathfrak{f}$,

$$P_{\mathsf{Ç} \to \mathfrak{f}} = [i' \;\; j'], \; P_{\mathfrak{f} \to \mathsf{Ç}} = P_{\mathsf{Ç} \to \mathfrak{f}}^{-1}. \tag{3}$$

Having established the method to translate between spaces, points from $\int$ can be translated to ς to construct ℓ_j. To determine which section of the contour is part of a curve, matching can be done for contour points that match the starting and ending point of the curve. Since the contour is made up of ordered points $\vec{p_{i_t}}$, $i \in K$ and K is the number of points for the section, we can almost evenly sample the contour. In our case, we pick four points and then translate them to L for constructing l_j (0th, 33rd, 66th and 100th percentile) such that $\vec{p_{\varsigma_i}} = (\vec{p_{\varsigma_i}} - \vec{p_{\varsigma_1}}) \cdot P_{\int \to \varsigma}$. From here, by sampling

$$C(t) = L(t) \cdot P_{\varsigma \to \int} + \vec{p_{\int_1}} \tag{4}$$

with $t \in [0, 1]$, the curve C in $\int$ can be obtained. The process is illustrated in Fig. 3.

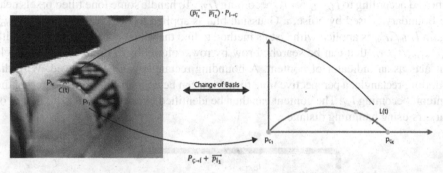

Fig. 3. The change of basis between the image $\int$ and curve ς spaces. To model the curve C, reference points $\vec{p_{\int_i}}$ from $\int$ are projected into ς for constructing a Lagrange polynomial L. To sample C at time t, $L(t)$ is sampled and projected back to $\int$.

3.3 Identifying Curved Markers

With the marker candidate properly modeled, the path opens for identifying the curved marker. The marker cannot be easily identified in the image space as it is likely to be stretched. So, the process of identifying a fiducial marker starts with projecting the content of the candidate to a normalized space. Specifically, the content may be sampled into a 32×32 marker content image $I_{\mathcal{M}}$. For quads, the process is straightforward, by applying a perspective transformation with the 4-side polygon's points as reference. For curved markers, on the other hand, it is not possible to simply apply perspective transformation as the content is not in a linear space. Instead of a linear projection, the following sampling method is used,

$$\vec{p_{\int}} = S(u_s, v_s) = (1 - u_s) \cdot C_0(v_s) + u_s \cdot C_1(1 - v_s)$$
$$\vec{p_s} = B_I(\vec{p_{\int}}), \tag{5}$$

where C represent the curves of the candidate markers, B is the bilinear sampler for the image I and (u, v) is the uv-coordinate on $I_{\mathcal{M}}$. As can be seen, the sampling is done within the marker content on I as it is flanked by the two curves. The curves take a different v_s due to the anti-clockwise orientation of the polygon.

Originally, when the content is moved to the normalized $I_{\mathcal{M}}$, it can be converted into a bitmap for comparing with the markers in a dictionary. This part is more complex for the curved marker due to its nonlinear nature. The border will not be evenly distributed and thus the content may be shifted away from the center, preventing it from being correctly converted to its bitmap counterpart. To remedy this problem, a bounding rectangle approach is proposed (Fig. 4). The key idea is to search for the content via iteratively finding the first row and column that is partially filled. The content will first be sampled into $I'_{\mathcal{M}}$. The $I'_{\mathcal{M}}$ will be thresholded with Otsu's method [19] becoming I_{OSTU}. The rows and columns at the boundaries can be easily sampled with pixels outside the marker. They may be marked as filled by Otsu's method. Thus, fully filled rows and columns are removed according to I_{OSTU} for $I'_{\mathcal{M}}$ becoming I_{Cln}. To handle some lone filled pixels near the boundary caused by noise, a Gaussian blur is applied to I_{Cln}, becoming $I_{Cln \to Gus}$. Again $I_{Cln \to Gus}$ is applied with Ostu's method to find the actual content, leaving us with $I_{Cln \to Gus \to OSTU}$ that can be searched row by row, column by column for filled pixels that acts as an indicator of content. A bounding rectangle can be retrieved. With the bounding rectangle, a perspective transformation can be applied on I_{OSTU}, centering the content, becoming $I_{\mathcal{M}}$. The content can then be identified by searching in a dictionary of markers using hamming distance.

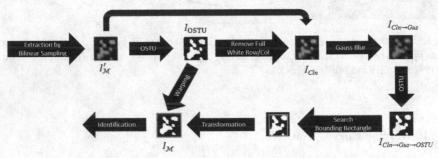

Fig. 4. Process for unwarping the curved marker's content. By centering the content correctly, it allows the content of a curved marker to be correctly identified.

3.4 Image Marker

A typical fiducial marker, like ArUco and AprilTag, is robust and efficient for tracking its pose. It is, however, visually limited due to their bit-based methodology. Our proposed image marker aims to complement this by replacing bits with expressive colored content. With a changed content comes a changed methodology. In order to identify the content, the image marker uses neighborhoods of distribution, which shares some similarity to the bit checking from other fiducial marker algorithms. For an image marker, the process in Sect. 3.2 and 3.3 is similar with an exception that the colored content is gray-scaled using the luminosity method for computing the bounding rectangle. However, after the content is extracted, the method for identification is different.

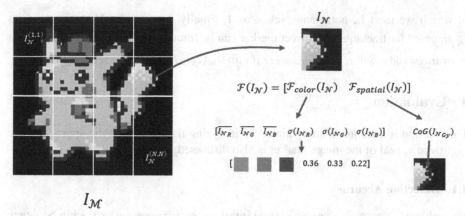

Fig. 5. The proposed image marker uses neighborhoods of distribution as features. Each image marker $I_{\mathcal{M}}$ is divided into cell neighborhoods $I_{\mathcal{N}}$. $I_{\mathcal{N}}$ captures color $\mathcal{F}_{color}(I_{\mathcal{N}})$ and spatial distributions $\mathcal{F}_{spatial}(I_{\mathcal{N}})$.

An image marker candidate's content will first be fit into a grid with each cell acting as its own neighborhood (Fig. 5). For the image marker, we pick $I_{\mathcal{M}}$ with a size of 64×64, and a 4-by-4 grid is chosen. Each neighborhood $I_{\mathcal{N}}$ is of size 16×16. Compared with the bit-based approach, each cell is like a bit, but instead of a binary feature, its features manifest as color and spatial distributions. Specifically, each neighborhood cell will compute encapsulated features of its mean and standard deviation of color, and center of gravity of shape. Each of the RGB channels computes its neighborhood mean and standard deviation individually, yielding six features $\mathcal{F}_{color}(I_{\mathcal{N}})= [\overline{I_{\mathcal{N}_R}} \quad \overline{I_{\mathcal{N}_G}} \quad \overline{I_{\mathcal{N}_B}} \quad \sigma(I_{\mathcal{N}_R}) \quad \sigma(I_{\mathcal{N}_G}) \quad \sigma(I_{\mathcal{N}_B})]$, where $I_{\mathcal{N}_R}$ is a red channel map. The center of gravity is computed as follows,

$$mass\big(I_{Gy}\big) = \sum_x^X \sum_y^Y I_{Gy}(x,y), \ CoG\big(I_{Gy}\big) = \frac{1}{mass\big(I_{Gy}\big)} \sum_x^X \sum_y^Y I_{Gy}(x,y) \cdot \begin{bmatrix} x \\ y \end{bmatrix}, \tag{6}$$

where I_{Gy} is a grayscale image and $I_{Gy}(x,y)$ is the intensity of a pixel at (x,y). The spatial feature of a neighborhood is $\mathcal{F}_{spatial}(I_{\mathcal{N}}) = CoG(I_{\mathcal{N}_{Gy}})$. The feature of $I_{\mathcal{N}}$ is $\mathcal{F}(I_{\mathcal{N}}) = [\mathcal{F}_{color}(I_{\mathcal{N}}) \quad \mathcal{F}_{spatial}(I_{\mathcal{N}})]$ while the feature of $I_{\mathcal{M}}$. is the aggregated feature from its neighborhoods $\mathcal{F}(I_{\mathcal{M}}) = [\mathcal{F}(I_{\mathcal{N}}^{(1,1)}) \quad \mathcal{F}(I_{\mathcal{N}}^{(2,1)}) \quad ... \quad \mathcal{F}(I_{\mathcal{N}}^{(N,N)})]$, in which $I_{\mathcal{M}}$ has N^2 neighborhoods. This aggregated feature is used for computing the similarity between a candidate and a marker. Given an image marker $\widehat{I_{\mathcal{M}}}$, and a candidate marker $I_{\mathcal{M}}$, their similarity is

$$D_{\mathcal{M}}\big(\widehat{I_{\mathcal{M}}}, I_{\mathcal{M}}\big) = \frac{1}{N^2} \sum_x^N \sum_y^N \left\| \mathcal{F}_{color}\left(\widehat{I_{\mathcal{N}}^{(x,y)}}\right) - \mathcal{F}_{color}\left(I_{\mathcal{N}}^{(x,y)}\right) \right\|_2^2 +$$
$$\lambda \left\| \mathcal{F}_{spatial}\left(\widehat{I_{\mathcal{N}}^{(x,y)}}\right) - \mathcal{F}_{spatial}\left(I_{\mathcal{N}}^{(x,y)}\right) \right\|_2^2, \tag{7}$$

in which we used *L2*-norm and pick λ as 1. Finally, let there be M image markers $\widehat{I_{\mathcal{M}}}_i$ targeted for tracking, the correct marker can be found with $\underset{i}{\operatorname{argmin}} D_{\mathcal{M}}(\widehat{I_{\mathcal{M}}}_i, I_{\mathcal{M}})$. An error threshold ϵ will reject the marker if $\underset{i}{\min} D_{\mathcal{M}}(\widehat{I_{\mathcal{M}}}_i, I_{\mathcal{M}}) > \epsilon$. We set ϵ as 0.15.

4   Evaluation

This section is a technical study aimed at analyzing the efficacy of the approach. The improved appeal of the image marker is also discussed.

4.1   Detection Accuracy

To evaluate the proposed bandage-based interface, experiments on its tracking efficacy are presented. Two stuffed toys fitted with bandages populated by markers are prepared, Pikachu (Fig. 6) and bear (Fig. 7). Videos of a user playing the toys are recorded. For both toys, we perform two actions: *rotation*, pivoting the toy at the center and rotating it; and *interaction*, moving the limbs of the toy. The purpose of these recorded actions is to test whether the tracking can enable AR interaction. The video lengths are 490 frames for Pikachu-rotation, 512 for Pikachu-interaction, 322 for bear-rotation and 363 for bear-interaction. The tracking of a part (body or limb) relies on the successful tracking of any of its marker. That is, a part is tracked if at least one of its markers is tracked. The proposed curvature-informed algorithm is evaluated against ArUco and AprilTag tracking implementation on OpenCV. The results are presented in Table 1.

Fig. 6. The Pikachu stuffed toy used for the experiments.

Fig. 7. The bear stuffed toy used for the experiments.

Table 1. Performance on limbs and body tracking (number of parts tracked/higher the better)

	Pikachu-rotation	Pikachu-interaction	Bear-rotation	Bear-interaction
ArUco - Traditional	1098	820	308	272
AprilTag	1332	941	313	244
(Ours) Curvature-aware only	**1596**	**1809**	**358**	**319**
(Ours) Image Marker + Curvature-aware	1373	1262	306	232
(Illustration Only) Image Marker Only	805	753	198	181

From the result, several observations can be made and some implications derived. First, by using the same set of fiducial markers, ArUco marker specifically in our case, the proposed curvature-informed algorithm (curvature-aware only) is able to achieve a significant improvement. For the pikachu-rotation, the parts are tracked 45.3% more compared to ArUco traditional and 19.8% more compared to AprilTag. The result is even more significant during interaction, going up to 120.6% for ArUco and 92.2% for AprilTag. With the bear video, it also shows improvement compared with ArUco (16.2% improvement for bear-rotation, 17.3% for bear-interaction) and AprilTag (14.3% improvement for bear-rotation, 30.7% for bear-interaction). This is an expected result as the shape of the toy forces most markers to be curved, and our algorithm is specifically designed in tracking curved markers. Another observation is that image marker (image marker only) trades visual effect with accuracy. By using it as an identification method, the tracking efficacy will become worse. However, by combining with the curvature algorithm, the detection rate will improve considerably (70.6% for Pikachu-rotation, 67.6% Pikachu-interaction, 54.5% bear-rotation and 28.1% bear-interaction), showing that the proposed curvature-aware method's improvement.

In Fig. 8, we showcase a curved marker for qualitative understanding. As we can see, our curvature approach is able to correctly manipulate the content such that it can be converted to a bitmap. This is the key reason for the success in Table 1. For ArUco traditional and AprilTag, they assume that the content is on a flat surface and therefore warp the content via perspective transformation. This will lead to distorted content as it will require a non-linear transformation to warp a map to a normalized space for identification. Furthermore, those two approaches assume that the marker candidates are quads. So, it is very possible that a curved marker cannot go past the detection phase with those methods.

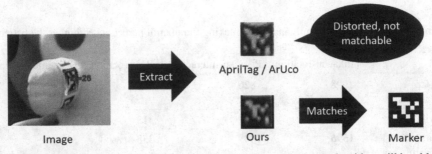

Fig. 8. By handling curvature explicitly, our proposed curvature-aware algorithm will be able to correctly warp the content for identification. ArUco traditional and AprilTag may not be able to handle curved markers as they expect flat ones.

4.2 Visual Appeal of Image Marker

Last, we surveyed 15 users (2 female) and are asked whether they prefer fiducial or image marker visually (Fig. 9). The result shown in Fig. 10 indicates there is a marked difference between the two markers in terms of appearances. This is important as a visually captivating bandage is likely important when AR is involved.

Bandage w/ Image Marker   **Bandage w/ ArUco Marker**

Fig. 9. The stuffed toys with image and fiducial markers are shown to the users.

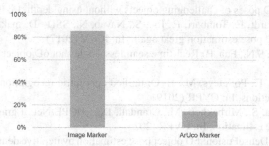

Fig. 10. Reported user visual preference between image and fiducial marker. Almost all users agree that image marker is visually more appealing.

5 Conclusion

The use of fiducial markers like ArUco is a popular choice that is low-cost and suitable for mobile devices. It has also been shown in the literature to be practical for handling articulation and interaction. An issue for the contemporary markers is that they are assumed to be flat and may not be tracked as accurately on uneven surfaces well. In this paper, we move towards enhancing uneven surfaces tracking with fiducial markers by proposing a curvature-aware algorithm. The keys to our algorithm are the extraction of polygon, curve modeling and sampling the nonlinear surface to a linear one. Further, to make the markers more appealing for AR applications, we also propose utilizing neighborhood of features that enables image markers. The quantitative evaluation shows that our method improves upon the handling of curved surfaces.

References

1. Cheng, K.-Y., Liang, R.-H., Chen, B.-Y., Liang, R.-H., Kuo, S.-Y.: iCon: utilizing everyday objects as additional, auxiliary and instant tabletop controllers. In: CHI (2010)

2. Drogemuller, A., Walsh, J., Smith, R.T., Adcock, M., Thomas, B.H.: Turning everyday objects into passive tangible controllers. In: TEI (2021)

3. Sin, Z.P.T., Ng, P.H.F., Leong, H.V.: Stuffed toy as an appealing tangible interface for children. In: ISM (2021)

4. Zheng, C., Gyory, P., Do, E.Y.-L.: Tangible interfaces with printed paper markers. In: DIS (2020)

5. Garrido-Jurado, S., Muñoz-Salinas, R., Madrid-Cuevas, F.J., Marín-Jiménez, M.J.: Automatic generation and detection of highly reliable fiducial markers under occlusion. Pattern Recogn. **47**(6), 2280–2292 (2014)

6. Olson, E.: AprilTag: a robust and flexible visual fiducial system. In: IEEE International Conference on Robotics and Automation (2011)

7. Wagner, D., Reitmayr, G., Mulloni, A., Drummond, T.: Pose tracking from natural features on mobile phones. In: ISMAR (2008)

8. DeGol, J., Bretl, T., Hoiem, D.: ChromaTag: a colored marker and fast detection algorithm. In: ICCV (2017)

9. Marchand, E., Uchiyama, H., Spindler, F.: Pose estimation for augmented reality: a hands-on survey. TVCG **22**(12), 2633–2651 (2016)

10. Rad, M., Lepetit, V.: BB8: a scalable, accurate, robust to partial occlusion method for predicting the 3D poses of challenging objects without using depth. In: ICCV (2017)

11. Kehl, W., Manhardt, F., Tombari, F., Ilic, S., Navab, N.: SSD-6D: making RGB-based 3D detection and 6D pose estimation great again. In: ICCV (2017)

12. Tekin, B., Sinha, S.N., Fua, P.: Real-time seamless single shot 6D object pose prediction. In: CVPR (2018)

13. Tekin, B., Bogo, F., Pollefeys, M.: H+O: unified egocentric recognition of 3D hand-object poses and interactions. In: CVPR (2019)

14. Doosti, B., Naha, S., Mirbagheri, M., Crandall, D.J.: HOPE-Net: a graph-based model for hand-object pose estimation. In: CVPR (2020)

15. Wang, C., et al.: DenseFusion: 6D object pose estimation by iterative dense fusion. In: CVPR (2019)

16. Li, X., Wang, H., Yi, L., Guibas, L., Abbott, A.L., Song, S.: Category-level articulated object pose estimation. In: CVPR (2020)

17. Suzuki, S., Abe, K.: Topological structural analysis of digitized binary images by border following. Comput. Vis. Graph. Image Process. **30**(1), 32–46 (1985)

18. Douglas, D., Peucker, T.: Algorithms for the reduction of the number of points required to represent a digitized line or its caricature. Can. Cartogr. **10**(2), 112–122 (1973)

19. Liu, D., Yu, J.: Otsu method and k-means. In: International Conference on Hybrid Intelligent Systems (2009)

Design Exploration for Better Security of Recognition-Based Image Authentication in Mobile Environment

Tetsuji Takada[1(✉)] and Daniel Schwarz[2]

[1] The University of Electro-Communications, Tokyo, Japan
zetaka@computer.org
[2] University of Bremen, Bremen, Germany

Abstract. Recognition-based image authentication (RbIA) has an advantage in terms of its memory retention of user credentials, which is one of the issues in knowledge-based user authentication (KUA). Therefore, RbIA is expected to serve as an alternative to conventional KUA. However, previous studies have reported that the security associated with RbIA schemes is comparable to that of four-digit personal identification number authentication. Therefore, the usage scene of RbIA schemes is considered to be limited. In this study, we propose two approaches for improving the security of an RbIA scheme without increasing the memory load of user credentials. We also conduct a user experiment to evaluate the login times of the proposed scheme for use in a mobile environment. The results reveal that the proposed scheme demonstrates potential in providing better security with a shorter login time than RbIA schemes proposed previously.

Keywords: Security · User authentication · Usable security · Graphical user authentication · Graphical password

1 Introduction

Recognition-based image authentication (*RbIA*) is one of image-based graphical user authentication schemes [1,2]. The RbIA scheme has the potential in improving credential memorability for knowledge-based user authentication. A user credential in RbIA is a set of images, and a user must set these images during user registration. In user authentication, the RbIA system presents a set of images on the screen. The presented images consist of both credential and non-credential images. The user is then required to identify all the credential images among the presented images. In this paper, we refer to the credential and non-credential images as the "pass-images" and "decoy images", respectively.

In the RbIA scheme, a user can make use of the "picture superiority effect" [3] and the Déjà Vu effect [4] for the retention of user credential. The former refers to the human ability of memorizing images better than symbols or words, whereas the latter refers to the human ability to recall visual scenes that one has seen

© The Author(s), under exclusive license to Springer Nature Switzerland AG 2022
P. Delir Haghighi et al. (Eds.): MoMM 2022, LNCS 13634, pp. 71–77, 2022.
https://doi.org/10.1007/978-3-031-20436-4_7

in the past. The RbIA scheme changes the operation from "a precise recall of a password or personal identification number (PIN)" to "a recognition of previously seen images". Therefore, the user does not have to recall the pass-images precisely. Even if a user has temporarily forgotten the pass-images, they may recall them by seeing the images displayed on the authentication screen.

RbIA also has usability advantages. These involve a simplified input operation and a load reduction of credential creation. The user operation of the RbIA scheme is to choose pass-images from the images displayed on the authentication screen, and the user is not required to type any text using a keyboard. Moreover, the creation of user credentials only involves the selection of images from existing or owned images.

However, only a few commercial products are available, and RbIA systems have not yet been widely used. This can be attributed to the false recognition that RbIA scheme can only provide the same level of security as four-digit PIN authentication. However, because RbIA scheme has certain design choices, it can provide better security depending on the design parameters, but no research has been conducted in this direction.

We propose two approaches for improving the security of RbIA scheme with a minimal impact on credential memorability. We also conducted a user experiment to determine the effect of such security improvements on the login time. The obtained results suggest that the proposed RbIA scheme has the potential of achieving an unprecedented balance between security and usability in the mobile context.

2   Related Work

Several previous studies have been conducted on RbIA schemes; however, extensive details cannot be provided owing to page limitations [4–10]. Based on a literature survey on such studies, an RbIA scheme can be represented by the following four parameters (m, n, p, q):

m) The number of images displayed on one authentication screen $(m > p)$
n) The number of authentication screens prepared for one authentication session $(n \geq 1)$
p) The number of pass-images a user has to select on one authentication screen $(p \geq 1)$
q) Is the answer sequence of pass-images verified?
   ($q =$ "yes" or "no". This parameter is valid only when $p > 1$.)

Table 1 lists the design choices for the proposed RbIA systems based on the four parameters. "NPC" in the second column of the table indicates the number of possible credentials. The larger the NPC value, the better the security provided by the RbIA scheme. Based on a survey, proposed RbIA schemes can be classified into two groups. One group has an NPC value of less than or equal to 10,000; accordingly, schemes in this group [5–7,9,10] can provide lower or equal levels of security as four-digit PIN authentication. The other group includes

Table 1. Design choices in RbIA systems can be represented by the four parameters.

	NPC	Login time(s)	(m, n)	(p, q)
UYI [9]	2,925	11.5–25.8	(27, 1)	(3, no)
Story scheme. [10]	3,024	–	(9, 1)	(4, yes)
Passfaces. [5]	6,561	20.0	(9, 4)	(1, –)
Awase-E [6]	9,999	24.6	(10, 4)	(1, –)
VIP (type 2) [7]	10,000	10.0	(10, 1)	(4, yes)
Deja Vu [4]	53,130	36.0	(25, 1)	(5, no)
Trevor et al. [8]	1,048,576	40	(4, 10)	(1, –)

schemes with NPC values greater than 10,000. However, the schemes in this group [4,8] have the issue of longer login times (>35 s).

3 Our Approach and Prototype System

We describe two ideas for improving the security of the RbIA scheme and introduce a prototype system based on these concepts. The formulas for the NPC of the RbIA scheme are as follows.

$$NPC = (_mC_1)^n \ _{(p=1 \ or \ p>1,q=no)} \ or \ NPC = (_mP_p)^n \ _{(p>1,q=yes)} \qquad (1)$$

In both equations, to improve the security of the RbIA scheme, we must increase the value of (m, n, p) or choose the $q = yes$ option. However, we assume that increasing the value of n, p and selecting the $q = yes$ option are not desirable. This is because aforementioned choices increase the credential memory load for users. Because the total number of pass-images (TNP) that a user must memorize is $TNP = n \times p$, increasing the values of these two parameters directly increases the TNP. In addition, Davis, et al. [10] reported that although users could remember the pass-images themselves, memorizing answer sequence of them was difficult.

Therefore, only parameter m has room to increase the value. We attempt to increase the value of m to improve the security of RbIA. However, this approach is expected to lead to an increase in the login time. Hence, we need to determine the m value to achieve better security and a reasonable login time. We also define the third value "first only" for parameter q as a different approach. This value implied that only the first selection of the pass-images is fixed to a specific pass-image, and subsequent pass-image selection could be performed in any order. This represents an idea establishing a compromise between both the "$q = $ yes" and "$q = $ no" options.

We implemented an RbIA prototype system based on the two approaches as Android application. We chose the following design option for the prototype system: $(m, n, p, q) = ((20/60/100), 1, 4, \text{"first only"})$. We also selected three values for parameter m to explore a better balance between security and usability.

Figure 1 shows the authentication screen of the prototype system. We defined a 4×5 image grid as a "page", and the image size was adjusted so that the all images on a page could be displayed on the screen simultaneously. When the value of m is in (60, 100), the system generates multiple pages and allows users to browse through all images using a page unit. The layout of the images on the page(s) is randomized for each authentication session.

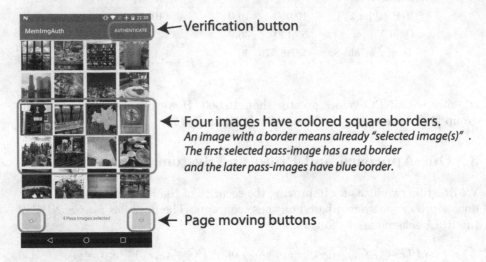

← **Verification button**

← **Four images have colored square borders.**
*An image with a border means already "selected image(s)".
The first selected pass-image has a red border
and the later pass-images have blue border.*

← **Page moving buttons**

Fig. 1. Screen snapshot of the credential input screen of the prototype system.

Table 2. Number of possible credentials (NPC) under the three q conditions ("yes", "first only", and "no") and three m conditions in $n = 1$ and $p = 4$.

	$q =$ "yes"	$q =$ "first only"	$q =$ "no"
$m = 20$	116,280	19,380	4,845
$m = 60$	11,703,240	1,950,540	487,635
$m = 100$	94,109,400	15,684,900	3,921,225

The third column in Table 2 lists the NPC values of the prototype system under the three m conditions. The formula for the NPC of the prototype system is as follows: $NPC_{proto} = m \times_{p-1} C_{m-1}$. The values in the second and fourth columns show the NPC under the "q=yes" and "q=no" conditions for comparison.

4   Usability Evaluation

A user experiment was conducted to evaluate possible changes in the login time owing to security improvements in the RbIA scheme based on the proposed

Table 3. Login times of the proposed scheme under three m conditions (left table), and a comparison between the proposed scheme and the schemes in previous studies in terms of the login time and the NPC value (right table).

	Login time (sec)			
	Mean	S.D.	Median	Shortest
m=100	22.02	12.82	17.86	5.42
m=60	15.52	8.60	12.85	5.20
m=200	5.87	2.35	5.45	2.35

	NPC	Login time (sec)
Proposed (m=100)	15,684,900	22.02
Proposed (m=60)	1,950,540	15.52
Trevor, et.al.	1,048,576	Over 30.0
Deja Vu	53,130	32.0
Proposed (m=20)	19,380	5.87
VIP (type 2)	10,000	10.0
UYI	2,925	11.5

approaches. We measured the login time under the following three m conditions: $m = (20, 60, 100)$. The experimental procedure was as follows: (Step 1) We explained the purpose and framework of the experiment to participants and obtained their consent for participation. (Step 2) The participants were asked to bring 100 self-taken photographs and used them for both pass-images and decoy images. (Step 3) We asked the participants to set up their credentials: they selected four pictures as pass-images and chose the first pass-image from among these four pass-images. The remaining 96 images were used as decoy images. (Step 4) Pre-training was conducted to reconfirm the authentication operation and the pass-images. (Step 5) Participants were asked to perform authentication repeatedly until they were successfully authenticated eight times under each of the three m conditions. The login time and authentication result were recorded by the prototype system. The reason for conducting the eight measurements was the following: as the image layout is randomly changed on each session, the results of only a few measurements were affected by the layout of the pass-images. We used "Nexus 5X" android phone, and 13 university students participated in the experiment.

Table 3 presents the results of the login times obtained under the three m conditions. In total, 106 sessions were conducted by the 13 participants, and only two sessions resulted in authentication failure. Thus, the authentication success rate was 98.1%.

5 Discussion and Conclusion

We discuss about the login times of the proposed scheme in the right table in Table 3. First, for all the three conditions, the median time was shorter than the mean login time. This implies that over half of the authentication attempts could be performed in a shorter time than the mean login time. Next, the shortest login times were less than 6 s under all the three conditions. We assume that this result depends on the layout of the pass-images, However, we cannot ignore the fact that the login time is equivalent to that of PIN authentication in certain cases while providing better security.

The left table in Table 3 presents the login time and the NPC values of some RbIA schemes for comparison. In this table, we classify the RbIA schemes into two groups according to the NPC values. In both groups, the proposed scheme achieves better security and a shorter login time than the RbIA schemes proposed in previous studies.

These results should be interpreted as the results of preliminary experiment aimed at demonstrating the potential of the proposed scheme. However, it should be noted that the experiment involved several biases: all participants were university students, and the results of the login time did not include the effect of memory degradation of pass-images. In addition, differences in the experimental methods and environments between our study and previous studies should also be considered in the comparative discussions.

In future studies, we aim to widen the scale of the experiment. Additionally, we aim to redesign the experimental method to reduce biases, which may have affected the results of our experiment. We will also conduct a comparative evaluation under the following three conditions.

- Proposed scheme with m = 20 vs. four-digit PIN
- Proposed scheme with m = 40 vs. Android pattern-lock
- Proposed scheme with m = 60 vs. six-digit PIN

References

1. Suo, X., Zhu, Y., Own, G.: Graphical passwords: a survey. In: 21st Annual Computer Security Applications Conference (ACSAC'05), p. 10 (2005). https://doi.org/10.1109/CSAC.2005.27
2. Biddle, R., Chiasson, S., Van Oorschot, P.C.: Graphical passwords: learning from the first twelve years. ACM Comput. Surv. 44(4), 1–41 (2012). https://doi.org/10.1145/2333112.2333114
3. Paivio, A.: Mental imagery in associative learning and memory. Psychol. Rev. 76(3), 241–263 (1969). https://doi.org/10.1037/h0027272
4. Dhamija, R., Perrig, A.: Deja vu - a user study: using images for authentication. In: 9th USENIX Security Symposium (2000). https://www.usenix.org/conference/9th-usenix-security-symposium/deja-vu-user-study-using-images-authentication
5. Brostoff, S., Sasse, M.A.: Are passfaces more usable than passwords a field trial investigation. People and Computers XIV - Usability or Else (2000). https://doi.org/10.1007/978-1-4471-0515-2_27
6. Takada, T., Koike, H.: Awase-E: Image-based authentication for mobile phones using user's favorite images. International Conference on Mobile Human-Computer Interaction (MobileHCI '03), pp. 347–351, (2003). https://doi.org/10.1007/978-3-540-45233-1_26
7. Angeli, A.D., Coventry, L., Johnson, G., Renaud, K.: Is a picture really worth a thousand words? exploring feasibility graphical authentication System. Int. J. Hum. Comput. Stud. 63(1–2), 128–152 (2005). https://doi.org/10.1016/j.ijhcs.2005.04.020
8. Pering, T., Sundar, M., Light, J., Want, R.: Photographic authentication through untrusted terminals. IEE Pervasive Comput. 2(1), 30–36 (2003). https://doi.org/10.1109/MPRV.2003.1186723

9. Hayashi, E., Dhamija, R., Christin, N., Perrig, A.: Use your illusion: secure authentication usable anywhere, 4th Symposium on Usable Privacy and Security (SOUPS '08), pp. 35–45 (2008). https://doi.org/10.1145/1408664.1408670
10. Davis, D., Monrose, F., Reiter, M.K.: On user choice in graphical password schemes. In: 13th USENIX Security Symposium, p. 13 (2004). https://www.usenix.org/conference/13th-usenix-security-symposium/user-choice-graphical-password-schemes

A Scheduling Method for Division-Based Broadcasting on Dynamic Video Delivery

Keita Katsuno[1] and Yusuke Gotoh[2(✉)]

[1] Graduate School of Natural Science and Technology, Okayama University, Okayama, Japan
[2] Faculty of Natural Science and Technology, Okayama University, Okayama, Japan
y-gotoh@okayama-u.ac.jp

Abstract. Due to the spread of multimedia broadcasting, such as digital terrestrial TV broadcasting and one-segment broadcasting, continuous media data broadcasting has been attracting great attention. In broadcasting, many clients can receive data at a fixed bandwidth, but clients have to wait between making their request to receive data and the start of data delivery. In order to reduce this waiting time, division-based broadcasting, in which the server divides data into several segments and delivers them on multiple channels, has been proposed. Conventional scheduling methods do not consider dynamic updating of the delivery environment by adjusting the available bandwidth. Consequently, the server cannot update the delivery schedule after delivery has started. In this paper, we propose a scheduling method for division-based broadcasting using dynamic video delivery. The proposed method reduces the waiting time for receiving video data by updating the delivery schedule so that all clients can receive the video data based on the change in the available bandwidth before and after the update. Simulation evaluations show that the proposed method reduces the waiting time compared to the conventional method.

Keywords: Division-based broadcasting · Dynamic video delivery · Scheduling · Waiting time

1 Introduction

Recently, with the rapid spread of smartphones, the number of Internet users using mobile terminals has been increasing. The methods of viewing video over the Internet have become more diverse, and services that distribute video data using Internet Protocol (IP) networks are increasing.

There are two types of delivery methods for video data: on-demand delivery and broadcast delivery. In on-demand delivery, the server allocates the bandwidth and delivers the video based on the client's request. Therefore, as the number of clients requesting video at the same time increases, the available bandwidth of the server increases proportionally. On the other hand, in broadcasting, although the server can deliver the same video repeatedly to clients at a certain bandwidth, the clients must wait until the requested data are delivered.

© The Author(s), under exclusive license to Springer Nature Switzerland AG 2022
P. Delir Haghighi et al. (Eds.): MoMM 2022, LNCS 13634, pp. 78–83, 2022.
https://doi.org/10.1007/978-3-031-20436-4_8

In order to reduce waiting time, we proposed division-based broadcasting to divide video data into multiple segments and deliver them using multiple channels [1–3]. In division-based broadcasting, many scheduling methods have been proposed to reduce the waiting time needed to receive data [4–9].

In video delivery services, the popularity of video data based on the number of simultaneous views by users changes dynamically during delivery depending on various factors such as the day of the week, the time of day, or the scale of the event. When a server broadcasts multiple videos, more users will watch the videos with higher popularity. By increasing the available bandwidth and dynamically updating the delivery schedule, the waiting time for the more popular videos should be reduced compared to the less popular videos. However, conventional scheduling methods assume that the delivery schedule is determined before the start of delivery and remains fixed until the end of delivery, and thus the server cannot dynamically update the delivery schedule.

In this paper, we propose a scheduling method that dynamically updates the delivery schedule based on changes in the available bandwidth for division-based broadcasting. The proposed method determines the ratio of the divided data according to the available bandwidth and the number of divisions of video data, and it dynamically changes the delivery schedule according to changes in bandwidth to reduce waiting time.

The remainder of this paper is organized as follows. We explain the dynamic update of delivery schedules in Sect. 2. We describe our proposed method in Sect. 3 and evaluate it in Sect. 4. Finally, we conclude in Sect. 5.

2   Dynamic Update of Delivery Schedules

For highly popular video delivery, clients can reduce waiting time by increasing the available bandwidth and decreasing the data size of the first segment. However, when the server makes a division-based broadcasting schedule using conventional methods, the server cannot change the delivery schedule determined before the start of delivering data.

An example of scheduling when the available bandwidth is increased using the conventional Bandwidth Equivalent-Asynchronous Harmonic Broadcasting (BE-AHB) method [10] is shown in Fig. 1. In the delivery schedule before the update, the server divides the video data into three segments S_1, S_2, and S_3 and repeatedly delivers each segment on three channels C_1, C_2, and C_3. In the delivery schedule after the update, the server divides the same video data into four segments S'_1, S'_2, S'_3, and S'_4 and repeatedly delivers each segment on four channels C_1, C_2, C_3, and C_4.

When the server updates the delivery schedule during delivery, the server suspends the delivery based on the schedule before the update and then resumes delivery based on the updated schedule. Clients that had received data when the delivery schedule was updated cannot receive the subsequent data in the delivery schedule before the update. The client needs to stop watching the currently playing video and start receiving the video data again from the beginning

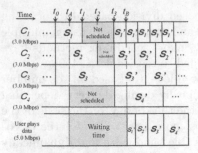

Fig. 1. Example of scheduling based on increasing the number of channels in BE-AHB method

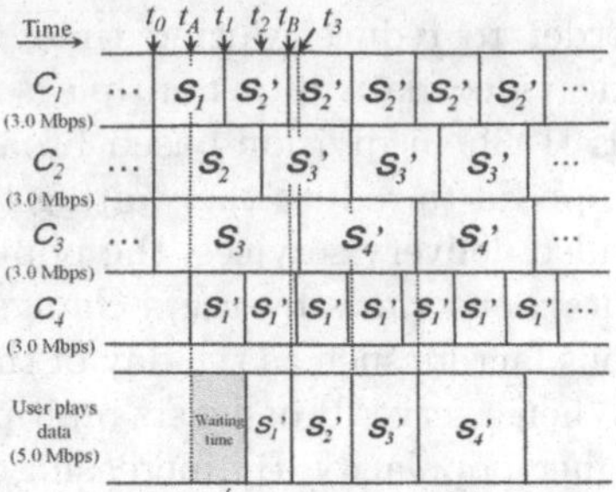

Fig. 2. Example of scheduling based on increased number of channels in proposed method

with the updated delivery schedule. In this case, the waiting time for the client becomes long.

In the example shown in Fig. 1, when the client requests an update of the delivery schedule at t_A, the server cannot use the updated schedule until t_3, which is the finishing time of delivering S_3. Therefore, the server cannot deliver segments between t_1 and t_3 using C_1, between t_2 and t_3 using C_2, and between t_A and t_3 using C_4. The waiting time of the client occurs between t_A and t_B, which is the finishing time of receiving S'_1.

In updating the video delivery schedule according to changes in popularity, when the server updates the delivery schedule after all segments have been delivered on all channels according to the delivery schedule before the update, the clients that were receiving video data at the time of the update will stop receiving it. The server needs to start from the beginning with the updated delivery schedule, and the waiting time for clients becomes long. Therefore, it is necessary to dynamically update the delivery schedule of video data so that clients do not stop receiving the video before and after the update, thereby reducing the waiting time for clients.

3   Proposed Method

3.1   Scheduling Procedure

In this paper, we propose a method that can update the delivery schedule during the delivery of video data and evaluate its effectiveness in reducing waiting time compared to the conventional methods. When updating the delivery schedule, the bandwidth of each channel changes according to the increase or decrease in the number of segments. We consider the case where the server creates an updated schedule by adding one new channel with the same bandwidth as the channel before the update.

In the proposed method, the following scheduling procedure is followed when the server updates the delivery schedule by increasing the number of channels.

1. At the update time t_A, the server creates a new channel C_{n+1} and allocates S_1'.
2. For $C_1, \cdots, C_n$, the server allocates the updated segment $S_2', \cdots, S_{n+1}'$ in the order of the channel with the earlier finishing time of segments.
3. For $C_1, \cdots, C_{n+1}$, the server repeatedly allocates $S_1', \cdots, S_{n+1}'$ in the order of the channel with the earlier finishing time of segments.

3.2 Implementation

We show an example of scheduling in the proposed method when the number of channels increases in Fig. 2. Between t_0 and t_1, we consider the case where the server updates the delivery schedule at t_A. The bandwidth of each channel is 3.0 Mbps, and the consumption rate is 5.0 Mbps. The numbers of channels and segments before the update are both 3. When updating the delivery schedule, the server adds one new channel with the same bandwidth as the channel before the update.

The server schedules segments according to the scheduling procedure described in Sect. 3.1. In step 1, at t_A, the server assigns S_1' to the newly created channel C_4. In step 2, the server assigns S_2', S_3', and S_4' to C_1, C_2, and C_3, which deliver segments in t_A, in order of the earlier time when the segment delivery is finished. In the case of Figure refProposed, the server allocates S_2' to C_1 at t_1, S_3' to C_2 at t_2, and S_4' to C_3 at t_3. Finally, in step 3, the server assigns S_1', S_2', S_3', and S_4' to the channel with the earlier end time on each channel. Thereafter, the server repeatedly allocates segments.

As shown in Fig. 2, compared with the scheduling of the conventional method, the proposed method delivers segments in all time periods. The waiting time of the client is only the receiving time of S_1'. The proposed method reduces the waiting time compared to the conventional method, which delivers the updated scheduling after the delivery of S_3, the last segment.

4 Evaluation

4.1 Evaluation Environment

In this work, we evaluated the usefulness of the proposed method using computer simulations. In the evaluation, we used the proposed method and a simple method that does not dynamically update the delivery schedule. When the number of channels is increased by dynamically updating the delivery schedule, the server updates the schedule by adding one new channel with the same bandwidth as the previous channel. The consumption rate is set to 5.0 Mbps.

4.2 Number of Segments and Amount of Waiting Time

We evaluated the waiting time according to the number of segments of video data. The results of the evaluation are shown in Fig. 3. The horizontal axis is

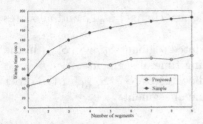
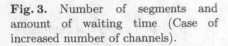
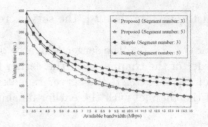

Fig. 3. Number of segments and amount of waiting time (Case of increased number of channels).

Fig. 4. Available bandwidth and waiting time (Case of increased number of channels).

the number of segments, and the vertical axis is the waiting time. The available bandwidth is 10 Mbps and the playing time is 180 s. The server increases the number of divisions by one after updating the delivery schedule. The delivery schedule is updated when half of the delivery cycle of S_1 has elapsed after starting to delivery it.

In Fig. 3, the waiting time of the proposed method is further reduced beyond that of the simple method. In the proposed method, the waiting time that occurs in the updated schedule is reduced by setting a new channel to deliver the segments. On the other hand, the simple method does not update the delivery schedule until the finishing time of delivering the last segment, which increases the waiting time. For example, when the number of segments is increased from 3 to 4, the waiting time of the proposed method is about 84.7 s, and that of the simple method is about 139.8 s. The proposed method reduces the waiting time by about 39.4% compared to the simple method.

4.3 Available Bandwidth and Waiting Time

We evaluated the waiting time according to the available bandwidth. The evaluation result is shown in Fig. 4. The horizontal axis is the available bandwidth, and the vertical axis is the waiting time. The number of segments is three and the playing time is 180 s.

In Fig. 4, the waiting time of the proposed method is further reduced beyond that of the simple method. In the proposed method, by scheduling new segments using the increased bandwidth, the overall waiting time is reduced by reducing the waiting time for S_1' after the update. For example, when the available bandwidth is 7.5 Mbps and the number of segments is 3, the waiting time is about 120.1 s for the proposed method and 176.9 s for the simple method. The proposed method reduces the waiting time by about 32.1% compared to the simple method.

5   Conclusion

In this paper, we proposed a scheduling method that considers the dynamic updating of video data in division-based broadcasting. The proposed method reduces the waiting time by allocating updated segments to the channels with the earliest finishing time of the segment being delivered. Simulation evaluation confirmed that the waiting time of the proposed method is further reduced beyond that of the simple method.

In the future, we plan to design and implement a scheduling method by considering the dynamic update of video data in a division-based broadcasting system and to evaluate the usefulness of the proposed method.

Acknowledgment. This work was supported by JSPS KAKENHI Grant Number JP21H03429 and JP22H03587, JSPS Bilateral Joint Research Project (JPJSBP120229932), and the JGC-S Scholarship Foundation.

References

1. Inoue, Y., Gotoh, Y.: A method to reduce waiting time for heterogeneous clients considering division ratios of video data. In: Proceedings of the 15th International Conference on Advances in Mobile Computing and Multimedia (MoMM 2017), pp. 92–96 (2017)
2. Kanamoto, S., Gotoh, Y.: A division-based broadcasting system considering dynamic updates of delivery schedule. In: Proceedings of the 17th International Conference on Advances in Mobile Computing and Multimedia (MoMM 2019), pp. 175–184 (2019)
3. Gotoh, Y., Nishino, K.: A scheduling method for division-based broadcasting considering consumption rate of multiple videos. In: Proceeding the Advances in Network-based Information Systems (NBiS-2020), pp. 327–337 (2020)
4. Juhn, L., Tseng, L.: Fast Data Broadcasting and Receiving Scheme for Popular Video Service. IEEE Trans. on Broadcasting **44**(1), 100–105 (1998)
5. Zhu, X., Pan, R., Dukkipati, N., Subramanian, V., Bonomi, F.: Layered Internet Video Engineering (LIVE): network-assisted bandwidth sharing and transient loss protection for scalable video streaming. In: Proceeding IEEE INFOCOM, pp. 226–230 (2010)
6. Xiao, W., Agarwal, S., Starobinski, D., Trachtenberg, A.: Reliable wireless broadcasting with near-zero feedback. In: Proceeding IEEE INFOCOM, pp. 2543–2551 (2010)
7. Fountoulakis, N., Huber A., Panagiotou, K.: Reliable broadcasting in random networks and the effect of density. In: Proceeding IEEE INFOCOM, pp. 2552–2560 (2010)
8. Wang, X., Cai, G., Men, J.: Wrap Harmonic Broadcasting and Receiving Scheme for Popular Video Service. IEEE Trans. Broadcast. **66**(1), 78–87 (2019)
9. Upreti, K., Verma, A., Jain, R., Bekuma, Y.: Broadcasting Scheme for Real Time Video in mobile Adhoc Network. Turkish J. Comput. Math. Educ. **12**(11), 3799–3803 (2021)
10. Yoshihisa, T., Tsukamoto, M., Nishio, S.: A broadcasting scheme for continuous media data with restrictions in data division. In: Proceeding IPSJ International Conference on Mobile Computing and Ubiquitous Networking (ICMU '05), pp. 90–95 (2005)

Mobile Computing and Wireless Sensors

Simulating Scenarios to Evaluate Data Filtering Techniques for Mobile Users

Sergio Ilarri[1]([✉])(iD), Raquel Trillo-Lado[1](iD), Ángel Arraez[2], and Alejandro Piedrafita[2]

[1] I3A, Universidad de Zaragoza, 50018 Zaragoza, Spain
{silarri,raqueltl}@unizar.es
[2] Universidad de Zaragoza, 50018 Zaragoza, Spain
{757203,757311}@unizar.es

Abstract. Citizens are nowadays being flooded with huge amounts of information, which will keep growing as the physical spaces become more intelligent, with the proliferation of sensors (e.g., pollution sensors, traffic sensors, etc.), mobile apps, and information services of different types (e.g., malls providing offers and other kinds of information to nearby customers). To actually become resilient modern citizens, people need to be able to handle all this highly-dynamic information and act upon it by taking suitable decisions. In this context, the development of suitable data management techniques to help citizens in their daily life plays a major role.

Motivated by this, we focus on the design of novel data management techniques for mobile users (pedestrians) and for drivers, which are two key areas in the daily life of citizens. More specifically, we consider the problem of recommending relevant items to pedestrians (e.g., tourists) and the challenges of drivers when they try to find an available parking space. As evaluating data management strategies in a real environment in a large-scale is very challenging, in this paper we propose suitable simulation approaches that facilitate the evaluation task. Through simulations, we obtain some initial experimental results that show the additional difficulties that appear when we want to satisfy additional constraints such as the desire to minimize the risk of virus spread in a COVID-19 scenario.

Keywords: Data management · Mobile computing · Recommender systems · Parking spaces

1 Introduction

The development of suitable data management techniques to help citizens in their daily life can provide significant benefits. People are usually overloaded with huge amounts of data (sensor data, information provided by mobile apps and information services of different types, etc.) that may be potentially relevant to take suitable decisions, but "finding the needle in the haystack" is difficult. As if that were not enough, modern cities can be involved in events that imply

© The Author(s), under exclusive license to Springer Nature Switzerland AG 2022
P. Delir Haghighi et al. (Eds.): MoMM 2022, LNCS 13634, pp. 87–101, 2022.
https://doi.org/10.1007/978-3-031-20436-4_9

sudden major changes in the way they need to interact with each other. This could be due to issues such as the climate change, natural disasters, or pandemics like the recent COVID-19.

Indeed, several key features characterize the current situation and demand novel approaches to facilitate the access by users to the data they require: 1) recent profound changes in the way that citizens behave, move, travel and socialize, due to the impact of the COVID-19, which calls for a redefinition of classical mobile information systems and data-oriented approaches; and 2) the need to raise social awareness among citizens so that they can adopt responsible behaviors to face current world-wide challenges such as the risk of spreading viruses like the COVID-19 and the environmental impact of daily activities such as spending time driving to try to find an available parking space.

While the world-wide context is imposing a high penalty on the quality of life of citizens, by designing appropriate data management techniques it is possible to contribute to a better daily life for people and also to foster suitable behaviors in such a way that the existing modern challenges that we face as a society can be tackled. Thus, we argue that traditional data management techniques used to develop information services and applications for mobile users need to be adapted to be useful, effective, and impactful in the current circumstances that permeate our lives due to the COVID-19 pandemic [10] and the existing environmental risks, and could also help to protect us from other future threats that we will need to face.

In this context, within the NEAT-AMBIENCE project (http://webdiis. unizar.es/~silarri/NEAT-AMBIENCE/), we aim at developing a general framework for the distributed management of data to tackle the challenges of the modern citizen in several scenarios and advance the state of the art regarding the design of next-generation data management strategies for mobile users. Moreover, we envision different use cases to consider, related to tourism, resources for drivers, health data, and agriculture. More specifically, we currently focus on the design of novel data management techniques for mobile users (e.g., pedestrians) and for drivers, which are two key areas to cover in the project. However, evaluating those techniques in the real-world is challenging, as we would need many users behaving in specific ways in order to verify if the techniques applied are really effective and provide a benefit.

In this paper, we present simulation tools that can be used to evaluate data management approaches in those two situations, as well as some illustrative initial experimental using those tools. The structure of the rest of the paper is as follows. Firstly, in Sect. 2, we present the two types of scenarios considered in the paper: recommending items to mobile users and helping drivers to find a resource such as an available parking space. Secondly, in Sect. 3, we describe our approach to simulate environments for the evaluation of recommender systems for mobile users. Thirdly, in Sect. 4, we present a simulation approach to evaluate data management techniques to help drivers in the difficult task of finding a suitable available parking space. Fourthly, in Sect. 5, we present some initial experimental results that illustrate the potential use of the simulators. Finally, in Sect. 6, we summarize our conclusions and lines of future work.

2   Data Filtering-Based Mobile Information Services

In this section, we present two representative types of information services for mobile users, that are the current focus of our work: mobile context-aware recommender systems (Sect. 2.1) and information services for drivers (Sect. 2.2).

2.1   Social-Distance and Context-Aware Mobile Recommender Systems

To tackle the problem of information overload in the current Big Data era, recommender systems (RS) [5], have acquired a great importance and attracted the attention of researchers and practitioners as well as companies and other organizations. When faced with a myriad of possible choices about a certain type of items (e.g., books to read, movies to watch, music to listen to, hotels to stay, restaurants to have dinner, etc.) or activities (e.g., different types of activities that can be performed while visiting a city as a tourist), a personalized recommender system can help the user to choose an option that suits his/her specific personal preferences. For that purpose, recommender systems can consider attributes of the user (like his/her age, gender, etc.) and data about user preferences collected through explicit feedback (e.g., when the user consumes an item, he/she can provide an assessment/rating in a numeric scale, for example, giving a rating in a scale of 0 to 5, or at least indicate whether he/she liked or not that item) and/or implicit ratings (i.e., actions performed by the user, such as watching a movie in its entirety or quickly abandoning its viewing, that can lead to inferences about his/her interests).

From an abstract perspective, a recommender system could be conceived as an intelligent piece of software that receives two inputs, the identifiers of a user and of an item, and returns the predicted rating that the user is expected to provide for that item. If the predicted rating is above a minimum relevance threshold, then it could be recommended to the user; otherwise, it is assumed not to be of enough interest to that user, and therefore it should not be recommended to him/her. This is a simplified vision, given the huge variety of techniques proposed in the field of recommender systems, but enough for our purposes.

Traditional recommender systems operate in a two-dimensional space (User x Item → Rating). However, more recently, research has been invested in the development of Context-Aware Recommender Systems (CARS) [1,5], which also incorporate the context (leading to a User x Item x Context → Rating space) to provide suggestions that are well adapted to the current circumstances of the user and the items (typical context variables include the location of the user, his/her current mood, if he/she is accompanied by other persons or not, the weather conditions, the hour of the day, etc.). CARS are particularly relevant to mobile computing scenarios [13], where users move and their context can quickly change. Popular application scenarios include the area of tourism, where a mobile recommender system can suggest relevant Points of Interest (POIs) or activities to perform when visiting a city.

Given the current COVID-19 pandemic, we believe that a new type of mobile CARS is needed, which we call Side-CARS (SocIal-Distance prEserving CARS) [10]. This type of CARS should ensure the required social distancing between users when providing them with recommendations. In this paper, we consider the term "social distance" in a broad sense, as in some scenarios the crowdedness/congestion of an area could be more important than the direct physical distance between people. Considering these aspects may lead to suggestions that are suboptimal in terms of the estimated overall benefit to the user, but on the other hand the probability of risk for the user and other pedestrians is minimized, which is an essential element that must be maintained.

As an example, imagine a scenario where a tourist enters a museum and has only a limited amount of time to visit it (e.g., one hour). In this scenario, he/she could benefit from the use of a recommender system that suggests specific pieces of art to contemplate in the museum. Such a recommender system should plan a trajectory that tries to maximize the satisfaction of the user during his/her visit to the museum, but that at the same time minimizes the risk of violating the social distance that must be kept with other visitors. COVID-19 regulations and others established due to health concerns could also limit the maximum number of persons in certain areas. Besides, different contextual variables could also be considered when providing the recommendations, such as the current mood of the user, the purpose of his/her visit (leisure, knowledge expansion, etc.), and other features (e.g., his/her age, if he/she moves in a wheelchair, etc.).

2.2   Social-Distance-Preserving Information Services for Drivers

The second type of data management techniques that we consider are those useful for the development of information services for drivers. We consider particularly services that provide information about resources on the roads that can be of interest to drivers (these might also be considered recommender systems for drivers). Examples of such resources are available parking spaces, gas stations, specific spots to refuel/recharge the vehicle within a given gas/charging station, restaurants and coffees shops on highways, drop-off areas for passengers using a ride-hailing company (such as Uber), etc. Some of these resources are scarce, and so different drivers may need to "compete" to use them (in this case, if a specific resource is being used by a driver, it cannot be used by another driver at the same time), like in the case of parking spaces. Other resources, such as a restaurant in a service area, could allow multiple users at the same time, as long as their maximum capacity is not exceeded.

A typical example is searching for available parking spaces, which is the type of resource that we consider in this paper, due to its relevance. The problem of searching for an available parking space is a time-consuming and unpleasant task for drivers, subject to many difficulties due to the high number of vehicles, particularly in big cities. Besides, due to the large amounts of time invested in searching for parking, this task leads to considerable fuel consumption and the associated atmospheric pollution, which in turn negatively affects the health of people. Studies such as those cited in [15] indicate that a significant percentage of cars wandering the roads are just searching for parking (as much as 30% in some scenarios, according to those studies). The use of private transportation could increase in a virus-spreading situation, as people will be afraid of contacts with others or with surfaces potentially infected in public transportation means such as buses or trams, which besides in some cases may be overcrowded. This could aggravate the problem of finding available parking spaces even more, due to a higher number of private cars traveling through the roads. Moreover, there seems to be a worrying correlation between air pollution and the dissemination of respiratory infections (like COVID-19) [6]; more specifically, it seems that more pollution entails more risk of a respiratory disease, so minimizing the air pollution (e.g., by reducing the time to park) may help to reduce the spread of those types of diseases.

Therefore, the development of smart parking solutions that can help drivers to find an available parking space is a relevant task to tackle. Although this is not a new topic, we believe that the existing proposals are not suitable in the current scenario, as they do not explicitly incorporate the notion of social distance or crowdedness; therefore, they could provide the driver information about available parking spaces that, if taken, could lead to risks concerning the need to keep a suitable interpersonal distance when leaving the car (and when walking towards the final destination). We think that it is important to keep in mind that a parking space is in many cases the initial point from which social distancing must be preserved. For example, when leaving a car that has just been parked, the driver and other passengers are likely to spend some time to pick up things from the car trunk. This is especially critical for an underground parking, as the probability of dispersion of the virus increases in indoor environments and these kinds of parking usually have deficient ventilation (direct ventilation through windows is not possible in the case of underground parking structures); moreover, in some occasions there are also air conditioning systems that can contribute to further dissemination of the virus by recirculating the air [14]. According to [16], "normal speech generates airborne droplets that can remain suspended for tens of minutes or longer and are eminently capable of transmitting disease in confined spaces" and talking can spread more than 1000 COVID-19 particles per minute. Considering [16], five minutes of speaking face-to-face can be enough to become infected, and according to [12] it is possible to get infected even with five minutes at a distance higher than six meters and without any direct or indirect contact, so it is always a good idea to minimize exposure.

Finally, as far as we know, existing approaches for the problem of parking do not consider other context data (e.g., the weather conditions, if the purpose of the trip is leisure or work, if the passengers would not mind walking a little bit until the final destination, etc.) or the characteristics and needs of the people traveling in the car (e.g., some passengers could be children, old people, people needing a wheelchair, etc.) to offer a suitable parking space.

Developing novel data management solutions to help drivers to find available parking spaces can provide clear benefits against the current challenges, as this activity leads to huge amounts of fuel consumption, drivers' dissatisfaction, and above all unneeded atmospheric pollution, which can in turn have an effect on health and the propagation of virus infections; besides, by guiding drivers to suitable and safe parking spaces, risky areas can be avoided. Although we focus on parking spaces, similar benefits can be obtained if appropriate data management techniques are developed for other types of resources. For example, some cities have started regulating the areas where the vehicles of ride-hailing companies can drop their passengers, and so a drop-off area can also be seen as a competitive resource; moreover, the passengers themselves can be considered as resources for the drivers of these companies and appropriate data management strategies could be developed to try to minimize the amount of time spent traveling in the vehicle at the same time by passengers belonging to different households. The problem of mobile resource search is still an open research problem and the current virus-related challenges make it even more relevant and complex.

3   Simulation of Scenarios to Evaluate Mobile Recommenders

In previous work, we developed an ad hoc simulator to represent two floors of the Museum of Modern Art in New York (MoMA) and users moving around the museum and providing ratings about the works of art they visualize [3,4]. That simulator served its purposes, but it was too limited in scope, as it does not allow simulating other scenarios and easily performing tests in other situations that may be required. Besides, its performance was limited, as the simulations were very time-consuming. Motivated by this, we have developed a generic simulator that supports defining other types of scenarios, called *RecMobiSim* (see website at [9]). Furthermore, the new simulator incorporates editing facilities, in such a way that it is possible to build and define maps of scenarios by using the same tool (see Fig. 1). Some of the key features of the simulator include:

– *Definition and edition of scenarios.* The simulator includes an editor, which allows defining maps of scenarios and editing existing maps (e.g., drawing, erasing, selecting, moving and editing the attributes of elements in the scenario). Maps can represent the layout of buildings with several floors, connected through stairs/lifts. A floor can be composed of several rooms (represented by polygons) connected to each other through doors; floors can be stored independently and combined in a single map, if desired. Besides, it is possible to populate the rooms with objects/items that can be visited and rated by the users (e.g., works of art in the case of a museum), either automatically or by indicating explicitly the location of each of these objects; these visitable objects are painted using an icon (that depends on its specific type) and can be stored and loaded independently of the scenario map (assuming that their location is compatible with the scenario map, as every object must

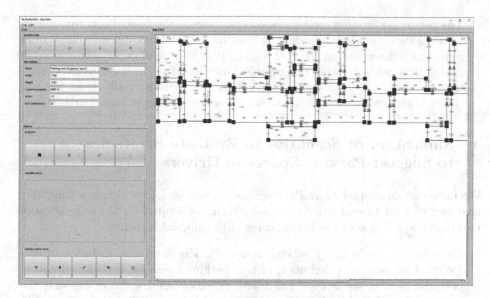

Fig. 1. RecMobiSim: map editor

be located within a room in the scenario). Several functionalities are provided
to facilitate the designing/editing task (e.g., it is possible to zoom in/out and
specify the desired proportion between pixels and meters).

– *Simulation of scenarios.* The simulator allows simulating (previously-defined)
scenarios. A wide set of configuration parameters can be set in order to determine how the simulation will evolve along time. Some parameters affect more
directly the simulation (e.g., the amount of time to simulate, the speed of the
mobile users simulated, etc.) and others the experimentation (e.g., the recommendation algorithm that will be used by the mobile users simulated that
use a recommender application, parameters of the recommendation algorithm,
and the type of communication used by the mobile users –if it is relevant for
the selected recommender algorithm–, which could be peer-to-peer –P2P– or
client/server using a centralized approach). For example, through the configuration it is possible to set a fixed random seed (affecting the generation of
random numbers in the simulator) in order to enable repeatable simulations.
Furthermore, the tester can start, stop, pause and resume the simulation at
any time. In each scenario, a set of mobile users will move around (respect-
ing expected rules of movement, such as the impossibility to traverse walls),
visit items and rate them, as required. The user ratings must be provided as
an input to the simulator (they could be part of an existing dataset [11] or
generated synthetically by using a tool such as DataGenCARS [2]).

– *Support for the evaluation of recommender systems.* The final goal of the
simulator is to facilitate the evaluation of the performance of different types
of recommender systems. Therefore, several statistics are collected during
the simulation, that allows comparing the recommender systems evaluated.

The person performing the evaluation can indicate the desired correspondence between the simulated time and the real time (e.g., one second simulated could represent ten seconds in the real world). It is also possible to perform batch evaluations, without using the graphical user interface, in order to have unattended evaluations and collect multiple results automatically (e.g., varying the recommender system used and/or the selected configuration parameters).

4   Simulation of Scenarios to Evaluate Strategies to Suggest Parking Spaces to Drivers

We have also developed *SimulParking* (see website at [8]), which is a simulator that can be used to evaluate data management techniques for the suggestion of parking spaces. Some of the key features of the simulator include:

- *Definition and edition of parking scenarios.* The simulator includes an editor, that supports the definition of new parking scenarios and the edition of previous parking scenarios defined with this tool (see Fig. 2). It supports the construction of parking structures composed by several floors (connected to each other through ramps that lead from one floor to another), as it is typical, for example, in a mall's parking. Templates can be used to quickly create a parking lot with the features provided (number of rows and columns, size of each parking space, etc.). Alternatively, a toolbar includes tools to define parking lots by drawing each of the elements required (horizontal and/or vertical parking spaces, exits for pedestrians, ramps, road arrows to mark the direction of the traffic flow on each road, sidewalks, entries and exits for vehicles, etc.). Several functionalities are included to facilitate the definition of scenarios, like the possibility to modify the zoom level, the possibility to select several items at the same time and move them around the scenario, etc.
- *Simulation of scenarios.* The simulator allows simulating parking lots that have been previously defined with the tool. For this purpose, it is possible to set several parameters that control how vehicles enter the parking lot, mark a number of parking spaces as occupied, mark specific parking spaces as available or occupied, simulate the existence of pedestrians in the scenario (e.g., placing them randomly in the scenario or defining hot spots where the density of pedestrians is particularly high), etc. It is possible to perform GUI-based simulations, where you can see how the simulation evolves in the graphical user interface, and also batch-based simulations with no GUI.
- *Detection of risky areas.* It is possible to use two different approaches to detect areas that entail potential risk from the perspective of spreading of a virus (like the COVID-19), presented in [7]: the *centroid-based method* adds a penalty if the distance between the center of the parking spot and the centroid of a cluster of pedestrians is smaller than the required safety distance, and the *intersection and density-based method* obtains the fragment of each parking space intersected by a risky area around a cluster and also considers the density of the cluster to compute a *cluster-specific safety distance* for that

cluster (the required safety distance plus an extra safety margin depending on the risk of that cluster).

- *Support for the evaluation of parking suggestion strategies.* The final goal is to be able to evaluate the performance of different strategies to suggest parking spaces to drivers entering the parking lot. For this purpose, different algorithms can be evaluated. Currently, we have implemented a strategy that initially tries to recommend a parking space that is completely risk-free (by using the method selected to detect risky areas), and if this is not possible then the method tries to recommend a parking space with low (but non-zero) risk. When there are several candidate parking spaces that are equally valid, one out of four different strategies can be applied to determine the parking space that will be recommended: *random*, which simply returns one parking space among the candidates; *closest-to-driver*, which suggests the candidate parking space that is the closest to the driver; *closest-to-pedestrian-exit*, which recommends the candidate parking space that minimizes the walking distance from the parking space to the pedestrian's exit of the parking lot (e.g., in the case of a mall, a parking space that is near the customers' entrance to the mall); and *first-floors-first*, which tries to fill the different floors of the parking lot one by one, starting with the first floor.

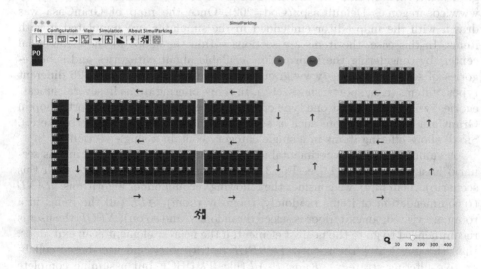

Fig. 2. SimulParking: example of a one-floor parking lot

Thanks to the previous functionalities, we can perform experimental evaluations like the ones presented in [7] (where we defined parking lots manually and evaluated strategies in a static way using *Matlab*) much more easily and flexibly. Furthermore, SimulParking can be integrated with a new version of the MAVSIM simulator [17, 18], which is a simulator of vehicular ad-hoc networks for the evaluation of mobile agent-based data management strategies, where we are also currently developing an extension that allows simulating on-street parking spaces in a city.

5   Experimental Evaluation

In this section, we present an initial experimental evaluation performed using the two simulators described in the paper. First, in Sect. 5.1, we present some experiments using RecMobiSim. Then, in Sect. 5.2, we show experiments with SimulParking.

5.1   Experiments with RecMobiSim

First of all, we performed some experiments with the MoMA scenario, to verify that the experimental results obtained with the new simulator are similar to our previous experimental results presented in [3,4]. Then, we performed experiments with a second scenario. Specifically, we edited a map to represent a commercial center, GranCasa, which is located in Zaragoza (Spain). To define the map, we considered data provided in the website of GranCasa (https://www.grancasa.es/mapa) and the Official College of Architects of Aragón (https://www.coaaragon.es/Default.aspx?Cod=202). Once the map of GranCasa was drawn with the map editor embedded in the simulator, we populated it with items. In this case, the items are sections within the shops in the commercial center; by considering the information available about categories and subcategories of services (https://www.grancasa.es/tiendas/?), we defined 26 different types of items (e.g., sports, shoes, etc.). In shops offering items in several subcategories, we create at least one type of item per category (e.g., one sports shop in GranCasa includes sections such as soccer, mountain climbing, basketball, etc.). Small shops offering items in a single category contain a single section.

A summary of the experimental settings used for the evaluation in this scenario is shown in Table 1 (see Fig. 3 for a snapshot of the simulator with this scenario). As in [3,4], we consider the following recommender algorithms: *RAND* (recommendation of items randomly, room by room), *ALL* (all the items in a room are visited, an exit/door is selected randomly, and so on), *NPOI* (the user is recommended to go to the nearest element; if the nearest element is an exit/door, then the user leaves the room), *T&UBCF* (a trajectory and user-based collaborative filtering strategy), *Know-It-All* (like T&UBCF but assuming complete knowledge about all the real ratings that the other visitors would provide), and *K-Ideal* (an ideal solution, where the k items that will receive the highest user ratings are recommended, ordered by the shortest trajectory visiting them).

As an example, Fig. 4 shows the average satisfaction of the user with each recommendation strategy, computed as the average of the ratings provided by the user for the items recommended and visited in the commercial center (in a scale of 0 to 5). T&UBCF provides the best average satisfaction, leaving aside the two unrealistic alternatives (Know-It-All and K-Ideal). Similar conclusions

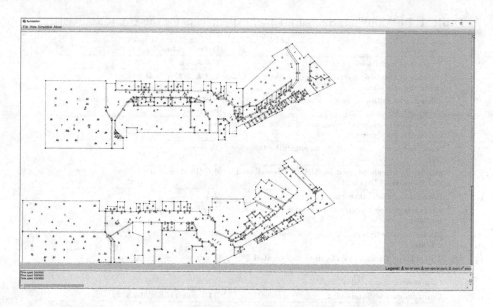

Fig. 3. RecMobiSim: simulation running in the GranCasa scenario

to those shown in [3, 4] for the scenario of the MoMA Museum can be obtained; nevertheless, in this case the size of the scenario is much larger and, as we keep the same number of users as in the museum simulator (176), this has an impact on some aspects of the evaluation. The currently-tested recommendation algorithms can lead to situations where the safety distance is not respected or to overcrowded areas, so alternative recommendation approaches can be proposed.

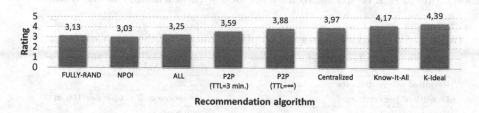

Fig. 4. RecMobiSim: average satisfaction with the items observed (GranCasa)

5.2   Experiments with the Parking Simulator

In this section, we present an example of an evaluation performed with Simul-Parking. Again, we consider the commercial center GranCasa (https://www.grancasa.es/), but in this case we focus on the three floors of a segment of its parking lot (as an example, see floor P2 in Fig. 5), with the basic experimental

Table 1. RecMobiSim: configuration of experiments for the *GranCasa* scenario

Parameter	Default value
Number of mobile users & Visit time	176 & 1 h
Number of items & Average speed of users & Time observing the items	283 & 5 Km/h & 30 s
Trajectories followed by users not using a recommender	NPOI (go to the Nearest Point of Interest)
Time needed to change from one floor to another (using the stairs or lift)	60 s
Number of recommended items shown to the user (K)	10 items
Similarity threshold used for UBCF (User-Based Collaborative Filtering)	0.5 (Pearson correlation)
Recommendation threshold (1–5)	2.5
Knowledge base increment threshold (to re-learn models)	40 new ratings
Minimum time interval between recommendation updates	30 s
TTL (Time To Live) of the data propagated through P2P	3 min
Communication latency	1 s
Communication bandwidth	54 Mbps (IEEE 802.11g)
Communication range in P2P mode	250 m
Time between user's mood updates	1800 s (30 min)

settings summarized in Table 2. We defined two entries in the parking lot; when a new vehicle arrives, we assumed that it enters through one of the two entries randomly. For simplicity, in this section, we focus on the metric that indicates the *parking time* needed by a vehicle entering the parking (excluding the time needed for parking maneuver). Each simulation was repeated 50 times and average values were computed; we also obtained the 95% confidence intervals (not shown due to lack of space), to have an idea of the variability of the results.

Table 2. SimulParking: configuration of experiments for the *GranCasa* scenario

Parameter	Default value
Required safety distance	2 m
Density of pedestrians	Average of 2 people per 100 m^2
Speed of vehicles	20 Km/h
Strategy to select among the candidate parking spaces	*closest-to-driver*
Repetitions to report average values	50 repetitions per experiment

As an example, in Fig. 6, we show the average parking time needed by a vehicle when we apply a centroid-based risk detection method, depending on the percentage of already-occupied parking spaces. Besides, we also show the parking time needed when the risk is not considered and the vehicle just tries to park in the closest parking space instead. As expected, the time to park increases when the parking lot is fuller. However, we can see that the parking times are

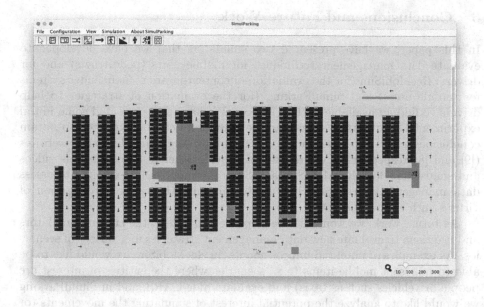

Fig. 5. SimulParking: parking with three floors – floor P2

quite limited in any case, which shows that in this scenario it is possible to consider the risk of parking spaces without much impact on the time needed to find a parking space. Other experiments show that increasing the density of pedestrians leads to higher parking times when risky areas are to be avoided, but not dramatically. Similarly, when several vehicles enter the parking space during a period of time, they contribute to decreasing the availability of parking spaces, which affects the parking time.

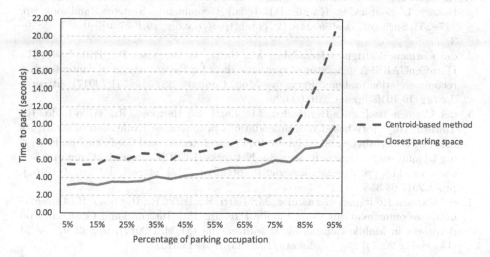

Fig. 6. SimulParking: evaluation of the time to park

6   Conclusions and Future Work

In this paper, we have presented two simulators that we have developed to evaluate data management techniques for mobile users (pedestrians) and for drivers: RecMobiSim (for the evaluation of context-aware recommender systems for mobile users) and SimulParking (for the evaluation of strategies to help drivers to find an available parking space). We have also presented some initial experimental results that show how the simulators can be exploited to obtain conclusions in a variety of scenarios. The simulators are available in their websites ([9] and [8], respectively), where we also provide other resources such as videos and snapshots. Both RecMobiSim and SimulParking can be exploited to assess data management strategies that try to minimize the risk of propagation of viruses such as the COVID-19.

As future work, we would like to improve and extend the current simulators and use them to evaluate new data management strategies in a variety of scenarios. As examples of potential improvements, in RecMobiSim we would like to be able to represent mobile items (e.g., scenarios where the entities of interest are people or vehicles such as taxis) and evaluate Side-CARS, and in SimulParking we would like to analyze the potential interest of simulating the movements (or specific behaviors) of pedestrians within the parking lots.

Acknowledgements. This work belongs to the project PID2020-113037RB-I00, funded by MCIN/AEI/ 10.13039/501100011033. We also thank the support of the Departamento de Ciencia, Universidad y Sociedad del Conocimiento del Gobierno de Aragón (Government of Aragon: Group Reference T64_20R, COSMOS group).

References

1. Adomavicius, G., Tuzhilin, A.: Context-aware recommender systems. In: Ricci, F., Rokach, L., Shapira, B., Kantor, P.B. (eds.) Recommender Systems Handbook, pp. 217–253. Springer, Boston, MA (2011). https://doi.org/10.1007/978-0-387-85820-3_7

2. del Carmen Rodríguez-Hernández, M., Ilarri, S., Hermoso, R., Trillo-Lado, R.: DataGenCARS: A generator of synthetic data for the evaluation of context-aware recommendation systems. Pervasive Mob. Comput. **38**, 516–541 (2017). https://doi.org/10.1016/j.pmcj.2016.09.020

3. del Carmen Rodríguez-Hernández, M., Ilarri, S., Hermoso, R., Trillo-Lado, R.: Towards trajectory-based recommendations in museums: Evaluation of strategies using mixed synthetic and real data. In: Eighth International Conference on Emerging Ubiquitous Systems and Pervasive Networks (EUSPN). Procedia Computer Science, vol. 113, pp. 234–239. Elsevier (September 2017). https://doi.org/10.1016/j.procs.2017.08.355

4. del Carmen Rodríguez-Hernández, M., Ilarri, S., Trillo, R., Hermoso, R.: Context-aware recommendations using mobile P2P. In: 15th International Conference on Advances in Mobile Computing & Multimedia (MoMM 2017), pp. 82–91. ACM (December 2017). https://doi.org/10.1145/3151848.3151856

5. del Carmen Rodríguez-Hernández, M., Ilarri, S.: AI-based mobile context-aware recommender systems from an information management perspective: Progress and directions. Knowl. Based Syst. **215**, 106740 (2021). https://doi.org/10.1016/j.knosys.2021.106740
6. Conticini, E., Frediani, B., Caro, D.: Can atmospheric pollution be considered a co-factor in extremely high level of SARS-CoV-2 lethality in Northern Italy? Environ. Pollut. **261**, 1–3 (2020). https://doi.org/10.1016/j.envpol.2020.114465
7. Delot, T., Ilarri, S.: Let my car alone: Parking strategies with social-distance preservation in the age of COVID-19. In: 11th International Conference on Emerging Ubiquitous Systems and Pervasive Networks (EUSPN 2020). Procedia Computer Science, vol. 177, pp. 143–150. Elsevier (November 2020). https://doi.org/10.1016/j.procs.2020.10.022
8. Ilarri, S., Arraez, A.: SimulParking website (July 2022). http://webdiis.unizar.es/~silarri/prot/SimulParking/
9. Ilarri, S., Piedrafita, A.: RecMobiSim website (July 2022). http://webdiis.unizar.es/~silarri/prot/RecMobiSim/
10. Ilarri, S., Trillo-Lado, R., Delot, T.: Social-distance aware data management for mobile computing. In: 18th International Conference on Advances in Mobile Computing & Multimedia (MoMM 2020), pp. 138–142. ACM (November-December 2020). https://doi.org/10.1145/3428690.3429164
11. Ilarri, S., Trillo-Lado, R., Hermoso, R.: Datasets for context-aware recommender systems: Current context and possible directions. In: First Workshop on Context in Analytics (CiA 2018), in conjunction with the 34th International Conference on Data Engineering (ICDE 2018), pp. 25–28. IEEE Computer Society (April 2018). https://doi.org/10.1109/ICDEW.2018.00011
12. Kwon, K.S., Park, J.I., Park, Y.J., Jung, D.M., Ryu, K.W., Lee, J.H.: Evidence of long-distance droplet transmission of SARS-CoV-2 by direct air flow in a restaurant in Korea. J. Korean Med. Sci. **35**(46), e415 (2020). https://doi.org/10.3346/jkms.2020.35.e415
13. Liu, Q., Ma, H., Chen, E., Xiong, H.: A survey of context-aware mobile recommendations. Int. J. Inf. Technol. Decis. Making **12**(1), 139–172 (2013). https://doi.org/10.1142/S0219622013500077
14. Lu, J., et al.: COVID-19 outbreak associated with air conditioning in restaurant, Guangzhou, China, 2020. Emerg. Infect. Dis. **26**(7), 1628–1631 (2020). https://doi.org/10.3201/eid2607.200764
15. Shoup, D.C.: Cruising for parking. Transp. Policy **13**(6), 479–486 (2006). https://doi.org/10.1016/j.tranpol.2006.05.005
16. Stadnytskyi, V., Bax, C.E., Bax, A., Anfinrud, P.: The airborne lifetime of small speech droplets and their potential importance in SARS-CoV-2 transmission. Proc. Natl. Acad. Sci. **117**(22), 11875–11877 (2020). https://doi.org/10.1073/pnas.2006874117
17. Urra, O., Ilarri, S.: MAVSIM: Testing VANET Applications Based on Mobile Agents, chap. 10, pp. 199–224. CRC Press - Taylor & Francis Group (2016). https://doi.org/10.1201/b19351-14
18. Urra, O., Ilarri, S.: MAVSIM website (May 2017). http://webdiis.unizar.es/~silarri/prot/MAVSIM/

BetterPlanet: Sustainability Feedback from Digital Receipts

Simeon Pilz[1]([✉])[iD], Jing Wu[1][iD], Sybilla Merian[2][iD], Simon Mayer[1][iD], and Klaus Fuchs[3][iD]

[1] University of St. Gallen, St. Gallen, Switzerland
pilz.simeon@gmail.com
[2] University of Zurich, Zurich, Switzerland
[3] ETH Zurich, Zurich, Switzerland

Abstract. The global food system accounts for 25–30% of anthropogenic greenhouse gas emissions. A large share of these emissions is due to individual food shopping patterns. Despite the rising concern about the environment, many individuals fail to act upon it and change their food consumption. In this study, we attempt to motivate individuals to reduce their food-shopping-induced environmental footprint. To narrow the intention-behavior gap, we propose a novel technical system that gives automated near-term sustainability feedback on individuals' food shopping recorded on digital receipts and communicates this feedback through the mobile application *BetterPlanet*, Based on a small sample (n = 8), we find a directional decrease in the overall CO_2-Scores. Therefore, our study demonstrates the technical feasibility of automated sustainability feedback from digital receipts. The proposed energy-weighted CO_2-Scoring Model contributes to the growing knowledge body of sustainability assessment.

Keywords: Greenhouse gas emission · Digital receipts · Data portability · Food shopping behavior

1 Introduction

Today, our food system is responsible for roughly 25–30% of global greenhouse gas emissions [5]. Particularly in high-income countries such as Switzerland, transforming current consumption practices is promising for reaching the stated global sustainability goals [8]. Although a shift in higher-order consumer values towards more sustainability has been observed [2], this does not automatically translate into more sustainable behavior. This pattern is commonly known as the intention-behavior gap [7]. One of the key determinants of behaving sustainably is motivation [9], which might be supported by providing customers with feedback about their diets. Existing efforts in this field typically rely on consumers to scan products (e.g., CodeCheck[1] or Yuka[2]). The substantial manual effort is

---

[1] https://www.codecheck.info/.
[2] https://yuka.io/.

© The Author(s), under exclusive license to Springer Nature Switzerland AG 2022
P. Delir Haghighi et al. (Eds.): MoMM 2022, LNCS 13634, pp. 102–107, 2022.
https://doi.org/10.1007/978-3-031-20436-4_10

a main explaining factor of the limited success of these systems [3]. We hence claim that a fully automated system is required to motivate consumers to shop more sustainably in the long run.

In this paper, we present the *BetterPlanet* mobile app and infrastructure, a system that provides feedback about the sustainability of individual food shopping behavior and attempts to motivate consumers to shop more sustainably. It automatically evaluates food purchasing data (recorded through loyalty cards) with a novel CO_2-Scoring model and communicates this information to users via the app interfaces. Self-Determination Theory [6] was used as the theoretical baseline for the design of the application. With *BetterPlanet*, we demonstrate the feasibility of a system that provides *fully automated* sustainability feedback about individual food purchasing, and usability of the proposed CO_2-Scoring Model. We present initial results from testing this system with 8 users.

2 The BetterPlanet System and Study

Two recent regulatory mandates by the European Union (EU) – mandated declaration of nutrients on food products sold online[3] and the General Data Protection Regulation[4] – led to a growing availability of structured product data and individual (grocery) shopping data. Against this backdrop, the *BetterPlanet* study has been conducted in Switzerland, where the two leading retailers cover a large share of the market[5] and both have popular loyalty card schemes. To simplify the process of requesting user shopping data, we work with BitsaboutMe[6] (BAM), a Swiss GDPR-compliant service that requests, stores, and shares user grocery data with users' consents. As digital receipts typically use abbreviated product names or broad category labels (e.g., "carrots"), the study team has been maintaining a food composition database EatFit[7], which contains product nutritional information and uniquely identifies products via Global Trade Item Numbers (GTINs). As of June 2022, EatFit contains 53'780 products across 126 categories. The 6'472 most frequently purchased item names have been matched to products identified by GTINs. Thereby, our study covers roughly 50% of all purchased products.

Sustainability information about products is only starting to become publicly available and there is not yet a widely accepted standard of how such sustainability information shall be summarized for consumers. A large number of heterogeneous models and labels exist (e.g., Eaternity Score[8], Eco-Score[9] and

---

[3] https://eur-lex.europa.eu/legal-content/EN/TXT/PDF/?uri=CELEX:
32011R1169.
[4] https://eur-lex.europa.eu/eli/reg/2016/679/oj.
[5] With respective market shares of with 35.1% and 34.8%, see https://www.statista.com/statistics/787298/.
[6] https://bitsabout.me/en/.
[7] https://eatfit-service.foodcoa.ch/static/swagger/.
[8] https://eaternity.org/score/.
[9] https://tinyurl.com/yts49fxj.

Eco Impact[10]). These models use CO_2-eq per kilograms as the baseline, which potentially leads to misinterpretations as heavier foods are not necessarily more calorie-dense. Therefore, our *BetterPlanet* system, which is described in the next chapter, includes a new CO_2-Scoring Model that takes energy content of products (in kilocalories) into account.

2.1 Application Architecture and Design

Application Architecture. The dataflow of the *BetterPlanet* app works as follows. First, the updated shopping data was provided on a daily basis by BAM. Next, the individual article names on receipts were sent to the EatFit database, which returned detailed product information, most importantly the product image URL, the product category, the energy per 100 g product in kilocalories, and the product weight if accessible. This information was then used to calculate the CO_2-Scores and the total impact of food products, as described in Sect. 2.2. The aggregated information was then sent to the back-end (a firebase server), from where the app fetched the data.

Application Design. Main pages of the app are shown in Fig. 1). More can be found on the GitHub repository[11]. In overview (Überblick), ones' food shopping behavior in the last 30 days was illustrated with different charts. Personal Product Range (Persönliches Produktsortiment) displayed all products bought during this time-frame, sorted by their CO2-Scores. Shopping History (Einkäufe) listed all receipts and their aggregated CO_2-Scores chronologically, starting from the most recent one. By clicking on one receipt, user can see all shopped items and their attributes (picture, name, amount, price, and CO_2-Score). Product Details (Produkt Details) displayed more detailed product information (the emission impact of the product (in $kgCO_2$-eq/kg and gCO_2-eq/kcal), the seasonality, the amount of times the user has bought, and details about what is included in the CO_2-Score and its calculation). In Community Challenge (Community Challenge), the average gCO_2-eq/kcal values of users' home cantons were shown to increase participants' relatedness.

2.2 CO_2-Data and CO_2-Scoring Model for *BetterPlanet*

The $kgCO_2$-eq/kg values of products that were used as the basis of calculating CO_2-scores in *BetterPlanet* were primarily taken from the World Food LCA (WFLDB) Database[12]. If products cannot be found in the WFLDB, the Eaternity database[13] was used alternatively. To account for different amount of emissions of organic and non-organic products, emission values from a study of the *Forschungsinstitut für Biologischen Landbau* (FIBL)[14] were taken.

---

[10] https://tinyurl.com/4xr3uf7u.
[11] https://github.com/Interactions-HSG/2022MoMM.
[12] https://simapro.com/products/quantis-world-food-lca-database/.
[13] https://co2.eaternity.ch/.
[14] https://www.fibl.org/de/themen/projektdatenbank/projektitem/project/1486.

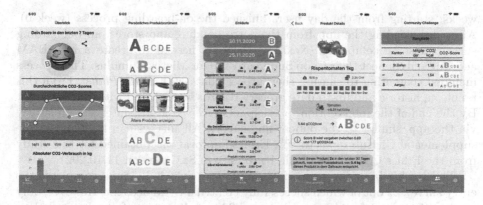

Fig. 1. Overview of the *BetterPlanet* app

We present a novel CO_2-Scoring system that is similar to the well-established Nutri-Score [1] system. The detailed scoring system can be found in Table 1. The CO_2-Score ranges from A (the best) to E (the worst), based on the unit gCO$_2$-eq/kcal. The distribution of the values was determined based on an existing sample (cf. [4]). Specifically, the mean of score C corresponds to the sample's mean (2.214 gCO$_2$-eq/kcal). Scores were then assigned linearly starting from 0 and with no upper bound on score E (see Table 1).

Overall, *BetterPlanet* differentiates between 209 food categories (i.e., 126 EatFit categories combined with our own name matching model). Among these 209 categories, there were 53 with two CO_2-eq-values each, differentiating organic and conventional products.

Table 1. CO$_2$-Scoring Model used in *BetterPlanet*

Score	CO$_2$ Equivalent
A	$\leq$ 0.880 gCO$_2$-eq/kcal[a]
B	< 1.771 gCO$_2$-eq/kcal
C	< 2.657 gCO$_2$-eq/kcal
D	< 3.542 gCO$_2$-eq/kcal
E	>= 3.542 gCO$_2$-eq/kcal

[a] grams of carbon dioxide equivalent per kilocalories.

2.3 Study Participants

Participants were recruited from September 15, 2021 until January 10, 2022 via newsletters, social media, and word of mouth. The intervention lasted three weeks, starting from the day users finished the on-boarding process (week 0). After downloading the app from the corresponding app stores, an onboarding survey must be completed. Next, participants needed to create a new BAM account and connect their Coop Supercard and/or Migros Cumulus. This process included consenting to sharing their grocery data with *BetterPlanet*. From this point on, historic and up-to-date grocery records were shared with *BetterPlanet*. By the end of the intervention, participants received a post-intervention survey via the app, similar to the onboarding survey. All surveys can be found in the supplemental GitHub repository[15]. Ethics approval was obtained for this study from the Ethics Committee of the University of St.Gallen on 11.10.2021.[16].

The app has been downloaded 98 times in total; 36 individuals completed the entry survey, 29 out of which successfully created a BAM account. However, only 8 users (5 male, 3 female, aged between 23 and 45) successfully donated their data, due to technical problems during the consent and data transfer processes. All 8 users who managed to enable the data flow completed the post survey.

3   Results and Discussion

In this paper, a working system was presented that collected food shopping data, provided fully automated feedback about sustainability of food shopping to users, and assessed users' motivation to change their food shopping behavior through an in-app survey. A novel energy-weighted CO_2-Scoring Model was proposed. With 8 participants, we observed a small directional decrease in the average CO_2-eq/kcal values when comparing the pre-intervention phase (week -3 to 0, mean = 1.23 (std = 0.57), purchases = 74) to the intervention phase (week 0–3: mean = 1.07 (std = 0.72), purchases = 43). After the intervention phase, we observed a directional but not significant increase (week 3–6: mean = 1.26 (std =1.06), purchases = 43; week 6–9: mean:1.17 (std = 0.57), purchases = 31). Further studies with bigger samples are needed to reassess these effects.

4   Limitations and Outlook

This novel system comes with multiple limitations. First, the tedious sign-up process and limited recruitment effort led to a small and potentially biased sample. Second, limitations come along with the usage of digital receipts. The biggest challenges are a) loyalty card data represents only people's partial food shopping behavior b) we can only identify around 50% of products (also see [4,10]). We have been dedicated to improving the data quality of the Eatfit database. Further, we encountered several technical issues with the data flow. The data delivery was sometimes significantly delayed because of BAM and required manual fixing. To solve these issues, we are building a modularized and self-sustainable infrastructure. Last, our CO_2-eq-values do not include all emissions from farm to fork (data about transportation, storage, and cooling are missing), are calculated on a category level, and only represent one sustainability-dimension.

---

[15] https://github.com/Interactions-HSG/2022MoMM.
[16] Reference Number: HSG-EC-20210901A.

5 Conclusion

We demonstrated the feasibility of automatically providing users with an overview of the CO_2-eq-oriented sustainability impact of their grocery shopping behavior using the mobile application *BetterPlanet*, and proposed a novel energy-based CO_2-Scoring model. We collected, identified and combined digital receipts with category-specific CO_2-eq data. Leveraging the new CO_2-Scoring model, we communicated the sustainability information to users via the mobile application. We furthermore conducted a validation study with 8 users. The application seemed to have a positive impact on our user base, but the results are, due to the low sample size, not generalizable. In summary, we believe that our research opens up highly interesting avenues towards enabling individuals to better understand, and modify, their behavior regarding sustainability.

Acknowledgements. This research is supported by the Swiss National Science Foundation (grants #188402, *FoodCoach*, and #197633, *ShopHero*). The *BetterPlanet* study could not have taken place without many colleagues who supported several preceding and accompanying studies, and we would like to thank Prof. Judith Walls for her inputs in the sustainability domain of the project.

References

1. Chantal, J., Hercberg, S.: Development of a new front-of-pack nutrition label in France: the five-colour nutri-score. Public Health Panor. **3**(4), 712–725 (2017)
2. Gollnhofer, J.F., Weijo, H.A., Schouten, J.W.: Consumer movements and value regimes: fighting food waste in Germany by building alternative object pathways. J. Consum. Res. **46**(3), 460–482 (2019)
3. Mateo, G.F., et al.: Mobile phone apps to promote weight loss and increase physical activity: a systematic review and meta-analysis. J. Med. Internet Res. **17**(11), e4836 (2015)
4. Mönninghoff, A., Fuchs, K., Wu, J., Albert, J., Mayer, S.: The effect of a future-self avatar mhealth intervention on physical activity and food purchases: the future me randomized controlled trial. J. Med. Internet Res. **24**(7), 1–4 (2022)
5. Olsson, L., et al.: Land Degradation. Intergovernmental Panel on Climate Change (2019)
6. Ryan, R.M., Deci, E.L.: Self-determination theory and the facilitation of intrinsic motivation, social development, and well-being. Am. Psychol. **55**(1), 68–78 (2000)
7. Sheeran, P., Webb, T.L.: The intention-behavior gap. Soc. Personal. Psychol. Compass **10**(9), 503–518 (2016)
8. Vermeir, I., et al.: Environmentally sustainable food consumption: a review and research agenda from a goal-directed perspective. Front. Psychol. **11**, 1603 (2020)
9. Webb, D., Soutar, G.N., Mazzarol, T., Saldaris, P.: Self-determination theory and consumer behavioural change: evidence from a household energy-saving behaviour study. J. Environ. Psychol. **35**, 59–66 (2013)
10. Wu, J., et al.: Estimating dietary intake from grocery shopping data-a comparative validation of relevant indicators in Switzerland. Nutrients **14**(1), 159 (2021)

Context-Aware Human Activity Recognition (CA-HAR) Using Smartphone Built-In Sensors

Liufeng Fan[1]([✉]), Pari Delir Haghighi[1], Yuxin Zhang[2],
Abdur Rahim Mohammad Forkan[3], and Prem Prakash Jayaraman[3]

[1] Monash University, Melbourne, VIC, Australia
lfan0012@student.monash.edu
[2] Deakin University, Melbourne, VIC, Australia
[3] Swinburne University of Technology, Melbourne, VIC, Australia

Abstract. Context-awareness has the potential to enhance human activity recognition (HAR) by identifying daily activities such as driving, studying, cooking, or showering. Most existing context-aware HAR approaches that utilize smartphone sensors assume that the phone is placed on certain locations on the body such as trouser pockets, attached to the waist or arm, or held by hand. However, when the smartphone is no longer worn by the person, recognizing human activities becomes a challenging task. This paper proposes a context-aware human activity recognition (CA-HAR) approach to recognize human activities even when the smartphone is no longer placed on the body. The CA-HAR approach performs aggregation of multiple sensor data from the smartphone to recognize human activities by applying deep learning and ripple-down rules (RDR). It uses a context-activity model to build and formulate the RDR rules that consider additional contextual information to deal with the on-body location problem. The paper presents a proof-of-concept implementation of the CA-HAR as an Android app and discusses two types of evaluations that were conducted to validate the performance of CA-HAR.

Keywords: Human activity recognition · Physical activities · Context-aware computing · Ripple-down rules

1 Introduction

Human Activity Recognition (HAR) is a research area that focuses on identifying the human activities [1]. With the rapid development in mobile technology, smartphones have the robust computing power and built-in sensors such as an accelerometer that can be used to identify basic physical activities including walking, sitting, lying, or standing on the phone [2]. In addition to acceleration, other built-in sensors in smartphones (e.g., Global Positioning System, camera, microphones, Bluetooth, etc.) provide an opportunity to capture useful contextual information such as location information (latitude, longitude), speed, sound level, and Wi-Fi signal strength [3, 4]. Context is defined as any information that can be collected and used to identify the situation of an entity [5]. A holistic context-aware human activity recognition approach using smartphones could

© The Author(s), under exclusive license to Springer Nature Switzerland AG 2022
P. Delir Haghighi et al. (Eds.): MoMM 2022, LNCS 13634, pp. 108–121, 2022.
https://doi.org/10.1007/978-3-031-20436-4_11

enable identifying human activities such as driving, studying, cooking, or showering regardless of the location of the smartphone on the body. This capability could benefit many mobile and IoT applications in health monitoring, smart cities, transportation, retail, and education to name a few. However, most existing studies perform HAR when the smartphone is placed on certain on-body locations such as trouser or shirt pockets, attached to the waist or arm, or held by hand [6]. There is a paucity of studies that have attempted to use multiple sensor data from the smartphone to identify human activities when the phone is not attached or kept close to the body, for example, when the phone is left on a table.

This paper aims to address this challenge by proposing a CA-HAR approach that uses additional contextual information from the smartphone sensors to identify human activities when the phone is no longer worn on the body. The proposed approach introduces a context-activity model that represents different types of contexts and activities, and their relationships. The context-activity model is integrated into CA-HAR using ripple-down rules (RDR). The paper makes the following contributions:

- Propose a context-activity model to classify contextual information collected from smartphones and represent their relationships with different activities of daily living (ADLs),
- Propose a CA-HAR approach that aggregates multiple sensor data from the smartphone for human activity detection regardless of the location of the smartphone on the body by applying deep learning and ripple-down rules (RDR),
- Implement the CA-HAR approach as an Android app, and evaluate it via a scenario-based demonstration on a real smartphone to recognize daily activities (without using external sensors).

The rest of the paper is organized as follows. Section 2 provides a review of the related work. Section 3 introduces the proposed context-activity model. Section 4 describes the proposed context-aware human activity recognition (CA-HAR) approach. Section 5 details the implementation of proposed approach. Section 6 presents the selection of the deep learning (DL) model. Section 7 presents the scenario-based demonstration, evaluation, and discussion. Finally, Sect. 8 concludes the paper.

2 Related Work

The goal of HAR is to detect human activity through a series of observations of the user behavior [7]. HAR mainly refers to human body posture-action recognition (such as walking, standing, sitting, lying, walking downstairs and upstairs) [1, 8, 9], but has been also used to recognize other human activities (such as vacuuming, cooking), known as activities of daily living (ADLs) [10]. The HAR algorithms can be divided into two categories: conventional machine learning (ML)-based classification algorithms and deep learning (DL)-based classification algorithms. Compared with traditional ML methods, DL classification algorithms are more robust and have higher recognition accuracy in the HAR domain [11, 12]. With regard to sensors, HAR can be divided into three categories of ambient sensor-based HAR, wearable sensor-based HAR, and hybrid sensor-based HAR (combined with ambient and wearable sensors) [13].

Smartphone-based HAR can be considered as a subclass of wearable sensor-based HAR [1]. Because of smartphones' high availability, multiple built-in sensors, and afford-able prices, more researchers have begun to focus on the smartphone-based HAR [14, 15]. A number of these studies apply context-aware computing to improve accuracy by collecting contextual information from the smartphone or other wearable sensors, in addition to the accelerometer and gyroscope data [11, 16–23]. Yet, there is a lack of stud-ies that use a general context model to represent context (only using smartphone sensor data) and their relationships with human activities. Using a context-activity model can provide a unified representation of context and associated activities that can be shared across different smartphone-based HAR applications.

In smartphone-based HAR studies, the location of the smartphone on the body is a crucial factor that influences the quality of data collection and the accuracy of activity recognition [14]. Therefore, in most studies, the smartphone needs to be kept close to the user's body or positioned at a certain location on the body chosen by researchers. There are remarkably few context-aware HAR studies that are able to detect human activities while the smartphone is no longer worn on the body.

This research aims to address the above-mentioned gaps by proposing a smartphone-based CA-HAR approach that recognizes human activities regardless of the position of the phone, and includes a context-activity model to represent a wide range of context types and activities, and their relationships. The context-activity model is described in the following section.

3 Proposed Context-Activity Model

An overview of the proposed context-activity model is presented in Fig. 1. The model is comprised of two parts, one representing different types of contexts and the other representing basic human activities (e.g., sitting or walking) and complex daily activities (e.g., gardening or showering). The context part includes mainly the context collected from smartphone sensors and the smartphone's operating system (e.g., battery level or screen status). The context could also include the demographic information of the smartphone's owner such as occupation. The model divides smartphone context into the five context categories: phone resources, movement, environmental, location, and user social context. Based on location context, complex daily activities are further divided into indoor and outdoor activities.

Indoor Activities - Home Activities: This type of activity recognition first needs to obtain basic location context (i.e., latitude and longitude and Wi-Fi information) to confirm that the location is 'home'. Additional contexts can then be used to identify types of home activities. The sound captured from the microphone as environmental context can be fused with the basic physical activities (e.g., standing) to identify cooking, vacuuming, showering, sleeping, watching TV, and studying/ working/web surfing [24, 25]. Different types of sounds collected from various activities are used to train deep learning (DL) models to identify complex activities such as cooking and showering [26]. In addition, Bluetooth information can also be integrated with the movement context to identify home activities such as watching TV and working/studying/web surfing. The Bluetooth status of smart TVs and laptops provides this contextual information.

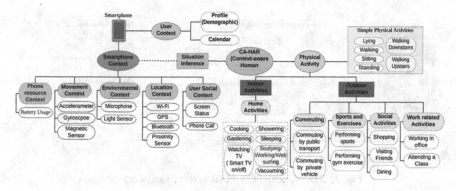

Fig. 1. The proposed context-activity model

Outdoor Activities - Commuting: An outdoor activity is first determined according to the location context. It then uses movement context (i.e., a simple physical activity) and additional location context (speed or Bluetooth) to identify if it is a commuting activity and whether it is by public transport or by private vehicle. The sound level can also be used to identify different commuting activities [24].

Outdoor Activities - Sports and Exercise Activities: It uses movement context (physical activity) combined with basic location context and user context (calendar information) to recognize activities, like performing sports or gym exercises.

Outdoor Activities - Social Activities: It uses movement context combined with location, user, and environmental context (e.g., sound) to identify outdoor social activities, such as shopping, visiting friends, and dining [24, 25].

Outdoor Activities - Work-Related Activities: It uses movement context combined with location context (i.e. latitude, longitude, Wi-Fi, Bluetooth), user context (calendar information), and the screen status information that can be obtained from smartphone's operating system using the native libraries.

The information about different categories of context represented in the proposed model and their relationships with indoor and outdoor activities are used to create RDR rules. The RDR rules allows aggregation of context information with the basic HAR results (i.e., lying, standing, walking, or sitting) to infer activities of daily living.

4   Context-Aware Human Activity Recognition (CA-HAR)

The architecture of the proposed CA-HAR approach is shown in Fig. 2. The CA-HAR approach collects context from different built-in sensors of smartphones and integrates it with deep learning-based physical activity recognition using the RDR rules to detect daily activities. The following subsections discuss the main components of the proposed architecture.

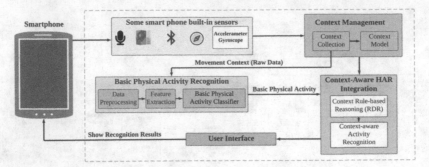

Fig. 2. The proposed CA-HAR system's architecture

4.1 Basic Physical Activity Recognition

This component is responsible for performing basic physical activity recognition that includes the following steps: data collection from built-in 9-axis inertial measurement units of the smartphone, data preprocessing, feature extraction, and classification. This study uses deep learning (DL) for the classification to identify six basic physical activities, including lying, sitting, standing, walking, and walking downstairs and upstairs. The DL-based classification model was selected after a series of experiments to evaluate the performance of different models (discussed in Sect. 6). The model training was conducted offline (on a laptop). Then the trained model (a mobile lite version) was transferred and deployed on the smartphone to detect user activities.

4.2 Context Management

This component has two subcomponents. Context collection is responsible for collecting context from the smartphone's built-in sensors and the operating system's native libraries. The context model is used to identify the type of context and its relationship with activities according to the context-activity model and is later used to formulate the RDR rules to recognize complex activities.

4.3 Context-Aware HAR Integration

This component consists of two sub-components. Context Rule-based Reasoning uses Ripple-Down Rules (RDR) to aggregate results of basic physical activity recognition (using a pre-trained DL model) and other collected contexts (as rule conditions) to infer complex activities. The RDR rule combines the basic physical activity condition with the context related conditions based on the context-activity model. RDR is an effective method to acquire and maintain rule-based systems [27]. RDR enables creating and maintaining knowledge structures incrementally building them using well-defined contexts [28, 29]. RDR forms binary decision trees, which are different from decision trees, where compound clauses are used to determine the rule branches. Furthermore, there are two main frameworks for RDR, including single-class RDR (SCRDR), which uses binary trees, and multi-class RDR (MCRDR), which applies multi-way trees (classify more cases from a single node). Since this study focuses on multi-activity recognition, the number of activities identified will be more than two. Therefore, MCRDR is more suitable than SCRDR and is used in the CA-HAR integration part.

5   Implementation

This study used a smartphone to collect context and identify human activities. A prototype android application was developed to validate the proposed CA-HAR approach. The smartphone used in the experiments is the MI 6X with Android version 9. The basic HAR model (a DL model) was trained offline on a laptop (MacBook Pro, 2020, M1, 16 GB) using python (3.9.7) environment. The trained model was then converted to a mobile lite version using the TensorFlow Lite library available in python and finally deployed to the smartphone. Table 1 shows the Android APIs and libraries used in the proposed CA-HAR and their associated contexts, context types, and sampling rate.

Table 1. Context-related Android API in this study

Android API and libraries	Context	Context types	Sampling rate
Sensor	3-axis acceleration data, 3-axis linear acceleration data, 3-axis rotation (gyroscope) data	Movement context	50 Hz
Location	GPS information (latitude, longitude, speed)	Location context	0.2 Hz
NetworkInfo	Network status (Wi-Fi or cellular)	Location context	0.2 Hz
WifiInfo	Wi-Fi information (SSID, BSSID, RSSI)	Location context	0.2 Hz
MediaRecorder	Sound	Environmental context	2 Hz
Intent	Screen status	User social context	0.2 Hz
BatteryManager	Charging Status	Phone resource context	0.2 Hz
CalendarContract	Calendar information	User context	0.2 Hz
Bluetooth	Bluetooth (BT) device information	Location context	0.2 Hz

The evaluation of CA-HAR consists of two parts. The first part includes the selection of a suitable DL model through experimental evaluations. The second part involves a scenario-based demonstration to verify the capabilities of the proposed CA-HAR.

6   Selection of Deep Learning (DL) Model

There are several DL models used in the literature for HAR. This study compares three widely used vanilla DL models and selects the best performing one for implementation, including the convolutional neural network (CNN) model [30], the deep neural network (DNN) model [31], and the recurrent neural network (RNN) model [32].

These models were chosen for three reasons: 1) easy to be converted into mobile platform compatible format; 2) low on-device processing latency due to the vanilla structure; 3) high accuracy on the UCI HAR dataset (See Table 2). UCI HAR dataset is one of the standard datasets for benchmarking HAR algorithms that uses smartphone sensors data [33].

Table 2. The performance results for the UCI dataset with different DL models

	Precision	Recall	F1	Accuracy
CNN [34]	93.2%	92.8%	92.9%	92.7%
DNN [35]	96.9%	96.8%	96.8%	96.8%
RNN [32]	96.8%	96.7%	96.0%	96.7%

The UCI HAR dataset was collected in a controlled indoor experimental scenario, while our test scenario is in the wild. The positions of the phone were different as well. In the UCI HAR study, the participants were instructed to put the phone on their waist. Therefore, in this study we collected a new HAR dataset for DL model training using the same preprocessing and feature calculation of UCI dataset [36]. The data collection setup is shown in Table 3.

Table 3. Data collection setup of self-labeled dataset

Settings	Description
Activities	Lying, walking, sitting, standing, walking downstairs and upstairs
Phone position	Hand Palm (Hold by hands)
Data collected	3-axis acceleration data and 3-axis angular velocity data
Devices	MI 6X
Sensors	Smartphone built-in accelerometer, gyroscope
Sample rate	50 Hz (0.02 s per reading)
Windows size	2.56 s (50% overlap)
Duration per activity	At least 46.9 min (1100×2.56 s $= 2916$ s)

The data collection and activity recognition were implemented and tested on the smartphone based on the approach used in [36] (shown in Fig. 3). All data was saved in a CSV file. The self-labeled data was then used to train all the DL models on the laptop with post-training quantization for the TensorFlow Lite format convention, and the optimal DL model was selected for the implementation. The results are shown in Table 4. It can be seen that the RNN model has the best performance (highest accuracy).

To evaluate the RNN model for our proposed tasks, an on-device DL benchmarking app [37], was used for testing. A shorter duration of 10 min (at least 235 windows) was considered for each activity. The results are shown in Table 5, with an average precision of 84%, a recall of 81%, an F1 score of 79%, and an accuracy of 81%. This performance is commonly acceptable in smartphone based HAR research studies [1, 6]. Hence, the RNN model was selected for this study.

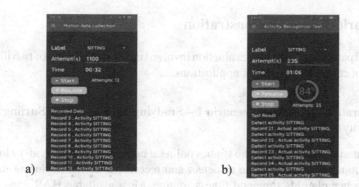

Fig. 3. (a) Data collection screen, (b) Activity recognition test screen

Table 4. The performance results for self-labeled dataset with different DL models

	60/40 train/test ratio				70/30 train/test ratio				80/20 train/test ratio			
	P	R	F1	Acc	P	R	F1	Acc	P	R	F1	Acc
CNN	92%	92%	92%	92%	92%	91%	91%	92%	95%	95%	95%	95%
DNN	88%	87%	87%	87%	90%	89%	89%	89%	87%	87%	87%	87%
RNN	93%	93%	93%	93%	93%	93%	93%	93%	97%	97%	97%	97%

Abbreviations: P = precision, R = recall, F1 = F1-score, Acc = accuracy.

Table 5. Results of actual testing RNN models using the self-labeled dataset

	Precision	Recall	F1-score	
Lying	93%	98%	95%	
Sitting	98%	100%	99%	
Standing	97%	33%	49%	
Walking	79%	94%	86%	
Walking downstairs	78%	73%	75%	
Walking upstairs	61%	92%	73%	
Accuracy				81%
Average	84%	81%	79%	

7   Scenario-Based Demonstration

The second part of the CA-HAR evaluation involved the demonstration of two illustrative scenarios of context-aware HAR applications.

7.1   Illustrative Simulation Scenario 1 – Studying/Working/Web Surfing (Home Activity)

Keith is a master student of IT who studies online at home due to the Covid-19 lockdown. He wants to use his smartphone to detect and record his activities during the day to help him better plan his time and fitness routine. Most available HAR apps can only identify basic physical activities, such as walking and sitting. The proposed CA-HAR approach can recognize daily activities, such as sleeping, studying/working/web surfing at home, regardless of the smartphone's position on the body. CA-HAR uses ripple-down rules (RPR) for identifying home activities, as shown in Fig. 4. At the beginning of the classification, it first determines whether the activity is an indoor activity based on location context (location is home). When a case was classified as a home activity, more rules are applied to identify more details about the home activity.

In this scenario, Keith is at home doing his homework using a laptop in the morning, and his smartphone is left on the desk (no longer worn on the body). Using the proposed CA-HAR approach, the activity can be identified as studying (home activity), as shown in Fig. 5. The CA-HAR app's screen shows the recognition results in the centre and the collected context on the top. The recognition process is based on the proposed ripple-down rules for home activities, and rules 1, 3, and 5 were used, as shown in Fig. 4. The activity was first classified as home (indoor) activities. Then, the RDR includes other rules and conditions: the DL based physical activity recognition result indicates "lying", the screen status is off, the activity lasted more than 30 min, the time is daytime, and Laptop BT is connected. After combining these context and activity related rules, the CA-HAR is able to identify the activity as "Studying (Home activities)". If the CA-HAR approach was not used in this scenario, the activity would have been recognized as "lying" which is an incorrect recognition of the user activity.

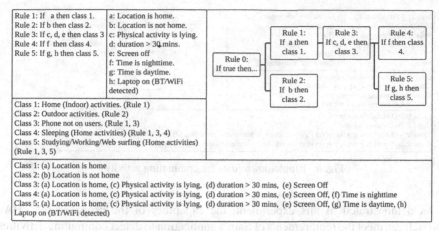

Rule 1: If a then class 1. Rule 2: If b then class 2. Rule 3: If c, d, e then class 3 Rule 4: If f then class 4. Rule 5: If g, h then class 5.	a: Location is home. b: Location is not home. c: Physical activity is lying. d: duration > 30 mins. e: Screen off f: Time is nighttime. g: Time is daytime. h: Laptop on (BT/WiFi detected)
Class 1: Home (Indoor) activities. (Rule 1) Class 2: Outdoor activities. (Rule 2) Class 3: Phone not on users. (Rule 1, 3) Class 4: Sleeping (Home activities) (Rule 1, 3, 4) Class 5: Studying/Working/Web surfing (Home activities) (Rule 1, 3, 5)	
Class 1: (a) Location is home Class 2: (b) Location is not home Class 3: (a) Location is home, (c) Physical activity is lying, (d) duration > 30 mins, (e) Screen Off Class 4: (a) Location is home, (c) Physical activity is lying, (d) duration > 30 mins, (e) Screen Off, (f) Time is nighttime Class 5: (a) Location is home, (c) Physical activity is lying, (d) duration > 30 mins, (e) Screen Off, (g) Time is daytime, (h) Laptop on (BT/WiFi detected)	

Fig. 4. Ripple-down rules for home activity

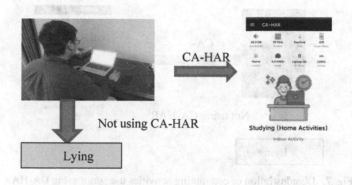

CA-HAR

Not using CA-HAR

Lying

Studying (Home Activities)

Fig. 5. Demonstration of Home activity using/not using CA-HAR

7.2 Illustrative Simulation Scenario 2 – Commuting by Private Vehicle

Sam is an IT developer for an auto insurance company. He needs a smartphone app to record how often users commute in the car. The app should also determine whether the user is in a private car or public transport. The proposed CA-HAR approach can help Sam to detect two different types of commuting (by private car or public transport), only using his smartphone and without the need to purchase any extra sensor. Also, Sam does not need to worry about the position of the phone on the body. In this scenario, we consider Sam is driving to work and his phone is placed on the passenger seat. Using the CA-HAR approach and RDR rule inference (see Fig. 6), the activity is first recognized as an outdoor activity based on location context (i.e., location is not home). Then, since the speed is greater than zero and CarPlay BT is detected as connected, the activity is identified as "commuting by private vehicle". RDR rules 1, 3, and 4 are used for inferring commuting activities (see Fig. 6). The actual result that is "commuting by private vehicle" is shown on the smartphone (see Fig. 7).

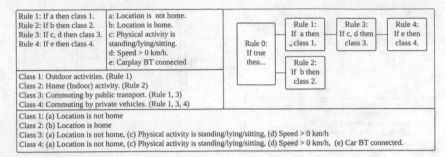

Rule 1: If a then class 1.	a: Location is not home.
Rule 2: If b then class 2.	b: Location is home.
Rule 3: If c, d then class 3.	c: Physical activity is
Rule 4: If e then class 4.	standing/lying/sitting.
	d: Speed > 0 km/h.
	e: Carplay BT connected

Class 1: Outdoor activities. (Rule 1)
Class 2: Home (Indoor) activity. (Rule 2)
Class 3: Commuting by public transport. (Rule 1, 3)
Class 4: Commuting by private vehicles. (Rule 1, 3, 4)

Class 1: (a) Location is not home
Class 2: (b) Location is home
Class 3: (a) Location is not home, (c) Physical activity is standing/lying/sitting, (d) Speed > 0 km/h
Class 4: (a) Location is not home, (c) Physical activity is standing/lying/sitting, (d) Speed > 0 km/h, (e) Car BT connected.

Rule 0: If true then...
→ Rule 1: If a then class 1.
→ Rule 3: If c, d then class 3.
→ Rule 4: If e then class 4.
Rule 2: If b then class 2.

Fig. 6. Ripple-down rules for commuting activity

As demonstrated in this experiment, the capability of the proposed CA-HAR approach can meet the requirements of Sam's application to detect commuting activities.

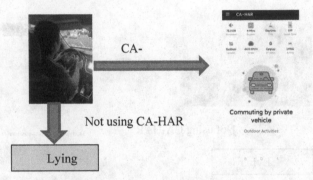

CA-

Not using CA-HAR

Lying

Commuting by private vehicle

Outdoor Activities

Fig. 7. Demonstration of commuting activities using/not using CA-HAR

7.3   Analysis of Results and Discussions

The comparison of activity recognition results considering the simple HAR and our proposed CA-HAR for the two scenarios is summarized in Table 6. Simple HAR uses only movement context (accelerometer and rotation data), and can detect basic activities like sitting or lying. However, considering additional contextual information (such as GPS, time, speed, screen status, and Bluetooth) enables CA-HAR to infer daily activities like studying. The results also show that CA-HAR provides more accurate information about the user's activity of daily living, without requiring the user to carry the smartphone at certain on-body locations.

Table 6. Comparison of activity recognition for commuting with and without CA-HAR

Simple HAR		CA-HAR	
Context used	Recognized activity	Context used	Recognized activity
Acceleration data, rotation data	Lying	Acceleration data, rotation data	Lying
	Lying	Acceleration data, rotation data **GPS (latitude, longitude, speed)**	Commuting by public transport
	Lying	Acceleration data, rotation data **GPS (latitude, longitude, speed) Bluetooth status**	Commuting by private vehicle
	Lying	Acceleration data, rotation data **GPS, screen status, activity duration, time, Bluetooth status**	Studying/working/web surfing (home activities)

8   Conclusion and Future Work

In this paper, we presented CA-HAR, an approach that applies deep learning and RDR rules to identify human activities from smartphones' sensor data even when the smartphone is no longer worn on the body. We implemented CA-HAR as an android application and tested it via two illustrative scenarios that show, CA-HAR has the potential to improve detection of human activities in cases where the smartphone is not placed on different on-body locations.

In future, we aim to expand this work by conducting user evaluations and usability testing to further validate the CA-HAR approach. We also plan to apply the CA-HAR approach for the detection of other daily activities such as showering, cooking, and vacuuming by training DL models using sound datasets.

References

1. Lara, O.D., Labrador, M.A.: A survey on human activity recognition using wearable sensors. IEEE Commun. Surv. Tutor. **15**, 1192–1209 (2013). https://doi.org/10.1109/SURV.2012.110 112.00192
2. Incel, O.D., Kose, M., Ersoy, C.: A review and taxonomy of activity recognition on mobile phones. BioNanoScience **3**, 145–171 (2013). https://doi.org/10.1007/s12668-013-0088-3
3. Bricon-Souf, N., Newman, C.R.: Context awareness in health care: a review. Int. J. Med. Inf. **76**, 2–12 (2007). https://doi.org/10.1016/j.ijmedinf.2006.01.003
4. Yurur, O., Liu, C.H., Sheng, Z., et al.: Context-awareness for mobile sensing: a survey and future directions. IEEE Commun. Surv. Tutor. **18**, 68–93 (2016). https://doi.org/10.1109/ COMST.2014.2381246

5. Dey, A.K.: Understanding and using context. Pers. Ubiquitous Comput. **5**, 4–7 (2001). https://doi.org/10.1007/s007790170019
6. Morales, J., Akopian, D.: Physical activity recognition by smartphones, a survey. Biocybern. Biomed. Eng. **37**, 388–400 (2017). https://doi.org/10.1016/j.bbe.2017.04.004
7. Cook, D.J., Krishnan, N.C.: Activity Learning: Discovering, Recognizing, and Predicting Human Behavior from Sensor Data. Wiley, Hoboken (2015)
8. Bao, L., Intille, S.S.: Activity recognition from user-annotated acceleration data. In: Ferscha, A., Mattern, F. (eds.) Pervasive 2004. LNCS, vol. 3001, pp. 1–17. Springer, Heidelberg (2004). https://doi.org/10.1007/978-3-540-24646-6_1
9. Martin, H., Bernardos, A.M., Tarrio, P., Casar, J.R.: Enhancing activity recognition by fusing inertial and biometric information. In: 9th International Conference on Information Fusion, pp. 1–8. IEEE (2011)
10. Hayashi, T., Nishida, M., Kitaoka, N., et al.: Daily activity recognition with large-scaled real-life recording datasets based on deep neural network using multi-modal signals. IEICE Trans. Fundam. Electron. Commun. Comput. Sci. **E101.A**, 199–210 (2018). https://doi.org/10.1587/transfun.E101.A.199
11. Salakhutdinov, R.: Learning deep generative models. Annu. Rev. Stat. Appl. **2**, 361–385 (2015). https://doi.org/10.1146/annurev-statistics-010814-020120
12. Mohamed, A., Dahl, G.E., Hinton, G.: Acoustic modeling using deep belief networks. IEEE Trans. Audio Speech Lang. Process. **20**, 14–22 (2012). https://doi.org/10.1109/TASL.2011.2109382
13. Wang, Y., Cang, S., Yu, H.: A survey on wearable sensor modality centred human activity recognition in health care. Expert Syst. Appl. **137**, 167–190 (2019). https://doi.org/10.1016/j.eswa.2019.04.057
14. Sousa Lima, W., Souto, E., El-Khatib, K., et al.: Human activity recognition using inertial sensors in a smartphone: an overview. Sensors **19**, 3213 (2019). https://doi.org/10.3390/s19143213
15. Straczkiewicz, M., James, P., Onnela, J.-P.: A systematic review of smartphone-based human activity recognition methods for health research. NPJ Digit. Med. **4**, 148 (2021). https://doi.org/10.1038/s41746-021-00514-4
16. Cao, L., Wang, Y., Zhang, B., et al.: GCHAR: an efficient Group-based Context—aware human activity recognition on smartphone. J. Parallel Distrib. Comput. **118**, 67–80 (2018). https://doi.org/10.1016/j.jpdc.2017.05.007
17. Anguita, D., Ghio, A., Oneto, L., et al.: Human activity recognition on smartphones for mobile context awareness. In: Advances in Neural Information Processing Systems 26: Proceedings of the 2012 Conference, pp. 1–9. Lake Tahoe, Nevada (2012)
18. Wannenburg, J., Malekian, R.: Physical activity recognition from smartphone accelerometer data for user context awareness sensing. IEEE Trans. Syst. Man Cybern. Syst. **47**, 3142–3149 (2017). https://doi.org/10.1109/TSMC.2016.2562509
19. Nath, S.: ACE: exploiting correlation for energy-efficient and continuous context sensing. In: Proceedings of the 10th International Conference on Mobile Systems, Applications, and Services, pp. 29–42. ACM (2012)
20. Ouchi, K., Doi, M.: Smartphone-based monitoring system for activities of daily living for elderly people and their relatives etc. In: Proceedings of the 2013 ACM Conference on Pervasive and Ubiquitous Computing Adjunct Publication, Zurich, Switzerland, pp. 103–106. ACM (2013)
21. Khan, A.M., Tufail, A., Khattak, A.M., Laine, T.H.: Activity recognition on smartphones via sensor-fusion and KDA-based SVMs. Int. J. Distrib. Sens. Netw. **10**, 503291 (2014). https://doi.org/10.1155/2014/503291
22. Villalonga, C., Razzaq, M., Khan, W., et al.: Ontology-based high-level context inference for human behavior identification. Sensors **16**, 1617 (2016). https://doi.org/10.3390/s16101617

23. Radu, V., Tong, C., Bhattacharya, S., et al.: Multimodal deep learning for activity and context recognition. In: Proceedings of the ACM on Interactive, Mobile, Wearable and Ubiquitous Technologies, vol. 1, pp. 1–27 (2018).https://doi.org/10.1145/3161174
24. Filios, G., Nikoletseas, S., Pavlopoulou, C., et al.: Hierarchical algorithm for daily activity recognition via smartphone sensors. In: 2015 IEEE 2nd World Forum on Internet of Things (WF-IoT), Milan, Italy, pp. 381–386. IEEE (2015)
25. Jung, M., Chi, S.: Human activity classification based on sound recognition and residual convolutional neural network. Autom. Constr. **114**, 103177 (2020). https://doi.org/10.1016/j.autcon.2020.103177
26. Wang, W., Liu, A.X., Shahzad, M., et al.: Understanding and modeling of WiFi signal based human activity recognition. In: Proceedings of the 21st Annual International Conference on Mobile Computing and Networking, Paris France, pp. 65–76. ACM (2015)
27. Compton, P., Jansen, R.: A philosophical basis for knowledge acquisition. Knowl. Acquis. **2**, 241–258 (1990). https://doi.org/10.1016/S1042-8143(05)80017-2
28. Gaines, B.R., Compton, P.: Induction of ripple-down rules applied to modeling large databases. J. Intell. Inf. Syst. **5**, 211–228 (1995). https://doi.org/10.1007/BF00962234
29. Breiman, L., Friedman, J.H., Olshen, R.A., Stone, C.J: Classification and Regression Trees (1983)
30. LeCun, Y., Bengio, Y., Hinton, G.: Deep learning. Nature **521**, 436–444 (2015). https://doi.org/10.1038/nature14539
31. Hammerla, N.Y., Halloran, S., Ploetz, T.: Deep, Convolutional, and recurrent models for human activity recognition using wearables (2016)
32. Murad, A., Pyun, J.-Y.: Deep recurrent neural networks for human activity recognition. Sensors **17**, 2556 (2017). https://doi.org/10.3390/s17112556
33. Dua, D., Graff, C: UCI machine learning repository (2017)
34. Wan, S., Qi, L., Xu, X., Tong, C., Gu, Z.: Deep Learning models for real-time human activity recognition with smartphones. Mob. Netw. Appl. **25**(2), 743–755 (2019). https://doi.org/10.1007/s11036-019-01445-x
35. Bozkurt, F.: A comparative study on classifying human activities using classical machine and deep learning methods. Arab. J. Sci. Eng. **47**, 1507–1521 (2021). https://doi.org/10.1007/s13369-021-06008-5
36. UCI Machine Learning Repository: Human Activity Recognition Using Smartphones Data Set. https://archive.ics.uci.edu/ml/datasets/human+activity+recognition+using+smartphones. Accessed 7 Sept 2021
37. Qiang, Z., Zhang, Y., Haghighi, P.D., et al: MobileDLSearch. ontology-based mobile platform for effective sharing and reuse of deep learning models. In: 2021 IEEE International Conferences on Internet of Things (iThings) and IEEE Green Computing & Communications (GreenCom) and IEEE Cyber, Physical & Social Computing (CPSCom) and IEEE Smart Data (SmartData) and IEEE Congress on Cybermatics (Cybermatics), Melbourne, Australia, pp. 51–58. IEEE (2021)

An Improved 3DIHDV-H0P Localization Algorithm Using for Smart Irrigation Applications

Halima Ghribi[1]([✉]) [ID] and Abderrazak Jemai[2] [ID]

[1] SERCOM-Lab., Tunisia Polytechnic School, Carthage University,
B.P. 743-2078 Marsa, Tunisia
halima.ghribi@ept.u-carthage.tn
[2] INSAT, SERCOM-Lab., Tunisia Polytechnic School, Carthage University,
1080 Tunis, Tunisia
Abderrazak.Jemai@insat.rnu.tn

Abstract. Smart irrigation systems are defined as a large number of sensor nodes working together to provide a specific service. Thus, accurate localization of sensors is crucial for covering the area of interest, as well as for the self-organization of networks and reducing node power consumption. In order to correctly interpret the detected communication information between nodes, positioning systems are installed on each node. However, using GPS is unsatisfactory for localization due to high cost, high power consumption, and environmental constraints. Moreover, the manual configuration of sensor nodes is impractical in large-scale deployment. Extensive research is being done to address these problems by integrating the range-free localization algorithm (i.e. DV-Hop algorithm) into node sensors to determine their geographical coordinates and improve localization accuracy. In this paper, we propose an improved algorithm named 3DIHDV-H0P which contains an error factor, a weighting coefficient, and a 3-dimensional hyperbolic method to estimate the position.

Keywords: Wireless sensor networks(WSN) · Localization · Minimum mean square error(MMSE) · Node coordinates · Location accuracy improvement

1 Introduction

Smart irrigation systems are defined as a large number of sensor nodes working together to provide a specific service like monitoring soil moisture, humidity [1], temperature, data collection, and decision-making in irrigation. Several solutions have been proposed to deal with sensor localization problems i.e. manual configuration but this is impractical in large-scale deployment. The other possible way for node localization is to equip each sensor node with a GPS receiver. Given the drawbacks of these two approaches self-localization by using various

© The Author(s), under exclusive license to Springer Nature Switzerland AG 2022
P. Delir Haghighi et al. (Eds.): MoMM 2022, LNCS 13634, pp. 122–130, 2022.
https://doi.org/10.1007/978-3-031-20436-4_12

localization algorithms is used in our context. It is an exchange solution of GPS or manual pre-programming of sensor nodes during the deployment. The existing localization algorithms can be mainly divided into two categories: range-based algorithms and the range-free algorithms [2]. On the one hand, range-based algorithms are based on calculating the absolute distance between sensor nodes [3]. They provide more accurate location results, but they are expensive to implement in large systems and require additional hardware support. Some well-known range-based schemes are: RSSI, ToA, AoA, and TDoA [4]. In the range based methods, the location can be calculated using either the method of trilateration, triangulation or multilateration. On the other hand, range-free algorithms [5] don't require calculating the distance between the sensor nodes. They use the hop count information or the connectivity between anchor nodes and unknown nodes to determine the location of each nodes. The ranges-free localization Algorithms [6] are known as a cost-effective alternative for low-cost applications. The most well-known range-free distributed localization algorithm is the DV-hop which holds many decided advantages of simplicity, low cost, feasibility and high coverage. Achieving better accuracy with some improved algorithms remains a matter of research. In this article, we propose an improved location algorithm, named 3DIHDV-HOP, to improve the location accuracy of sensor nodes. The rest of this article is organized as follows: in Sect. 2, the classical DV-Hop algorithms is described. In Sect. 3, we introduce the related work of some existing DV-Hop versions. Section 4 describes in detail our innovative version of the DV-HOP algorithm. Section 5 contains the simulation results of our improved version of the DV-HOP algorithm. Then, we have discussed the impact of the change of the anchors' number and the unknown nodes number on the MMSE location error in the 3DIHDV-HOP and some location algorithms. Finally, a conclusion is drawn in Sect. 6.

2   The DV-HOP Localization Algorithm

DV-HOP is a classic localization method, proposed by Dragos Niculescu and et al. [19]. It is similar to the traditional routing algorithm based on a distance-vector, and works well in isotropic networks. DV-HOP consists of three steps: broadcast information and calculation of the minimum hop number, distance calculation, and position estimation [7]. In the first step, anchor nodes broadcast an information packet containing their positions (x_i, y_i) and a hop number that is set to 0. Then, each sensor node receives the information packet and checks whether the hop number is minimal or not. If the hops number is less than the existing value, then the value will be replaced by the received hops number, otherwise the hop number will be rejected. After that, the information packet will be sent in the network and the hop number counter will be incremented by one [17]. According to this calculation method, all nodes of the network have a minimum hop number for each anchor node.

3   Related Works

The localization of sensor nodes is an interesting area of research and many algorithms based on DV-hop have been recently developed to improve its performance. In [7], the improved algorithm introduces threshold M, it uses the weighted average hop distances of anchor nodes within M hops to calculate the average hop distance of unknown nodes. Subsequently, a weighted algorithm WDV-HOP [8] was implemented to enhance the accuracy of the DV-Hop algorithm. It was based on the use of weighted average hop size to calculate the hop size of unknown nodes [9]. In [10], authored by Abdelali Hadir and al, developed an improved HWDV-Hop, which focuses on the use of a weighting coefficient for each average hop size to calculate the average hop size of nodes. In this version, the MMSE technique is used to estimate the average hop size distance. In paper [12], authors focused on the merging of the WDV-Hop algorithm, and the weighted hyperbolic localization algorithm(WH). It includes weights to the correlation matrix of the estimated distances between the anchor nodes and the unknown nodes in order to improve precision and accuracy. The authors in [13] proposed a new version of DV-HOP which consists of defining two classes of nodes according to the number of anchors in the neighborhood, then applying the localization methods proposed to each node class. In 2019 [14], an improved version of the DV-HOP algorithm is proposed based on the re-evaluation of the average hop distance of the anchor node by an error factor, correcting the minimum hop number of the unknown node and the anchor node by a correction coefficient and using a mean square error method to estimate the position of unknown nodes. In serval application areas, like irrigation monitoring, and environmental monitoring, WSNs are deployed in a Three-Dimensional (3D) plane. The authors in [15] proposed a novel distributed approach to enhance the accuracy of traditional hop-based algorithms for 3D environments. The proposed Three-Dimensional Distance-Error-Correction-based hop localization algorithm is based on the distance error correction factor. The authors of [11], proposed a localization algorithm based on DV-Hop and EDV-Hop techniques for mobile nodes in 3D. The proposed algorithm uses the average hop size weighted mean to estimate the average hop size for networks and the 2D hyperbolic technique. In paper [18], a multi-objective particle swarm optimization based DV-Hop localization is proposed in 3-dimensional wireless sensor networks. The authors in [16] proposed a MA*-3DDV-Hop algorithm that integrates the improved A* algorithm and the 3DDV-Hop algorithm. In MA*-3DDV-Hop algorithm, the hop-count value of nodes is optimized to improve the error of calculating the average distance per hop. Then, the multi-objective NSGA-II is adopted to optimize the coordinates locally.

4   A Proposition of 3DIHDV-H0P Algorithm

- **The Average Hop Distance of Anchor Nodes**: The 3DIHDV-Hop algorithm is divided into three improved steps: the anchor nodes flood their positions, the estimate of the average distance is changed and the hyperbolic technique is used to calculate the node's location. The first step of 3DIHDV-Hop is similar to 3DDV-Hop. Each anchor node of our algorithm broadcasts an information packet which contains their parameters (position, number of hops, and their ID) to these neighborhood nodes (anchor nodes and unknown nodes). After the receiver nodes verify the packet information, they increment the hop count. This packet has been sent to each neighbor node until each node has obtained the minimum hop number set by the anchor node.

Table 1. Formula of 3DIHDV-H0P Algorithm

The Average Hop Distance of Anchor Nodes	Weighting Coefficient for the Minimum Hops Number	Hyperbolic Estimation Method
$HopSize_i = \dfrac{\sum i \neq j^M \left(\sqrt{(x_i - x_j)^2 + (y_i - y_j)^2 + (z_i - z_j)^2}\right)}{\sum_{i \neq j}^M (h_{ij})}$ (1)	$h_{ij}^{est} = \dfrac{d_{ij}}{HopSize_i}$ (2)	$d_{iu}^2 = (x_i - x_u)^2 + (y_i - y_u)^2 + (z_i - z_u)^2$ (3)
$d_{ei} = d_{ij} - HopSize_i * h_{ij}$ (4)	$w_i^{est} = \dfrac{h_{ij}^{est}}{h_{ij}}$ (5)	$d_{iu}^2 = x_i^2 + z_i^2 - 2x_i x_u + y_i^2 + y_u^2 - 2y_i y_u - 2z_i z_u + z_i^2 + z_u^2$ (6)
$E_i = \dfrac{\sum i \neq j^M (d_{ij} - HopSize_i * h_{ij})}{(M-1) \sum_{i \neq j}^M (h_{ij})}$ (7)	$hnew_{ui} = w_i^{est} * h_{ui}$ (8)	$A_i = x_i^2 + y_i^2 + z_i^2 \, and \, B_u = x_u^2 + y_u^2 + z_u^2$ (9)
		$d_{iu}^2 = A_i - 2x_i x_u - 2y_i y_u - 2z_i z_u + B_u$ (10)
		$d_{iu}^2 - A_i = -2x_i x_u - 2y_i y_u - 2z_i z_u + B_u$ (11)
$HopSize_{new} = HopSize_i + E_i$ (12)	$d_{ui} = HopSize_{new} * hnew_{ui}$ (13)	$Z = HG ;\ Z = \begin{bmatrix} d_{1u}^2 - A_1 \\ d_{2u}^2 - A_2 \\ \vdots \\ d_{n_u}^2 - A_n \end{bmatrix}$ (14)
		$H = \begin{bmatrix} -2x_1 & -2y_1 & -2z_1 & 1 \\ -2x_2 & -2y_2 & -2z_2 & 1 \\ \vdots & & & \\ -2x_n & -2y_n & -2z_n & 1 \end{bmatrix} ;\ G = \begin{bmatrix} x_u \\ y_u \\ z_u \\ B_u \end{bmatrix}$ (15)

The average hops distance of anchor nodes is calculated by combining the position information of other anchor nodes with the minimum hop number. The equation for the average hop distance of anchor nodes is described as formula 1. The real distance between the anchor nodes i and j is fixed. However, the estimated distance is expressed by the product between the average hop distance of the available anchor nodes and the minimum hop number. The expression of the difference between the two distances can be summarized as formula 4. where d_{ij} is the real distance between anchors i and j. h_{ij} is the minimum hop number from anchor i to anchor j. Each anchor node has an error factor between their real distance and their estimated distance. The average error factor per hop is determined by formula 7. where d_{ij} is the distance between anchors i and j, h_{ij} is the minimum hop number from anchor i to anchor j. M is the number of anchor nodes. Therefore the $HopSize$ is corrected as formula 12.

– **Weighting Coefficient for the Minimum Hops Number**: The flooding
  of packet information from the anchor node to these available anchors doesn't
  necessarily follow a direct path. It is possible that the information packet can
  follow an indirect path to get from one node to another one. For this reason, we
  assign a weight to each path hop. Therefore, we use the average hop distance
  of the nearest anchor node to determine the minimum hop number(see Fig. 1).
  So, the minimum hop number is described by formula 2.

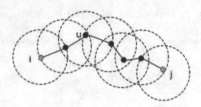

Fig. 1. Nonlinear transmission path between anchor nodes

In order to calculate the minimum hops number between the anchor i and j,
it is possible to find the weighting coefficient by the difference between the
theoretical minimum hops number and the real minimum hops number. This
weighting coefficient can be used from the unknown node to the anchor node.
It is represented in formula 5. With h_{ij}^{est} the theoretical minimum hop number
of the anchor node. h_{ij} is the real minimum hop number. A weight coefficient
is used to correct the minimum hop number. The correct minimum hop number is represented as formula 8. The distance between the unknown nodes
and the anchor nodes is calculated from the weighted minimum hop number
and the corrected hop distance. It is represented as shown in formula 13.

– **Hyperbolic Estimation Method**: To calculate the positions of nodes, we
  propose to apply a hyperbolic method to improve the accuracy of the DV-Hop
  algorithm. We suppose that (x_i,y_i,z_i) the coordinates of the anchor nodes,
  (x_u,y_u,z_u) the coordinates of the unknown nodes and d_{iu} the distance between
  them.

5   Simulation Result

In this section, MATLAB R 2016a numerical tool is used to implement our
proposed algorithm and then compared with the DV-HOP algorithm and other
improved variants in the literature. We perform these simulations to evaluate the
localization accuracy of our improved version named 3DIHDV-HOP according to
the variation of the number of anchors, the variation of the number of unknown
nodes, and the variation of the communication range.

– **MMSE According to the Variation of the Number of Anchors**: In this experimental result, we use a total number of nodes equal to 100, and an anchors node number varies between 11 and 21 nodes. The nodes are distributed with a communication range equal to 80 m. The simulation scenario is repeated 100 times to get readable curves. Figure 2-(a) shows the simulation of the DV-HOP algorithm and some improved versions of DV-HOP existing in the literature as well as our proposed algorithm. When the number of anchors increases from 11 to 21 anchors, we see that the MMSE of all the algorithms decreases slowly until reaches a value below 0.53. In addition, we notice that the MMSE value of the 3DIHDV-HOP algorithm is more lower than the MMSE values of the ImprovebothDV-Hop and 3DeDV-Hop algorithms, which are the most innovative. The MMSE value of the 3DIHDV-HOP algorithm is slowly decreased until reaching a minimum value equal to 0.22. From the simulation result shown, we deduce that our proposed algorithm 3DIHDV-HOP, is more efficient in terms of MMSE localization value and precision values compared to other implemented algorithms.

– **MMSE According to the Variation of the Communication Range**: A total number of nodes equal to 300 nodes is used with a communication range that varies between 35 m and 55 m and an anchors number equal to 30 nodes. This scenario is performed 100 times. According to Fig. 2-(b) below, the MMSE localization of all implemented algorithms tends to decrease if the communication range increases. According to the simulation result, we notice that the values of 3DeDV-Hop and Improveboth-Hop are very close as well as the value of the 3DIHDV-Hop algorithm is lower than the values of these algorithms. The graph shows that compared to the DV-Hop algorithm, the improved algorithms have added some calculations that increase the accuracy of localization and decrease the MMSE. When the communication range R equals 35 m, the MMSE of the DV-Hop algorithm is 1.19, compared to the HDV-Hop algorithm is 1.11, the WHDV-Hop Algorithm [11] is 0.33, the 3DeDV-Hop Algorithm [12] is 0.31, and the Improveboth-Hop Algorithm [14] is 0.31 respectively. When the communication range R is 55 m, the MMSE of the 3DIHDV-Hop algorithm is reduced from 0.31 to 0.28 compared to other algorithms. As explained, we find that our improved version of the DV-HOP algorithm is more efficient than the other simulated variants.

– **MMSE According to the Variation of the Number of Unknown Nodes**: As depicted in Fig. 2-(c), the number of nodes is 200, and the number of unknown nodes belongs to the interval[160:5:185] with a communication range equal to 75 m. The simulation result shows that the proposed algorithm has a smaller MMSE than the MMSE of the other implemented location algorithms. The 3DIHDV-HOP algorithm has a high accuracy compared to other algorithms. If the number of unknown nodes is equal to 160, we find that the ImprovebothDV-Hop, 3DeDV-Hop, and WHDV-Hop algorithms have MMSE values equal to 0.25, 0.23, and 0.27, respectively, while the proposed algorithm 3DIHDV-Hop has an MMSE value equal to 0.19. This value is smaller compared to the values of the other algorithms. The original DV-Hop and HDV-HOP algorithms have an MMSE value about 0.53 and

0.51, respectively. The values of these latter are significantly different from
the MMSE value of the 3DIHDV-HOP algorithm.

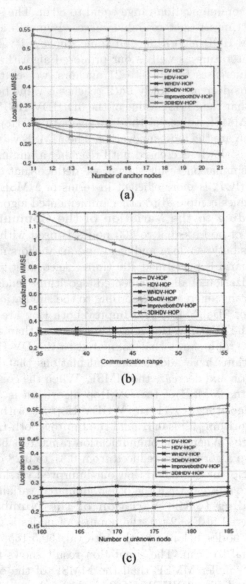

(a)

(b)

(c)

Fig. 2. MMSE According to the Variation of the Number of Anchors, the Communication Range, the Number of Unknown Nodes.

6   Conclusion

The accuracy of location algorithms in WSNs is a fundamental challenge for all researchers. In this paper, we describe in detail the DV-HOP algorithm. Then, we proposed an improved 3DIHDV-HOP based on correcting the average hops distance of anchor nodes by an error factor, improving the minimum hop number of unknown nodes by a weighting coefficient and using three-dimensional hyperbolic method to determine the estimated position of unknown nodes for smart irrigation applications. A numerical simulation via Matlab was investigated to evaluate the localization accuracy of the proposed 3DIHDV-HOP algorithm as a function of the number of anchors, the variation of the number of unknown nodes, and the variation of the communication range. It is demonstrated that our proposal outperforms recent variants in the literature such as ImprovebothDV-HOP and 3DeDV-HOP algorithms based on DV-HOP in terms of MMSE localization. In future work, we propose to implement our algorithm in sensors node (motes micaZ) and test it in a real smart irrigation system.

References

1. Yick, J., Mukherjee, B., Ghosal, D.: Wireless sensor network survey. Comput. Netw. **52**(12), 2292–2330 (2008)
2. Nazir, U., Shahid, N., Arshad, M.A., Classification of localization algorithms for wireless sensor network: A survey. In: International Conference on Open Source Systems and Technologies, pp. 1–5. IEEE (2012)
3. Dargie, W., Poellabauer, C., et al.: Fundamentals of wireless sensor networks: theory and practice. John Wiley and Sons (2010)
4. Shakshuki, E., Elkhail, A.A., Nemer, I., et al.: Comparative study on range free localization algorithms. Proc. Comput. Sci. **151**, 501–510 (2019)
5. Ssu, K.-F., Ou, C.-H., Jiau, H.W.: Localization with mobile anchor points in wireless sensor networks. IEEE Trans. Veh. Technol. **54**(3), 1187–1197 (2005)
6. Zhang, J., Wu, Y.-H., Shi, F., et al.: Localization algorithm based on DV-HOP for wireless sensor networks. J. Comput. Appli. **30**(2), 323–333 (2010)
7. Hu, Y., Li, X.: An improvement of DV-Hop localization algorithm for wireless sensor networks. Telecommun. Syst. **53**(1), 13–18 (2013)
8. Li, J., Zhang, J., Xiande, L.: (2009) A weighted DV-Hop localization scheme for wireless sensor networks. In: 2009 International Conference on Scalable Computing and Communications; Eighth International Conference on Embedded Computing. IEEE, p. 9–272 (2009)
9. GUADANE, Mohamed, BCHIMI, Wassima, SAMET, Abdelaziz, Enhanced range-free localization in wireless sensor networks using a new weighted hop-size estimation technique. In, et al.: IEEE 28th Annual International Symposium on Personal, Indoor, and Mobile Radio Communications (PIMRC). IEEE 2017, 1–5 (2017)
10. Hadir, A., Zine-Dine, K., Bakhouya, M., El Kafi., J., et al.: , An optimized DV-hop localization algorithm using average hop weighted mean in WSNs. In, et al.: 5th Workshop on Codes, Cryptography and Communication Systems (WCCCS), pp. 25–29, IEEE (2014)
11. Hadir, A., Zine-Dine, K., Bakhouya, M., et al. Localization Algorithms for Mobile Nodes for Three-Dimentional WSNs. In: 2018 6th International Conference on Wireless Networks and Mobile Communications (WINCOM). IEEE, p. 1–8 (2018)

12. Mass-Sanchez, J., Ruiz-Ibarra, E., Cortez-González, et al.: Weighted hyperbolic DV-hop positioning node localization algorithm in WSNs. Wireless Personal Commun., 96(4), 5011–5033 (2017)
13. Gui, L., Val, T., Wei, A.: A Novel Two-Class Localization Algorithm in Wireless Sensor Networks. Netw. Protoc. Algorithms **3**(3), 1–16 (2011)
14. Fang, W., Xu, H., Yang, G.: Improved DV-Hop algorithm based on Minimum Hops correction and reevaluate Hop distance. In: 2019 5th International Conference on Information Management (ICIM). IEEE, pp. 102–107 (2019)
15. Prashar, D., Joshi, G.P., Jha, S., et al.: Three-Ddmensional distance-error-correction-based Hop localization algorithm for IoT devices. CMC-Comput Materia Continua **66**(2), 1529–1549 (2021)
16. Huang, X., Han, D., Cui, M., et al.: Three-dimensional localization algorithm based on improved A* and DV-Hop algorithms in wireless sensor network. Sensors **21**(2), 448 (2021)
17. Kumar, S., Lobiyal, D.K.: An advanced DV-Hop localization algorithm for wireless sensor networks. Wireless Pers. Commun. **71**(2), 1365–1385 (2013)
18. Kanwar, V., Kumar, A.: Range free localization for three dimensional wireless sensor networks using multi objective particle swarm optimization. Wirel. Pers. Commun. **117**(2), 901–921 (2021)
19. Niculescu, D., Nath, B.: Ad hoc positioning system (APS). In: GLOBECOM 2001. IEEE Global Telecommunications Conference (Cat. No. 01CH37270), pp. 2926–2931. IEEE (2001)

Online Teaching and Movements

Online Dance Lesson Support System Using Flipped Classroom

Shuhei Tsuchida[1]($\boxtimes$)(iD), Daichi Shimizu[1](iD), Kanako Shibasaki[2],
Tsutomu Terada[1](iD), and Masahiko Tsukamoto[1](iD)

[1] Kobe University, 1-1, Rokkodai-cho, Nada-ku, Kobe, Japan
t.sway.tmpp@gmail.com
[2] Sports Academy Tsuchiura, 1-11-5 Kawaguchi, Tsuchiura, Ibaraki, Japan

Abstract. Contemporary online lessons that use web-conferencing systems suffer from several issues, mainly because instructors engage in the same type of instruction as they do in conventional offline lessons. For example, it might be difficult for learners to grasp three-dimensional movements. Teaching through a video displayed on a screen is also limited, as opposed to teaching through physical bodies and showing movements in person. In addition, it is difficult for the instructors to teach one person at a time during a lesson with many students. This study proposes an online dance lesson support system that enables instructors to remotely but effectively teach multiple learners. We initially focus on the framework of online dance lessons and subsequently propose a lesson style that applies to flipped classrooms. We aim to provide a new lesson style for on-demand lessons and real-time lessons using deep learning techniques.

Keywords: Training · Dance lesson · Flipped classroom · Online

1 Introduction

Although the development of information technology has benefitted intellectual labor, telecommunications, and digital content dissemination, it has reduced the amount of physical activity in people's daily lives and proliferated health problems caused by inactivity. In modern society, the lack of exercise needs to be compensated for by incorporating sports and exercise into everyday life to maintain normal bodily functions. Moderate exercise is also accompanied by a sense of exhilaration and can improve mental health. Spaces where everyone can enjoy exercising to maintain a healthy state of mind and body, such as fitness gyms, are crucial in modern society.

During the COVID-19 epidemic, demand for spaces where people can gather shifted from the physical world to the virtual world. For example, the closure of fitness gyms offering dance and other exercises opened opportunities for online lessons using web conferencing systems, such as Zoom. However, current online lessons frequently provide identical instruction to that of conventional offline

© The Author(s), under exclusive license to Springer Nature Switzerland AG 2022
P. Delir Haghighi et al. (Eds.): MoMM 2022, LNCS 13634, pp. 133–142, 2022.
https://doi.org/10.1007/978-3-031-20436-4_13

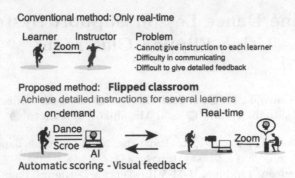

Fig. 1. Proposed online dance lesson applying flipped classroom.

lessons using an unmodified web conferencing system, causing diverse problems. For example, compared to instructions that use the physical body to show movements in person, instruction via video on a PC or other display makes it difficult to grasp three-dimensional movements and limits the methods of instruction. It is also difficult for instructors to instruct one person at a time in a large group lesson. Therefore, this study proposed an online dance lesson support system that enables instructors to remotely but effectively teach multiple learners. This study initially focuses on the framework of online dance lessons and thereafter proposes a lesson style that applies to flipped classrooms.

In particular, this study focuses on the flipped classroom as the basis of the framework. A flipped classroom is an educational method wherein learners work individually before the class on basic learning such as explanatory lectures, and engage with the instructor during the class on learning that is necessary for the retention of knowledge and development of application skills such as tutorials and project learning [2]. In conventional face-to-face and online dance lessons, "learning" (acquisition of individual movements) and "development/exercise" (acquisition and refinement of choreography with multiple movements, refinement of expressiveness to music) are usually interwoven. In our proposal, the flipped classroom structure is applied, and on-demand video lessons conduct the "learning" part of the lessons. In contrast, the "development/exercise" part is conducted by real-time online lessons (Fig. 1). By applying the aforementioned structure, the "learning" part, which requires repetition to understand the movements and make detailed corrections, can be studied repeatedly at the learners' own pace. In contrast, the "development/exercise" part, which develops and expands the expressive power of learners according to their characteristics and movements, can be conducted and explored through individual instruction and sharing with other participants. The advantage of this approach is that learners can devote time to developmental and exploratory activities such as individual instruction and sharing with other participants. We believe that the framework composed of repeated "learning" - "development/exercise" lessons enables us to provide effective lessons that develop the expressive ability of participants.

2   Related Works

Many support systems for learning dance skills have been proposed [18]. They vary from tactile [3,15] and auditory [9,14,23] systems to video presentations [1, 8,12], use of mobile robots [11,16,22], gamification [4,20], etc. In this study, we developed a dance lesson support system focusing on virtual reality(VR) technology to apply it to the flipped classroom of an online dance lesson.

Several VR-based support systems have been proposed [6,17,25]. Tsampounaris et al. [21] developed a system that allows users to change into different avatars, visualize traces of the movements of various body parts, and interact with virtual objects. Senecal et al. [19] developed a system for presenting virtual partners in salsa dance, where practicing with a partner is important. This study found that the motions of inexperienced participants converged with those of skilled participants upon practicing with the system. Kasahara et al. [10] found that showing a slightly futuristic video from the motion information of users made their bodies feel lighter. Various VR systems have been proposed; however, to the best of our knowledge, no systems apply flipped classrooms to an online dance lesson.

3   Preliminary Investigation

3.1   Lesson Design

This study has planned and implemented an online dance lesson employing the above framework and a dance instructor with immense teaching experience. The lesson is summarized below. The dance lessons were held on July 4, 15, and 22, 2020, with detailed improvements. The first lesson was an on-demand video lesson of approximately 15 min (the participants could watch the video repeatedly, and the actual duration depended on the participants). A video lesson was filmed and distributed to the participants, briefly explaining and demonstrating basic rhythms, dance steps, and simple choreographies combining them. The instructor filmed each movement/step and provided a detailed verbal explanation of the demonstration. The participants listened to the instructor's explanation and watched the demonstrated movements while imitating and learning the dance steps one by one. We sent the video via YouTube a few days before the real-time lesson. Subsequently, the real-time online lesson was conducted, which spanned approximately 45 minutes per lesson. In this lesson, all participants repeated the choreography that they had performed at the end of the on-demand lesson. The instructor commented on the quality, expressiveness, and areas for improvement. The participants also had time to ask questions about what they did not understand, share their impressions of the choreography in groups, and share and discuss their impressions of the dance themselves. We designed the lessons to encourage information sharing and interaction between instructors and participants. The real-time lessons were conducted using the online conference software "Zoom" (Fig. 2).

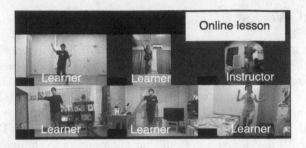

Fig. 2. A real-time lesson using Zoom. The participants attended from their own homes and nearby studios.

3.2 Participants' Impressions

In the post-lesson discussions, the participants expressed their appreciation of the framework's value. Some participants felt that it was valuable to work repeatedly on the parts of the lesson that did not go well in the on-demand lesson. Furthermore, they felt they could watch other participants dance in the real-time lesson and share their impressions and awareness when dancing.

Considering the instructor's findings and the participants' feedback after the preliminary investigation, we can discuss the establishment of teaching methods tailored to individual situations in on-demand video lessons. The level of mastery of the basic steps varied greatly between participants, both in terms of type and points for improvement. Currently, there is no way to overcome this disparity other than individual guidance in real-time lessons, and this shortened the time allocated to development. The content needs to be improved to enable robust learning of the basics. This can be done by preparing videos that include detailed correction methods for the steps that the participants have difficulties with.

4   Proposed Method

For preliminary investigation, we propose an online dance lesson style. The lesson style mainly consists of on-demand and real-time lessons (Fig. 3). This lesson style was structured considering a flipped classroom [13].

A flipped classroom is a teaching style that replaces the teaching traditionally conducted in the classroom (learning) with independent learning (development/exercise) modules assigned as homework. Usually, the learning occurs in the class, followed by self-learning through exercises. However, in a flipped classroom, the learning takes place through self-learning and the exercises are undertaken in the class. The advantages of this system are that learners can repeat the learning at their own pace and have more opportunities for output; further, the possibility of collaborative learning is increased, and instructors can easily monitor learners' progress. Owing to these advantages, we expected that flipped classrooms could be applied to online dance lessons for effective teaching.

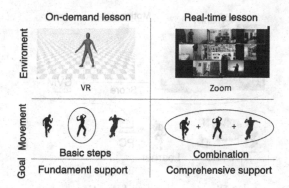

Fig. 3. Our proposed lesson style.

The application of the flipped classroom to online dance lessons is illustrated in Fig. 1. In conventional online lessons, real-time lessons using a web conferencing system such as Zoom are common. In the proposed method, the lessons are divided into two categories: on-demand and real-time. In the on-demand lesson, learners learn the basic dance steps on their own, and in the real-time lesson, they perform dance steps that combine the basic steps learned in the on-demand step. This lesson style allows detailed feedback to be returned to each learner individually, even when teaching many learners.

4.1 On-Demand Lesson: Basic Movement Learning Support Tool

System Design. The preliminary investigation found that mastery of the basic steps, both in terms of type and improvement, varies between participants. To address this, we need a system that can support participant-specific modifications in on-demand lessons. Specifically, a function that automatically scores which parts of the learner's body are similar to the reference movements and to what extent, and a function that provides feedback on the scoring results, would together solve this problem.

To achieve automatic scoring, we need to acquire the motion information of the learner in real time. Moreover, these functions are also necessary for the proposed system, based on related studies, such as the ability to practice with a mirror [5], the desirability of the largest possible display when imitating movements [7], and the ability to check movements from different angles in three dimensions [24].

System Configuration. Based on Sect. 4.1 describing the system design, we developed a support system for on-demand lessons. Figure 4 shows a system configuration. The system consists of a PC (G-Tune NM-S712SIR6SPZI), VIVE Pro Eye, and three VIVE Trackers. In addition to these devices, our system enables real-time motion tracking by utilizing the Final IK (Inverse Kinematics) library.

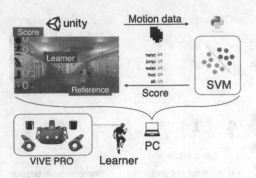

Fig. 4. System configuration.

We configured the VR lesson space in Unity and implemented the automatic scoring functionality described later in Python. Specifically, the system sends motion data from the VR lesson space to Python and automatically scores dance motions by applying them to a learning model.

Automatic Scoring. In the on-demand lessons, the learners learn dance movements using the proposed system that checks and supports the acquisition of basic steps, which is a fundamental part of improving one's dancing. Specifically, we envisage the use of automatic scoring of dance steps. In basic dance steps, each body part, for example, the hips and hands, needs to be moved accurately. Therefore, by presenting a score for each body part that is important for achieving the basic dance steps, learners can check how accurately they are moving their bodies, which supports self-learning.

To build the automatic scoring function, we first collected motions of basic dance steps from dancers. We adopted the motion "New Jack Swing", a basic movement in hip-hop dance. We collected 900 movements spanning approximately two seconds each. We created a tool to visualize, edit, and score the collected motions using openFrameworks to create the training dataset. A professional dance instructor subjectively scored the collected motions in three levels. We used these data as training datasets with the correct answers labeled. The learning model used the support vector machine (SVM) machine learning method. The differences between frames of the joint positions of the 3D motion were calculated for 120 frames, and we used the mean and standard deviation of the differences as a 40-dimensional feature vector. These vectors were divided into parts for each region, each of which is trained using SVM. This process could make models in which hand, waist, foot, and overall scores can be calculated on three levels. The classification accuracy of the scores was approximately 89% for the entire body, 84% for the feet, 89% for the hands, and 94% for the waist.

User Flow. This section describes the procedure for using the system from the user's perspective. The system utilization procedure is shown in Fig. 5. First,

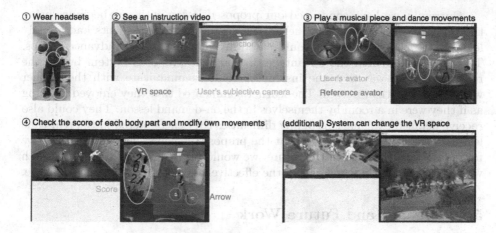

Fig. 5. User flow.

the user wears a headset and puts on trackers. Thereafter, the user enters the VR space. The user can move freely in the space by pointing to the position they want to move to while pressing a button on the controller. By pressing another button on the controller, the user can watch an instructional video, such as the one employed in the preliminary investigation. By practicing while watching this video, the user can first receive the same level of practice as the on-demand lessons in the preliminary investigation. Furthermore, the user can move on to practice using the automatic scoring function. Pressing the trigger on the controller starts the playback of the musical piece, and the reference avatar starts dancing. The user dances to the avatar's dance and watches the scoring change in real time. The user can refer to this score to understand which body parts are not being imitated accurately. In addition to the scoring display, low-scoring areas are highlighted with arrows so that the user can visually see which parts to focus on. Other advantages of VR include, for example, the possibility to place a large mirror in the open air and concentrate on practice.

4.2 Real-Time Lesson

The real-time lessons corresponding to the "development/exercise" in the flipped classroom focus mainly on the communication between the instructor and the learners. Specifically, the lessons will be conducted using an online conferencing system, such as Zoom, with the following flow: First, the learner demonstrates the basic steps learned in the on-demand lesson. Thereafter, the instructor instructs the learners one by one based on those basic steps. At this point, the instructor also introduces a longer choreography combining the basic steps. Comments are then shared among the participants. Finally, the instructor provides instructions on the following task, and learners return to the on-demand lesson. We believe that learners will learn more advanced steps by repeating this lesson style.

Currently, we have conducted our proposed lesson with one beginner using the proposed system. The instructor commented that the students had already learned the basic steps, and could smoothly move on to the advanced steps. They also commented the advantage of using the proposed system before the real-time lesson was that the instructor could communicate with the learner with their concerns resolved. The learner commented that they enjoyed learning as if they were in a room by themselves in the on-demand lesson. They could also receive detailed explanations of any difficulties they encountered in the real-time lesson. This feedback indicated that the proposed lesson style could be effective for online dance lessons. In the future, we would like to conduct further research with more participants and clarify the effectiveness of our proposed lesson style.

5   Summary and Future Work

In this study, we proposed an online dance lesson support system that enabled instructors to remotely but effectively teach multiple learners. We first focused on the framework of online dance lessons and subsequently proposed a lesson style that applied to flipped classrooms.

Structuring "development/exercise" content in real-time lessons remains challenging. Currently, the content is being closely examined based on the rich teaching experience of the lecturers. Further refinement of the content into more effective content based on clear theory remains to be achieved. In the future, we aim to construct more effective lessons for fostering expressive ability, considering the interaction between on-demand lessons and real-time lessons.

When building the proposed system, motion-capturing devices were selected considering device availability and accuracy. The minimum number of tracking devices required for learning dance steps has not been studied so far, and we could share the knowledge (six-point tracking) to help build a dance-step-learning support system in the future. We developed the proposed system on SteamVR, which can be released as an application.

Recently, VRChat has been widely used, and many users enjoy dancing on VRChat. We can use our proposed system to develop lessons for such users. There is a new type of user in VRChat that differs from those who attend traditional studio lessons. For example, we expect that many people would like to learn dancing but are embarrassed to attend a studio lesson because of the presence of many people. Our proposed system and lesson style allow VRChat users to take dance lessons and could be established as a new business model using machine learning techniques. Our system could also be used for purposes other than dance lessons, including rehabilitation and weightlifting.

Acknowledgements. This work was supported by Mitou Foundation, and JST, CREST Grant Number JPMJCR18A3, Japan.

References

1. Anderson, F., Grossman, T., Matejka, J., Fitzmaurice, G.: Youmove: Enhancing movement training with an augmented reality mirror. In: Proceedings of the 26th Annual ACM Symposium on User Interface Software and Technology, UIST 2013, pp. 311–320 (2013)
2. Bergmann, J., Aaron, S.: Flipped Learning: Gateway to Student Engagement. International Society for Technology in Education (2014)
3. Camarillo-Abad, H., Sánchez, A., Starostenko, O., Sandoval Esquivel, M.: A basic tactile language to support leader-follower dancing. J. Intell. Fuzzy Syst. **36**, 5011–5022 (2019)
4. Charbonneau, E., Miller, A., LaViola, J.J.: Teach me to dance: Exploring player experience and performance in full body dance games. In: Proceedings of the 8th International Conference on Advances in Computer Entertainment Technology, ACE 2011, p. 8 (2011)
5. Dearborn, K., Ross, R.: Dance learning and the mirror: Comparison study of dance phrase learning with and without mirrors. J. Dance Educ. **6**, 109–115 (2006)
6. Eaves, D., Breslin, G., Schaik, P., Robinson, E., Spears, I.: The short-term effects of real-time virtual reality feedback on motor learning in dance. J. Presence **20**, 62–77 (2011)
7. Elsayed, H., et al.: CameraReady: Assessing the Influence of Display Types and Visualizations on Posture Guidance, pp. 1046–1055 (2021)
8. Fujimoto, M., Terada, T., Tsukamoto, M.: A dance training system that maps self-images onto an instruction video. In: Proceedings of the 5th International Conference on Advances in Computer-Human Interactions, ACHI 2012, pp. 309–314 (2012)
9. Großhauser, T., Bläsing, B., Spieth, C., Hermann, T.: Wearable sensor-based real-time sonification of motion and foot pressure in dance teaching and training. J. Audio Eng. Soc. **60**(7/8), 580–589 (2012)
10. Kasahara, S., et al.: Malleable embodiment: Changing sense of embodiment by spatial-temporal deformation of virtual human body. In: Proceedings of the 2017 CHI Conference on Human Factors in Computing Systems, CHI 2017, pp. 6438–6448 (2017)
11. Kosuge, K., et al.: Partner ballroom dance robot -pbdr-. SICE J. Control Measur. Syst. Integrat. **1**(1), 74–80 (2008)
12. Kyan, M., et al.: An approach to ballet dance training through ms kinect and visualization in a cave virtual reality environment. J. ACM Trans. Intell. Syst. Technol. **6**(2), 37 (2015)
13. Lage, M.J., Glenn, J.P., Michael, T.: Inverting the classroom: A gateway to creating an inclusive learning environment. J. Econ. Educ. **31**(1), 30–43 (2000)
14. Landry, S., Jeon, M.: Interactive sonification strategies for the motion and emotion of dance performances. J. Multimodal User Interf. **14**, 167–186 (2020)
15. Nakamura, A., Tabata, S., Ueda, T., Kiyofuji, S., Kuno, Y.: Dance training system with active vibro-devices and a mobile image display. In: Proceedings of the 2005 IEEE/RSJ International Conference on Intelligent Robots and Systems, IROS 2005, pp. 3075–3080 (2005)
16. Nakamura, A., Tabata, S., Ueda, T., Kiyofuji, S., Kuno, Y.: Multimodal presentation method for a dance training system. In: Extended Abstracts Proceedings of the 2005 Conference on Human Factors in Computing Systems, CHI EA 2005, pp. 1685–1688 (2005)

17. Philo Tan Chua, et al.: Training for physical tasks in virtual environments: Tai chi. In: Proceedings of the Proceedings of the IEEE Virtual Reality Conference, VR 2003, pp. 87–94 (2003)
18. Raheb, K.E., Stergiou, M., Katifori, A., Ioannidis, Y.: Dance interactive learning systems: A study on interaction workflow and teaching approaches. J. ACM Comput. Surv. **52**(3), 37 (2019)
19. Senecal, S., Nijdam, N.A., Aristidou, A., Magnenat-Thalmann, N.: Salsa dance learning evaluation and motion analysis in gamified virtual reality environment. J. Multimedia Tools Appli. **79**(33), 24621–24643 (2020)
20. Smith, S., Sherrington, C., Studenski, S., Schoene, D., Lord, S.: A novel dance dance revolution (ddr) system for in-home training of stepping ability: Basic parameters of system use by older adults. J. Sports Med. **45**, 441–5 (2009)
21. Tsampounaris, G., El Raheb, K., Katifori, V., Ioannidis, Y.: Exploring visualizations in real-time motion capture for dance education. In: Proceedings of the 20th Pan-Hellenic Conference on Informatics, PCI 2016, p. 6 (2016)
22. Tsuchida, S., Terada, T., Tsukamoto, M.: A system for practicing formations in dance performance supported by self-propelled screen. In: Proceedings of the 4th Augmented Human International Conference, AH 2013, p. 178–185 (2013)
23. Yamaguchi, T., Kadone, H.: Supporting creative dance performance by grasping-type musical interface. In: Proceedings of the 2014 IEEE International Conference on Robotics and Biomimetics, ROBIO 2014, pp. 919–924 (2014)
24. Yan, S., Ding, G., Guan, Z., Sun, N., Li, H., Zhang, L.: Outsideme: Augmenting dancer's external self-image by using a mixed reality system. In: In Proceedings of the 33rd Annual ACM Conference Extended Abstracts on Human Factors in Computing Systems, . CHI EA 2015, pp. 965–970(2015)
25. Yang, U., Kim, G.J.: Implementation and evaluation of "just follow me": An immersive, vr-based, motion-training system. J. PRESENCE: Virt. Augmen. Reality **11**(3), 304–323 (2002)

Who Shapes the Network of a Pedagogical Space? Clues from the Movements in the Physical Places

Lai Wei and Kenny K. N. Chow[✉]

School of Design, The Hong Kong Polytechnic University, Hong Kong, China
sdknchow@polyu.edu.hk

Abstract. Researchers who study pedagogical space mostly look at physical space, such as the density of space usage and education-related material designs. The interaction of objects and the resulting network in the physical space, referred to as a secondary pedagogical spatiality, have received less attention. In a classroom setting, objects may refer to the lecturers and students. This study examines the representations of their body movements corresponding with concurrent verbal language, seat layout, and instructional equipment. We further examine the objects' movements and how they relate to the physical spaces and understand the process of interactions in the physical spaces. The findings, which support the Actor-Network Theory concerning the connectedness and fluidity of objects in physical places, help move toward a theory of pedagogical network.

Keywords: Network in physical spaces · Pedagogy · Actor-network theory · Multimodality · Bodily movement

1 Introduction

Several studies have shown that spaces (e.g., conventional classrooms, digital educational platforms, workshops, outdoor) affect the formation of the social consciousness of lecturers and students and prevent them from effective education-related activities [3, 4, 9, 12]. Researchers mainly focused on investigating the density of space usage [23] and education-related material design [11, 15]. In contrast, the physical interactions within pedagogical spaces are underexplored. Essentially, educational activities are dynamic assemblies of social actions, reactions, and interactions among lecturers, students, instructional equipment, and the sites [8]. Lecturers typically take the lead in educational activities and stand as the focal point in the spaces, and students sit around them during lectures. Thus, making sense of the physical interactions within pedagogical spaces and the relationship between lecturers and educational activities is essential.

Pedagogical space can be understood as Euclidean space, the common understanding of physical space. However, a second spatiality level also exists, formed by a network connected by *objects* [21]. This second level of spatiality is commonly known as *a fluid form of space* [21], which consists of 1) objects, including lecturers, students, and

© The Author(s), under exclusive license to Springer Nature Switzerland AG 2022
P. Delir Haghighi et al. (Eds.): MoMM 2022, LNCS 13634, pp. 143–153, 2022.
https://doi.org/10.1007/978-3-031-20436-4_14

instructional equipment [19, 20], and 2) The objects' movement [20]. From a linguistic point of view, the objects are multimodal carriers in pedagogical discourse [18, 31]. Kress indicated that humans' verbal expression serves as one of the primary multimodality in teaching discourse, gesture, gaze, bodily movement, and instructional equipment reveal unspoken information [17]. However, the impacts of using instructional equipment in educational activities have been relatively understudied. Thus, we propose that the formation of pedagogical space is related to the movements of objects, particularly instructional equipment use. The study is undertaken from Law's network space theory (NST) [21], Latour's Actor-network theory [20], and multimodal discourse [18] for examining the representations of instructional equipment, lecturers' gestures, and body movements corresponding with concurrent verbal language, and the seat layout of students. We further identify the objects through their movements and their correlations with the physical spaces. In this article, we will answer two questions:

- What are the representations of the objects' movements in physical spaces?
- How do the objects shape the pedagogical network in physical spaces?

2   Related Work

2.1   Pedagogical Space

Objects' Movements. The pedagogical space is revealed through the objects' educational events and their movements performed. Thus, the representations of objects' movements and the relations between objects are essential for understanding the pedagogical space. Their representations conform to *a syntax of consistent functionality* [21] and *move only within Euclidean space, remaining immobile within network space* [21]. Lecturers' and students' bodied movements (e.g., gestures, postures, mental states-related behaviors) and instructional equipment used (e.g., computers, projection screens, desks, chairs) are tagged. We defined two types of object movements, 1) *Active movement*. Lecturers' and students' bodied movements [6, 7] and bodily interactions [2] have been evaluated through their independent modalities—body movements and gestures. However, few studies analyze the movements of lecturers' and students' social actions. Lim speculated a social-related classification of gestures [24] according to Martinec's types of actions [25–27]. In a classroom context, he believes gestures are separated into communicative gestures (i.e., representing action and indexical action), which feature self-representation and linguistic correlation, and performative gestures (i.e., presenting action), which reflect people's states and behaviors [24]. Lecturers' and students' social actions are recognized by verbal content, gaze, gestures, postures, and body orientation, according to Lim's multimodal taxonomy in classroom discourse [22]. In addition to the preceding, the lecturers' movements and gestures scales are supposed to sketch the pedagogical network space. 2) *Passive movement*. The physical instructional equipment is typically set aside for easy accessibility, allowing for relative movement. Hence, the instructional equipment's movements are derived from bodily interactions with lecturers.

Objects' Relative Distance. Lecturers situating themselves in a teaching environment has been studied through physical space level [1, 5, 22, 30]. Yet, the relationship between lecturers' movements and physical spaces is rarely explored. Humans perceive space by measuring the distance between objects according to the framework of the interpersonal distance of man [13, 14]. However, applying Hall's interpersonal space set to evaluate the representations of lecturers' interpersonal space perception cannot interpret the lecturers' space use. Previc proposed the behavioural systems involved in 3-D spatial interactions [28] that humans perceive easy manipulation and their somatosensory and motor system are active in peripersonal space. This is similar to Hall's intimate space. In focal extrapersonal space referring to Hall's personal space, humans primarily use eye movement for object recognition. Humans' movement is target-orientated, and they tend to have more head movement in action extrapersonal space which is identical to Hall's social space. Consequently, their somatosensory perception is reduced but remains visual and auditory perception actively. Bodily movement is adopted in ambient extrapersonal space resembling Hall's public space, and the humans' intention approaches spatial orientation.

2.2 Multimodality in Pedagogical Spaces

Lecturers, as the center of educational activities, are mainly in charge of transmitting structured knowledge and directing the mobility of turn-taking. Students, the prominent participants in educational activities, are expected to comprehend novel knowledge and interact in educational communication [16]. Instructional equipment aids and facilitates effective communication between lecturers and students. As a result, lecturers are the primary objects in educational activities, while students and instructional equipment collaborate to carry out educational activities.

Lecturers' Multimodality: Lecturers' gaze, gestures, postures, and mental state-related behaviors as kinetics forms of multimodality carry unspoken and context-related information [31]. In the interim, lecturers' verbal language functions for narrating educational content and highlighting important information, reflecting their social and mental state [30]. The orchestration of those lecturers' multimodalities composes a dynamic system of teaching discourse. Analyzing those multimodalities and their composition is critical to comprehending lecturers' social actions and distinguishing the relationships with students, equipment, and physical space.

Students' and Instructional Equipment's Multimodality: Students and equipment primarily produce unspoken and passive multimodality. In a lecture setting, students usually play the roles of the audience, and their bodied movements are not particularly large. However, students bring lecturers unspoken information through their gaze and slight body movements. Lecturers widely reported that they perceive a sense of social presence while teaching in front of students [10, 28]. Instructional equipment, including computers, projection screens, desks, and chairs, are other types of unspoken multimodality. They support lecturers in presenting visualized and deconstructed information as semiotic resources. They demonstrate images, text, and videos, but lecturers are required to access and manipulate them actively. Hence, instructional equipment also obtains semiotic modality. In a later stage, we will examine the instructional equipment that has been identified and evaluate their relations with lecturers and students.

3 Methods

Given the theoretical propositions in the preceding sections, this paper applies the proposed conceptions of pedagogical spaces' formulation through the lecturers' and students' movements together with verb language and instructional equipment in three real-life teaching settings. Through the movements and correlations of the objects, the case study approach promises to reveal the representations of the objects' movements and gain an in-depth understanding of pedagogical spaces' formulation. As linguistic analysis and gestural analysis of the meanings were brought through the lens of Systemic Functional Theory [22], we apply systemic functional-multimodal discourse analysis in this study. Three case studies are adopted: offline, online, and hybrid teaching settings.

3.1 Measurements

Based on Previc's behavioral 3-D spatial interaction systems [29], we depict the spatial relation diagram of multimodal sources in lecturers' space in Fig. 1, in which three levels of lecturers' space were defined. It investigates the lecturers' relative distance perception by investigating their bodily movements. From a relative space aspect, the innermost level of lecturers' space is a space for them to manipulate teaching equipment and demonstrate instructional sources easily. The middle level of lecturers' space refers to action extrapersonal space with more expansive horizontal space for ease of target positioning, in which lecturers illustrate their visual and spatial attention patterns. Lecturers' whole-body movement is supposed to be fruitful to continually interact with students in the outermost level of lecturers' perception space. Lecturers produce three progressive scale gestures (i.e., small, medium, and large) that relate to the embodied spatial spreading of somatosensory perception in line with Previc's peripersonal space. Large gestures cover the greatest distance that humans are attempting to stroke. Medium gestures are human gestures that span between the head and the waist and are less than 0.5 m apart. In contrast, small gestures are movements that occur in front of a person's chest. Two-dimensional relative distance perception is designed for manifesting the correlations between lecturers and physical space.

3.2 Subject and Research Site

We conducted this study in three different types of daily usage classrooms based on the features of lecturers' natural activities in a real-life teaching situation. We recruited three male participants, given the pseudonyms of George (offline), John (online), and Tom (hybrid), who are university lecturers having around ten years of teaching experience for undergraduate courses and specializing in design and arts disciplines. We implemented around 60 min of observation for each lecture. Moreover, we observed lecturers' and students' speech, non-verbal movement, and teaching process; specifically, we recorded lecturers' movements and equipment usage.

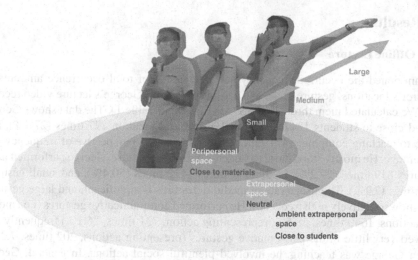

Fig. 1. A spatial relation diagram of multimodal sources in lecturers' space taking offline lecturer as an example

3.3 Equipment

The multimodal discourse analysis software ELAN was used to annotate 9611,357 ms valid video recordings, 3130,372 ms for offline mode, 3066,990 ms for online mode, and 3413,995 ms for hybrid mode. Three tiers were recorded, annotated, and analyzed, including lecturer action types and representing and presenting action types that revealed lecturers' social involvement, locations, and gesture scales[21]. We also transcribed lecturers' verbal language from video recordings and manually reexamined it through an online transcription service. Statistics software SPSS is applied to calculate the general data description.

3.4 Procedure

Before the class started, we notified the lecturers and the students that the teaching process would be video recorded. Then a camera was placed at a three-quarter angle about three meters away from the lecturers. During the class, one of our researchers sited in the classroom to observe the lecturers' and students' actions and material usage and monitor the camera consistently working without interrupting the regular teaching processing. We observed and recorded three one-hour-long lectures.

4 Results

4.1 Offline Lecture

We annotated the occurred frequency and percentage of total occurrence amounts of lecturer's locations, gesture scale, and action types from George's lecture video recording. We calculated them through SPSS (see Fig. 2 and Table 1). The data shows George stayed close to students 1347 times (48.1%), neutral location 777 times (27.7%), and close to teaching equipment 471 times (16.8%) from the perspective of frequency and percentage. He mostly stood close to students during his lecture. George performed large gestures 819 times (29.2%), medium gestures 1412 times (50.4%), and small gestures 201 times (7.2%). The usage rate of medium gestures is significant, and large gestures also show a relatively high frequency. He performed communicative gestures (i.e., indexical actions, 1640 times, 58.5%; representing action, 731 times, 26.1%) frequently and showed very little in the performative gestures (presenting actions, 202 times, 7.2%). When George was teaching, he involved plentiful social actions. In general, George used gestures effectively, which he mostly used to communicate with the students and the actual teaching site.

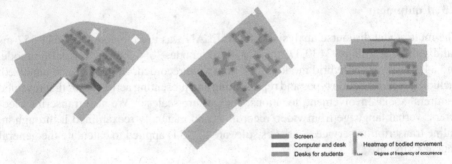

Screen
Computer and desk   Heatmap of bodied movement
Desks for students   Degree of frequency of occurrence

Fig. 2. A heatmap of lecturers' and students' bodied movements in offline lecture setting (left), online lecture setting (middle), and hybrid lecture setting (right).

Thirty-three students who wore masks attended the lecture and sat silently during the teaching process. They did not make noticeable movements and barely talked with George. Instructional equipment includes two projection screens, a computer, a laptop, and desks and chairs for placing belongings and students' use. George mainly utilized the laptop for presenting information on screens, and laptops were placed on students' desks. He occasionally strolled between the laptop and the screen behind him, but he generally stood near students. A two-meter-long microphone line limited George's range of motion because he had been lecturing with the microphone.

Table 1. Frequency and percentage of three features of George's Multimodal Use

Lecturer location		Close to students	Close to teaching equipment	Neutral	Null	Total
	Fre	1347	471	777	207	2802
	%	48.1	16.8	27.7	7.4	100.0
Lecturer gesture scale		Large	Medium	Small	Null	Total
	Fre	819	1412	201	370	2802
	%	29.2	50.4	7.2	13.2	100.0
Lecturer action type		Indexical action	Presenting action	Representing action	Null	Total
	Fre	1640	202	731	229	2802
	%	58.5	7.2	26.1	8.2	100.0

4.2 Online Lecture

We annotated the occurred frequency and percentage of total occurrence amounts of gesture scale and action types from John's lecture video recording. We calculated them through SPSS (see Fig. 2 and Table 2). Since John was online presenting, his location did not count. The data demonstrates that John stroked large gestures 29 times (1.8%), medium gestures 398 times (24.9%), and small gestures 926 times (58%). The usage rate of small gestures is significantly high. Large and medium gestures show relatively low frequency. He performed communicative gestures frequently (i.e., indexical actions, 539 times, 33.8%; representing action, 736 times, 46.1%) and showed relatively less in the performative gestures (presenting actions, 259 times, 16.2%). John's range of motion is limited, yet he makes clear communicative actions.

Twenty-four students attended the lecture who donned masks and sat silently during the session. Twenty-three students attended online. They did not make any apparent moves and had no communication with John. Instructional equipment includes a projection screen, a computer, and desks and chairs for placing belongings and students' use.

Table 2. Frequency and percentage of three features of John's Multimodal Use

Lecturer gesture scale		Large	Medium	Small	Null	Total
	Fre	29	398	926	244	1597
	%	1.8	24.9	58.0	15.3	100.0
Lecturer action type		Indexical action	Presenting action	Representing action	Null	Total
	Fre	539	259	736	63	1597
	%	33.8	16.2	46.1	3.9	100.0

John was online and had no full-bodied movements observed. He only used the screen to share instructional materials with students virtually.

4.3 Hybrid Lecture

We annotated the occurred frequency and percentage of total occurrence amounts of lecturer's locations, gesture scale, and action types from Tom's lecture video recording and calculated them through SPSS (see Fig. 2 and Table 3). The data reveals Tom stood close to students who attended in the physical classroom 0 times (0%), neutral location 1204 times (73.9%), and close to teaching equipment 307 times (18.8%) from the perspective of frequency and percentage. He mainly stood neutral position during his lecture. Tom performed large gestures 16 times (1%), medium gestures 400 times (24.5%), and small gestures 977 times (60%). The usage rate of small gestures is significantly high. Large and medium gestures show relatively low frequency. He performed communicative gestures (i.e., indexical actions, 1098 times, 67.3%; representing action, 194 times, 11.9%) frequently and showed very little in the performative gestures (presenting actions, 219 times, 13.4%). Tom did not make any noticeable motions, preferring to stand in a neutral posture amid educational equipment, students, and the physical teaching site.

Six students attended the lecture who wore masks and sat in silence during the talk. Thirty-three students participated in the class through the internet. They made no overt moves and did not communicate with Tom. Instructional equipment includes a projection screen, a computer, and desks and chairs for placing belongings and students' use. He stands in the center of the computer screen and the live students most of the time, with three-quarters of his side facing the live students and computer displays and the rest facing the computer screen directly. Because he had been teaching with the microphone, Tom's range of motion was constrained by a two-meter-long microphone cord.

Table 3. Frequency and percentage of three features of Tom's Multimodal Use

Lecturer location		Close to students	Close to teaching equipment	Neutral	Null	Total
	Fre	0	307	1204	118	1629
	%	0	18.8	73.9	7.2	100.0
Lecturer gesture scale		Large	Medium	Small	Null	Total
	Fre	16	400	977	236	1629
	%	1.0	24.5	60.0	14.5	100.0
Lecturer action type		Indexical action	Presenting action	Representing action	Null	Total
	Fre	1098	219	194	219	1629
	%	67.3	13.4	11.9	13.4	100.0

5 Discussion

The study aims to explore the formulation of a pedagogical network through under-standing the objects in physical spaces, the representations of objects' movements, and the process of movements' integrations. The results show the following. In the offline teaching scenario, the physical classroom space is large compared with the general class-rooms, and the class was in full attendance. There was no requirement for online teaching. George was utterly involved in the offline learning environment. George employed a lot of communicating gestures and concentrated on medium- and large-scale gestures. We speculate that George's bodied movements shaped a vast educational field and linked the students. Due to the students' presence and the teaching aids were situated close to the students. Even though George moved to the projector frequently to emphasize the important information projected on the screen, he swiftly returned to the location near the students and stayed closely with them. We hypothesize that in the offline scenario, although there was no verbal interaction, George perceived the students' gaze and used many large-scale gestures to build an educational information space. In the meantime, the placement of teaching aids between the students and the lecturer enhanced educational communication. The objects formed an educational network, including the lecturer, the students, and the teaching aids.

The classroom in the online teaching mode is larger than the conventional classroom, and the class had half attendance. John presented a strong desire for social interaction. John employed several communicative actions and concentrated on a minor range of movements. We assume that John could not sense the presence of the students and instructional equipment in the physical classroom. Moreover, the web camera restricted his teaching performance. Therefore, his movements drew a small educational space, and his connection with students was minimal. Despite the outstanding number of John's communicative actions, his bodily information was limitedly released to the students. It is maybe because he could not see the students' gaze, and there was no verbal interaction during the class. We speculate that he utilized a lot of small body movements to construct the educational space, and the space was isomorphic and heterotopic.

Under the hybrid teaching scenario, the classroom was a standard size, the physical attendance of students was low, and most of the students presented online. Tom stood in front of the computer and faced the computer screen most of the time. We assume he needed to pay attention to the students in two scenarios and may focus more on the online students. Tom used many small-scale communicative actions, and only inconspicuous movements were identified throughout the class. He stood between the computer and the students and formed a triangular educational space. We suspect that the computer screen, microphone, and teaching equipment limited Tom, and he barely interacted with students. There were no significant revelations regarding his movements' trace. When Tom was teaching in hybrid mode, the educational space was restricted by teaching aids and multimodal technologies.

This paper verifies the notions of ANT [20] and NST [21] about the connection and fluidity of objects in physical spaces to construct a second space. Although the instructional equipment had passive movements, they significantly affected three teach-ing scenarios. In this paper, we argue that 1) the lecturers' spatial perception is affected under different teaching scenarios, which may result in the failure of educational network formulation. The form of multimodal teaching scenario (e.g., hybrid teaching mode) was identified, and it negatively influenced the formulation of pedagogical space. 2) The use and placement of teaching aid significantly influenced educational networks' formulation. The students and the lecturer were closely bound in a pedagogical network, when the teaching aids were placed at the position between the students and the lecturer. We claim teaching aids play as active objects to promote the formulation of pedagogical network.

6   Conclusion

Today's educational institutions commonly use virtual learning environments like online classrooms or immersive VR classrooms, and the investigation of the use of educational space is underexamined. Our study can project on developing virtual learning environments. Our study analyzed the representations of objects' movements in three real-life classroom settings. The study found the pedagogical network formulations and the processes of the objects that shaped the spaces. Our study differs from previous studies on pedagogical spaces in that we identified the correlation between objects and physical spaces in the educational context. The analysis result shows the importance of studies on pedagogical spaces in the HCI community. Research is ongoing, and we are currently investigating more lectures and planning evaluations through in-depth interviews.

Acknowledgments. We acknowledge the University Grants Committee of Hong Kong for funding this research.

References

1. Anagnostopoulos, D., Basmadjian, K., Mccrory, R.: The decentered teacher and the construction of social space in the virtual classroom. Teach. Coll. Rec. **107**(8), 1699–1729 (2005)
2. Baraldi, C.: Structural variations of classroom interaction: implications for the education system. Int. Stud. Sociol. Educ., 1–22 (2021). https://doi.org/10.1080/09620214.2021.190 2371
3. Beckers, R., van der Voordt, T., Dewulf, G.: Learning space preferences of higher education students. Build. Environ. **104**, 243–252 (2016). https://doi.org/10.1016/j.buildenv.2016. 05.013
4. Beyrouthy, C., Burke, E.K., Landa-Silva, D., McCollum, B., McMullan, P., Parkes, A.J.: Towards improving the utilization of university teaching space. J. Oper. Res. Soc. **60**(1), 130–143 (2009). https://doi.org/10.1057/palgrave.jors.2602523
5. Byers, T., Imms, W., Hartnell-Young, E.: Making the case for space: the effect of learning spaces on teaching and learning. Curric. Teach. **29**(1), 5–19 (2014)
6. Cook, S., Mitchell, Z., Goldin-Meadow, S.: Gesturing makes learning last. Cognition (2008). https://doi.org/10.1016/j.cognition.2007.04.010
7. Dargue, N., Sweller, N., Jones, M.P.: When our hands help us understand: a meta-analysis into the effects of gesture on comprehension. Psychol. Bull. **145**(8), 765–784 (2019). https:// doi.org/10.1037/bul0000202
8. van Dijk, T.A.: Discourse as Social Interaction. Sage, Thousand Oaks (1997)

9. Fägerstam, E.: Space and Place: Perspectives on outdoor teaching and learning (2012). http://urn.kb.se/resolve?urn=urn:nbn:se:liu:diva-81318. Accessed 12 Jan 2022

10. Feldhammer-Kahr, M., et al.: It's a challenge, not a threat: lecturers' satisfaction during the Covid-19 summer semester of 2020. Front. Psychol. **12**, 638898 (2021). https://doi.org/10.3389/fpsyg.2021.638898

11. Gao, K.: Design and implementation for distant education system based on whiteboard. In: Proceedings of the 2018 International Conference on Distance Education and Learning (ICDEL 2018), pp. 171–175 (2018). https://doi.org/10.1145/3231848.3231883

12. Green, H.: Their Space. Education for a Digital Generation (2007). https://ictlogy.net/bibliography/reports/projects.php?idp=651&lang=es. Accessed 24 Jan 2022

13. Hall, E.T.: The Hidden Dimension. Doubleday, Garden City (1966)

14. Hall, E.T., Hall, T.: The Silent Language. Anchor Books (1959)

15. Halskov, K., Lundqvist, C.: Filtering and informing the design space: towards design-space thinking. ACM Trans. Comput. Hum. Interact. **28**(1), 81–828 (2021). https://doi.org/10.1145/3434462

16. Kember, D.: A reconceptualisation of the research into university academics' conceptions of teaching. Learn. Instr. **7**(3), 255–275 (1997)

17. Kress, G.: Literacy in the New Media Age. Routledge, London (2003). https://doi.org/10.4324/9780203299234

18. Kress, G.: Multimodality: A Social Semiotic Approach to Contemporary Communication. Routledge, London (2009). https://doi.org/10.4324/9780203970034

19. Latour, B.: On actor-network theory: a few clarifications. Soziale Welt **47**(4), 369–381 (1996)

20. Latour, B.: Drawing things together. In: The Map Reader, pp. 65–72. Wiley. https://doi.org/10.1002/9780470979587.ch9

21. Law, J.: Objects and spaces. Theory Cult. Soc. **19**(5–6), 91–105 (2002). https://doi.org/10.1177/026327602761899165

22. Lim, F.: A systemic functional multimodal discourse analysis approach to pedagogic discourse (2011)

23. Lim, F.V., O'Halloran, K.L., Podlasov, A.: Spatial pedagogy: mapping meanings in the use of classroom space. Camb. J. Educ. **42**(2), 235–251 (2012). https://doi.org/10.1080/0305764X.2012.676629

24. Lim, V.F.: Analysing the teachers' use of gestures in the classroom: a Systemic Functional Multimodal Discourse Analysis approach. Soc. Semiot. **29**(1), 83–111 (2019). https://doi.org/10.1080/10350330.2017.1412168

25. Martinec, R.: Construction of identity in Michael Jackson's Jam. Soc. Semiot. **10**(3), 313–329 (2000). https://doi.org/10.1080/10350330050136370

26. Martinec, R.: Interpersonal resources in action. Semiotica **2001**, 117–145 (2001). https://doi.org/10.1515/semi.2001.056

27. Martinec, R.: Gestures that co-occur with speech as a systematic resource: the realization of experiential meanings in indexes. Soc. Semiot. **14**(2), 193–213 (2004). https://doi.org/10.1080/1035033042000238259

28. Meishar-Tal, H., Levenberg, A.: In times of trouble: higher education lecturers' emotional reaction to online instruction during COVID-19 outbreak. Educ. Inf. Technol. **26**(6), 7145–7161 (2021). https://doi.org/10.1007/s10639-021-10569-1

29. Previc, F.H.: The neuropsychology of 3-D space. Psychol. Bull. **124**(2), 123 (1998)

30. de Saussure, F.: Course in General Linguistics. Columbia University Press, New York (2011)

31. Critical Analysis of Multimodal Discourse - Leeuwen - - Major Reference Works - Wiley Online Library. https://onlinelibrary.wiley.com/doi/full/10.1002/9781405198431.wbeal0269. Accessed 24 Jan 2022

Resolving Learners Misunderstandings Using an Adaptive Divide and Correct Technique

Alireza Tabebordbar[1], Amin Beheshti[1(✉)], Nabi Rezvani[1], Mohsen Asadnia[1], and Stephen Elbourn[1,2]

[1] Macquarie University, Sydney, Australia
{alireza.tabebordbar,amin.beheshti,mohsen.asadnia}@mq.edu.au,
nabiallah.rezvani@hdr.mq.edu.au, stephen.elbourn@itic.com.au
[2] ITIC Pty Ltd., Sydney, Australia
stephen.elbourn@students.mq.edu.au

Abstract. The education system is one of the main government sectors that has been affected by COVID-19 pandemic. Most governments around the world have temporarily closed educational institutions and distance learning imposed a massive impact on students' learning processes. In an online teaching and learning environment, handling students' misunderstandings is a challenging and time-consuming task. Many of the proposed solutions for handling students' misunderstandings are highly demanding on teachers, and suffer from lack of descriptively. In this paper, we propose a novel adaptive divide and correct technique to assist teachers in providing formative feedback to students. Additionally, we lower teachers' cognitive load in comprehending misunderstandings by measuring their semantical commonality. Our experiment results showed that our approach could significantly augment teachers in providing formative feedback to a large number of students.

Keywords: Resolving misunderstandings · Adaptive divide and correct · Expert-level feedback

1 Introduction

The COVID-19 pandemic has induced a great amount of loss and confusion on our societies and businesses. The pandemic crystallizes the dilemma decision-makers are facing between keeping businesses open to maintain the economy or closing them to save lives and control the outbreak. One of the sectors that many governments decided to close is schools and universities. However, homeschooling not only is a massive shock for students and their parents but also teachers[1] need to move online to deliver their courses on an untested and unprecedented scale [24]. This compelled teachers to postpone or cancel their assessments.

---

[1] In this paper, we use the terms teachers and instructors interchangeably and both refer to a person who helps students to acquire knowledge.

© The Author(s), under exclusive license to Springer Nature Switzerland AG 2022
P. Delir Haghighi et al. (Eds.): MoMM 2022, LNCS 13634, pp. 154–168, 2022.
https://doi.org/10.1007/978-3-031-20436-4_15

The role of teachers as the prime driver of learning systems in augmenting learner's comprehension is significant [4]. Teachers identify students' misunderstandings and provide feedback to aid students to make sense of their courses. Teachers also allowing students to confront their misunderstandings by reviewing and commenting on their works. However, in an online course with hundreds of enrolled students, there is a need for techniques that effectively handle students' misunderstandings as relying on the traditional one-to-one feedback model[2] is infeasible [21]. Over the past years as the number of students outgrows there have been increasing efforts to handle students' misunderstandings in large or online platforms. These solutions focused on utilizing instructors' feedback for a larger number of students by relying on techniques, such as propagating/broadcast [9], rubric [25], and similarity metrics [26]. Although disseminating instructors feedback to a larger number of students aids instructors to better resolve students' misunderstandings. These solutions (1) are highly demanding, as teachers need to comprehend and formulate new feedback for every misunderstanding; (2) they suffer from lack of descriptivity as many of the instructors' feedback is not justified and ineffective in resolving students mistakes [21]; (3) many of the provided feedback are not actionable and cannot provide a concrete step forward to resolve students' misunderstandings [21].

In recent years, an increasing number of research disciplines [2, 13, 19, 21, 26] have focused on augmenting instructors to provide formative feedback. An example of such a system is CRITIQUEKIT [21], which guides instructors to write specific and actionable feedback to enhance students' comprehension. In this context, we follow a similar trend by lowering instructors' cognitive load in comprehending and resolving students' misunderstandings. Instead, we rely on *Learning Analytics (LA)* [12] and fuse the instructor's knowledge with machine learning algorithms to identify and resolve students' misunderstandings. A learning analytic system aims at providing personalized recommendations and feedback concerning students learning objectives. Examples of such systems are measuring student engagement [14], predicting students' performance [7], and quantifying their learning experience [5].

In this paper, we propose a technique to resolve students' misunderstandings in online and large scale learning environments. While previous systems focused on supporting instructors when writing new feedback, we provide a different learning analytic approach. Our solution provides expert-level feedback to a large number of students by measuring the semantical commonality between students' questions. Additionally, we let instructors examine the effectiveness of their feedback using an adaptive divide and correct technique. Our solution is made up of two main technical achievements: *clustering*, which takes advantage of deep learning skip-gram embedded network and clusters similar students' misunderstandings using their *semantical commonality*. An *adaptive divide and correct technique*, which verifies the effectiveness of instructors' feedback over time. We utilize a machine learning algorithm for analyzing learners learning behaviour and guides instructors to identify the most effective feedback for resolving students' misunderstandings.

The rest of this paper is organized as follows: in Sect. 2, we discuss the previous works regarding handling students' misunderstandings and providing

---

[2] In a one-to-one feedback model instructors provided feedback case by case to students.

feedback. In Sect. 3, we discuss our proposed solution. First, we describe how we measure the semantical commonality of misunderstandings. Then, we explain how our proposed adaptive divide and correct technique helps instructors to provide formative feedback. In Sect. 4, we discuss our experiment results, before concluding the paper in Sect. 5.

2   Related Works

In this section, we discuss prior works related to providing formative (Sect. 2.1) and expert-level feedback (Sect. 2.2) for resolving students' misunderstandings. In particular, we discuss techniques proposed for providing feedback for online and large scale environments. Besides, we consider it appropriate to discuss approaches on learning analytics to position our proposed adaptive divide and correct technique (Sect. 2.3).

2.1   Formative Feedback

Providing fast and formative feedback is critical for improving students' learning. Providing formative feedback can facilitate students learning and highlight their strengths and weaknesses. Formative feedback can resolve learners misunderstandings by correcting their thinking or learning behaviours [19]. Ngoon et al. [21], characterised that feedback must be actionable, specific and justified in order to be effective. However, as the number of students outgrows providing feedback that effectively suggests a step forward to resolve students misunderstanding is becoming more challenging and time-consuming. Thus, many solutions (e.g., [13, 19, 21, 26]) focused on augmenting instructors formulating their feedback. For example, Martinez et al. [26] proposed a technique for providing feedback by asking instructors to label the most common wrong answers with the students' and clustering the misunderstandings using the statistical co-occurrence patterns. Head et al. [11] proposed a technique to cluster learners submissions and propagating instructors feedback to all submissions that can be fixed with the same transformation. Joyner [13] proposed a technique for providing cost-effective and formative feedback to a large number of students on online platforms. The approach selects teacher assistants among learners using their demographic information and experiences.

In this context, we aid instructors to provide formative feedback to a group of students with similar misunderstanding. However, our technique measures the semantical commonality between students misunderstandings using a deep learning skip-gram embedding network. Thus, lowering instructors cognitive load in comprehending the misunderstandings and providing feedback. In the next section, we accentuate different techniques proposed for providing feedback to learners.

2.2   Feedback Models

With the increasing interest in online programs, different solutions have been proposed to facilitate the interaction between learners and instructors. However, providing expert-level feedback dampen the scalability of courses due to the massive costs that institutions must incur for hiring instructors or teacher assistants [11]. Thus, many efforts in educational systems emphasize on removing expert-level feedback to justify the affordability. For example, many initiatives relied on automated systems (e.g., [8,23,32]) to provide individualised feedback to learners. Although automated feedback systems allow a rapid revision of students' misunderstandings, these systems are relatively expensive and cannot integrate well with open-ended and project-based courses. Another line of works has focused on peer feedback [6,10,18,29]. These solutions utilise the knowledge of learners to review and give feedback to other classmate works. Peer reviews substantially reduce the cost of giving feedback to learners. But, these solutions are often unmotivated [17], and unreliable [30]. Additionally, they suffer from perception issues, where learners works may not evaluate by experts. Alternatively, implicit techniques have been proposed as a cost-effective and scalable solution for reviewing learners works. An example of such system is supplying learners with an exemplary approach and allowing them to compare their works with the given solution [11]. However, it has been proven that implicit feedback raise more questions in the mind of students and only insists on preexisting meta-cognitive skills [11]

Alternatively, supplying learners with expert-level feedback can provide a greater level of supports for students. Because, not only experts have greater knowledge, experience, and ability to provide formative feedback, but also, it is more desirable for many courses that need to maintain accreditation or a standard [11]. In this context, we focus on facilitating the interaction between instructors and learners by augmenting instructors to provide formative feedback in a scalable fashion.

2.3   Learning Analytic

During the past years, researchers have put a considerable number of efforts on analysing the educational data to further support learners and increase their engagement. Examples of such educational tools include Course Management Systems (CMS) such as Moodle and e-class, which assists instructors during their lectures or student assessment. However, often the data generated in educational contexts is large and complex, making it difficult to derive insight and perform deep analysis [14,31]. In recent years, *Learning Analytic* (LA) as an emerging field among researchers, focused on utilizing predictive models as a source for extracting valuable insight. It aims at creating a personalized and collaborative learning environment to provide recommendations regarding students learning performance. Hence, learning analytic focuses on collecting and discovering information from instructors and learners to identify and amend the issues that affect the learning objectives [15,28]. Over the past years, the field learning

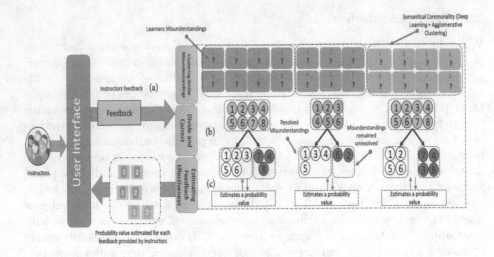

Fig. 1. Overview of the proposed approach for resolving learners' misunderstandings. The technique is made up of three stages: (1) Clustering, (2) Divide and Correct, (3) Estimating Feedback Effectiveness. (Color figure online)

analytic have received a large number of attentions, including [1,7,14,27]. In this context, we follow a similar trend by utilising a machine-learning algorithm to facilitate collaboration among learners and instructors. We demonstrate how machine learning can augment instructors to comprehend students' misunderstandings and to provide formative feedback in a timely manner.

3   Solution Overview

In this section, we describe our proposed solution: (1) We explain how our approach lowers instructors cognitive load to comprehend students' misunderstandings. We fuse a deep learning skip-gram embedding network [16,20] and an agglomerative clustering algorithm [22], to measure the semantical commonality existing between learners' misunderstandings. (2) We describe how our adaptive divide and correct technique enhances instructors to provide formative feedback. We rely on students verification and a machine-learning algorithm to measure the effectiveness of instructors feedback in resolving the misunderstandings. Overall, our approach is made up of three main stages (Fig. 1), *Clustering Similar Misunderstandings, Providing and Verifying Feedback, Estimating Feedback effectiveness*. Followings explain each stage in detail.

3.1   Clustering Similar Misunderstanding

The goal of this step is to offload instructors from constantly sending feedback for resolving similar misunderstandings. For example, we explain how our approach identifies two misunderstandings in a "Data Streaming" course, e.g., *"How a message is partitioned in a streaming system and how a consumer reads mes-sages"* and *"What is the role of partition and offset in consuming messages"* are semantically similar and can be answered with the same feedback. Identifying similar misunderstandings not only allows instructors to discover the frequent misunderstandings occurs among students but also facilitates learning by provid-ing feedback to a larger number of students. The following explains the proposed solution in detail.

The initial step to identify learners' misunderstandings is pre-processing. In this step, we extract the content bearing tokens to compute their semantical commonality. We perform pre-processing by removing the stopwords and filter-ing out of the ungrammatical and irrelevant tokens, e.g.imoji. Also, we used the WordNet lemmatizer over the extracted tokens to increase the probability of matching between words with the common base, e.g., "runny", "run", "running" all reduce to the base form "run". For pre-processing step, we used the system proposed by Beheshti et al. [3]. It provides a pipeline for different curation tasks, including named entity extraction, information linking, indexing and similarity computation. After pre-processing students misunderstandings, we measure their semantical commonality and cluster the similar ones by coupling a deep learning skip-gram network with an agglomerative clustering algorithm. Thus, we trained a skip-gram network to obtain neural embeddings of students misunderstand-ings. The neural embeddings construct a vector space model and represent each misunderstanding as a set of vectors. We used word2vec[3] neural embeddings model to map students misunderstandings onto a vector space model.

We represent each misunderstanding M onto a vector space model by tok-enizing their content bearing tokens $M = \{m_1, m_2, m_3, ..., m_n\}$. Then, for each token $m \in M$, we query the vector space model and extract the vector $V(m)$ corresponds to it. Next, we compute the mean of all vectors $V(m)$. The result-ing vector $V(M)$ represents the misunderstanding M in vector space model. We perform the same steps for other misunderstandings.

$$V(M) = \frac{\sum_{i=1}^{n} m}{||M||}$$

After representing the misunderstandings onto the vector space model, we cluster them using an agglomerative clustering algorithm. Initially, the algorithm considers all vectors $V(M)$ as a singleton cluster. Then, it successively split clus-ters into smaller ones based on their similarity. We have chosen cosine similarity as the similarity metric[4].

$$cos(\theta) = \frac{V(m_1) \cdot V(m_2)}{||V(m_1)|| \cdot ||V(m_2)||}$$

---

[3] https://github.com/tmikolov/word2vec.
[4] We consider misunderstandings over 75 % cosine measure as similar.

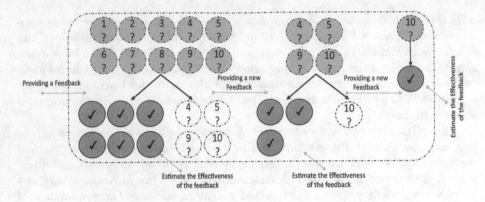

Fig. 2. Overview of the divide and correct technique: The diagram shows how the system determines the effectiveness of feedback and how instructors interact with students to resolve their misunderstandings.

where $V(m_1)$ and $V(m_2)$ representing vectors of attributes m_1 and m_2, and $||V(m_1)||$ and $||V(m_2)||$ are their lengths.

Example: Consider following questions that have been asked by students of a "Stream Processing" course (Fig. 2).

$M_1 \mapsto$ How a message is partitioned while streaming data and how a consumer reads messages?

$M_2 \mapsto$ What is the role of partition and offset in consuming messages?

$M_3 \mapsto$ How a producer operates in a stream processing system?

To cluster the misunderstandings based on their semantical commonality, first we perform a pre-processing task to identify the content bearing tokens. M_1 = { message, partition, data, stream, consumer, read}, M_2 = {role, partition, offset, consumer, message} and M_3 = {producer, operate, stream, process, system}. Next, we query a vector space model to represent each token as a vector. $V(M_1)$ = { $V_1(message)$, $V_2(partition)$, $V_3(data)$, $V_4(stream)$, $V_5(consumer)$, $V_6(read)$}, $V(M_2)$ = {$V_1(role)$, $V_2(partition)$, $V_3(offset)$, $V_4(consumer)$, $V_5(message)$}, and $V(M_3)$ = {$V_1(producer)$, $V_2(operate)$, $V_3(stream)$, $V_4(process)$, $V_5(system)$}. Finally, we compute the mean of all vectors, e.g. $V(M_1) = \frac{V_1+V_2+V_3+V_4+V_5+V6}{||V(m_2)||}$, and cluster them using an agglomerative clustering algorithm.

3.2   Providing and Verifying Feedback

Although providing feedback to a group of learners allowing instructors to resolve a larger number of misunderstandings, the instructors are still unaware of the effectiveness of their feedback. Thus, to augment instructors to produce formative feedback, we proposed an adaptive divide and correct technique. The approach iteratively examines the effectiveness of provided feedback from learners perspective and update the instructor about the performance of feedback in resolving students misunderstandings. The following explains the proposed divide and correct technique in detail.

Adaptive Divide and Correct Feedback Model: Typically, in a course with hundreds of enrolled students, an instructor needs to resolve a large number of misunderstands over time. However, in some cases, resolving a misunderstanding with single feedback is infeasible. This is either because, a misunderstanding might be entrenched in students thinking, or the instructor feedback is not enough formative. The divide and correct approach rely on learners verification to update the instructor about the effectiveness of her feedback. Each time an instructor sending feedback, students reply to verify whether their misunderstanding resolved or not. The system splits students misunderstanding based on their verification ($success$ = resolved and $fail$ = not resolved) and prompts the instructors to send new feedback to students that their misunderstandings remained unresolved. The system continuously involves the instructor to provide new feedback until all students reply that their misunderstanding disappeared.

Each time students verify the effectiveness of feedback, the system estimates a probability value (see Sect. 3.3) to update the instructor about the performance of the feedback in resolving students misunderstanding. The probability value continuously updated based on the learners' verification, augmenting the instructor to choose the feedback that identified as the most effective from the students' perspective. For example, consider Fig. 1, which shows a set of misunderstandings clustered based on their similarity. The instructors may examine the misunderstandings and provide students with feedback (Fig. 1a). Then, the system using the divide and correct technique to verify whether the feedback could resolve students' misunderstanding or not (the circles colored in red indicates misunderstanding remained unresolved (Fig. 1b). The system based on the students' verification estimates a probability value to update the instructors about the feedback effectiveness (Fig. 1c). For those students with unresolved misunderstanding, the instructor sends new feedback and again the system estimates a new probability value to indicate its effectiveness. Over time by interacting with students the system better learns the performance of feedback and assists the analyst to select the feedback that obtained the highest effectiveness.

3.3 Estimating Feedback Effectiveness

The goal of this step is to support instructors through collective wisdom and science while interacting with students to resolve their misunderstandings. Estimating the effectiveness of feedback augment instructors to reliably support students without spending significant time for formulating new feedback or vetting their past feedback to resolve students' misunderstandings. To determine the effectiveness of feedback, we relied on a reinforcement learning algorithm. Reinforcement learning is an area of machine learning that focused on taking the most suitable action to maximize the benefit. The algorithm is good for complex and dynamic environments and learns by observing the consequences of its actions. The algorithm conducts exploitation and exploration for selecting an action. In exploitation, the algorithm selects the action identified as the most suitable one. While in exploration the algorithm investigates the environment to understand the performance of other actions as well. Exploitation and exploration is essentially trial and error learning. The algorithm receives a success/failure as the outcome of its actions. It receives a reward for taking an action that identified as a correct/beneficial, and at the same time receives a demote for taking the wrong action. Over time the algorithm learns to select an action's that accumulated the highest reward.

We address the problem of estimating the effectiveness of feedback using a multi-armed bandit algorithm. The algorithm is a reinforcement learning algorithm, which represents the possible actions as a set of arms. The algorithm repeatedly estimates a probability for each arm by observing their performance. In our context, the instructors' feedback represents the action choices (arms), and the students' verification (whether the feedback could resolve their misunderstanding or not) updates the algorithm about the effectiveness of feedback. Over time by collecting students verification's the algorithm better learners the effectiveness of feedback in resolving a misunderstanding. Each time, students verify feedback sent by an instructor the algorithm estimates a probability θ to represent its effectiveness, where $0 < \theta < 1$. The algorithm estimates the effectiveness of feedback using beta distribution. The likelihood for this distribution is a Bernoulli distribution and the prior is a beta distribution. Thus, using the Bayesian formula, we can estimate the value of θ as below:

$$P(\theta \mid s) = \frac{P(s \mid \theta) \times P(\theta)}{P(s)} \propto P(s \mid \theta) \times P(\theta)$$

where $P(s \mid \theta)$ represents the likelihood (Bernulli distribution), and $P(\theta)$ is the prior (Beta distribution).

$$P(s \mid \theta) = \theta^r (1 - \theta)^{n-r}, r = \sum_{r=0}^{n} s$$
$$P(\theta) = \frac{\theta_n^{\alpha_n - 1}(1 - \theta_n)^{\beta_n - 1}}{\beta(\alpha_n, \beta_n)}$$

Eventually, the posterior is proportional to the product of the prior and the likelihood, with the likelihood updated continuously with students verification. This update is easy to implement because the beta and Bernoulli distributions are conjugate. More clearly consider a set of feedback $S = \{M_1, M_2, M_3, ..., M_n\}$, which an instructors sent to students in a divide and correct fashion. Initially, the prior distribution for the feedback reward is equal to $Beta(1, 1)$. Then, students verify feedback effectiveness by replying to instructors (whether the feedback could resolve their misunderstanding or not). Thus, the algorithm updates the probability value of $Beta(x, y)$ by $Beta$ (*x+ number of times feedback displayed to students and identified as effective, y+ number of times the feedback displayed to students, but couldn't resolve their misunderstandings*). In this manner, the algorithm based on the verification collected from students updates the effectiveness of feedback and augment instructors to select the feedback that best resolves students misunderstandings.

4   Experiments and Results

This section discusses the results obtained from evaluating the performance of our system for augmenting instructors to resolve learners' misunderstandings and providing formative feedback. We first explain the settings of the experiment and the dataset used. Then, we discuss the experiments scenarios for capturing participants feedback. Finally, we discuss the obtained results.

4.1   Experiments Settings

The core component of techniques described in the previous sections is implemented in Python. We also used MySQL for persisting our results. For evaluating the performance of our system, we conducted a controlled experiment by inviting 10 participants from a lab. All participants had a major in computer science, but with a different academic and industrial background. Four of the participants explained that they have more than five years of work experience in the industry. Three of the participants had more than five years of experience in academia. While the rest had less than five years of experience in both academia and industry. As an instructor, we required somebody with experience in both academia and industry. Thus, we invited a senior software engineer, which was conducting PhD and was TA during last trimesters to take the role of instructor. For evaluating students misunderstandings, we selected a general programming question from job interviews *(e.g., Write an algorithm that finds the two elements in a list of numbers where the sum equals to a specific value. Example: In the list [1, 2, 4, 6, 7] with given sum of 10, the algorithm should return 4, 6)* and asked the participants to solve the question. The task was not timed and participants submit their questions using the tool[5] (Fig. 3).

4.2   Experiment Scenarios

This section explains the experiments scenarios, we have designed to collect participants feedback. We defined two sets of experiments: (1) we followed a repeated measure ANOVA with two independent variables: *tool*: The proposed adaptive divide and correct technique (Fig. 3), and a conventional system that instructors send feedback to students[6]—and *feedback*. (2) A usage scenario, which explains how the system interacts with students and instructors to resolve their misunderstandings. The first scenario analysis the performance of our approach with conventional systems. To compare the performance, we asked the participants to fill a 7-point Likert scale questionnaire. The goal of the questionnaire was to evaluate the systems from students and instructors perspective.

Below are the factors that used in our experiments to evaluate systems performance. We asked the students to answer the below questions: (i) **Physical**

---

[5] All experiments are carried out on cloud platform (Amazon Web Service (AWS)).

[6] By writing feedback for every misunderstanding or choosing among the previously given feedback.

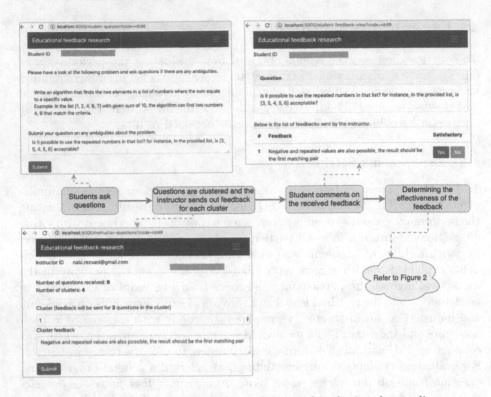

Fig. 3. The designed interface for resolving students' misunderstanding.

Demand: Which of the above systems are easier to work and understand (How physically demanding the system is); (ii) **Formative:** Which of the two systems could provide more formative and effective feedback; and (iii) **Performance:** Which systems could understand your misunderstanding better and resolve it.

Also, we asked the instructor to answer the below questions: (i) **Temporal demand:** Which of the two systems could help you to answer students misunderstandings in less time; (ii) **Effort:** Which system could help you to answer students' misunderstandings easier and with less effort (how hard was it to understand students misunderstandings); and **Mental Demand:** Which system could lower your cognitive load to comprehend students misunderstandings.

The above factors are derived from NASA TLX[7] questionnaire. The questionnaire is a multidimensional assessment tool that rates the perceived workload in order to assess a task or system. The second scenario conducts a study on the usability aspect of our approach. We discuss the weaknesses and strengths of our system from the participants perspective.

---

[7] https://en.wikipedia.org/wiki/NASA-TLX.

4.3   Results: Performance Analysis

We conduct statistical analysis (ANOVA test) to compare the performance of
our system with a conventional feedback system. A repeated-measures ANOVA
revealed the impact of our system on lowering participants overall workload
$F_{avg} = 1.28$. This tendency can be observed in detail in Fig. 4(a) which shows
students could receive more relevant feedback while interacting with our system.

Table 1. Mean and standard deviation of the questions given to student participants
for conventional feedback and adaptive divide and correct techniques.

	Physical demand	Formative	Performance
Mean (conventional)	4.3	5.3	4.0
Mean (adaptive)	3.3	3.0	3.4
Std dev (conventional)	1.87	3.57	2.64
Std dev (adaptive)	2.29	2.45	2.79

The results showed that our system could significantly improve performance
$F(1, 16) = 1.03, p = 0.33$. We also observed that using our system participants
could receive more effective (formative) feedback $F(1, 16) = 2.61, p = 0.12$. Additionally, Table 1, shows the mean and standard deviation obtained from participants interactions with both systems. The results revealed that both mean
and standard deviation reduced in our proposed approach, which indicates an
improvement in the workload experienced by participants. This is reasonable
because the quicker feedback our system could provide to participants for resolving their misunderstandings. In addition to previous experiments, we analyzed
the performance of tools by calculating the number of feedback and active time
instructors spent to resolve students misunderstandings (Fig. 4(b)). The study
showed that our proposed clustering approach could significantly reduce the
workload of instructors in both dimensions (time and number of feedback). In
terms of the number of feedback, using our system instructors sent 1.5 times less

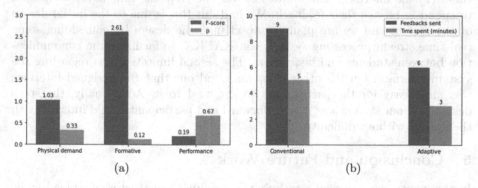

(a)   (b)

Fig. 4. (a) ANOVA F-score and p values for student questions. (b) Comparison of
number of feedbacks sent and the time spend in minutes by instructors.

feedback compared to the conventional feedback system. Besides, we analysed the time that instructors actively spent on both systems to resolve students' misunderstandings. Our results revealed that using our systems instructors could provide formative feedback in less time.

4.4   Results: Participants Analysis

At the end of the study, we asked participants to share their impressions on strengths and weaknesses of our system. The participants' comments confirmed the results we obtained using the ANOVA test. For example, one of the participants mentioned that she could get her response much quicker than the conventional system. Another participant explained that he got the impression that he can communicate with the instructor more conveniently. Also, some of the participants commented about the usability of the designed interface. For example, a participant explained that "The interface was fairly simple to work and the provided answer was fairly comprehensive". We also, examined the comments of the instructor to better understand the design flaws of our system. The instructor explained that the system seems to reduce his workload. He pointed out to the clustering feature of the system that allowing him to provide feedback to many students at the same time. On the other side, participants mentioned to some of the weakness of our systems, including (1) Some of the comments was regarding the time that participants had to wait to receive their response. For example, I had to wait to receive the initial feedback, or I was expecting to receive my feedback quicker. (2) one of the participants complained about the quality of the feedback and mentioned that "both provided feedback state almost the same thing. In other words, I was expecting more clarification by the second time not just restate the first responses". However, the participants had a positive impression over the designed system compared to the regular feedback approach and all they were agree that our system could provide formative and comprehensive feedback in less time.

Limitations and Discussions. Based on our obtained results and participants feedback, we have divided this section into two categories: (1) the response time, (2) the interface. The limitation was the response time students needed to spend to receive their feedback. We find out this is due to the initial design of the system and we are planning to change the design by embedding some real-time stream processing system, e.g. KAFKA, to facilitate the communication between students and instructors. The second limitation was regarding the system interface. On the other side, we found out that the designed interface was fairly easy for the participants to get used to it. Additionally, the steps designed in our system was straightforward and participants could interact with the system without difficulty.

5   Conclusion and Future Work

In this paper, we proposed a technique for reducing instructors workload while interacting with students on online and large scale environments. Our approach reduces instructors cognitive load in responding to students misunderstandings by computing their semantical commonality using a skip-gram embedding network and an agglomerative clustering algorithm. Additionally, we proposed an adaptive divide and correct technique to allow instructors to learn the effectiveness of their feedback. Our approach continuously estimates a probability value to represent the performance of feedback in resolving instructors misunderstandings. The experiment results showed that our solution could significantly lower instructors workload while interacting with a large number of students.

Acknowledgement. We acknowledge the AI-enabled Processes (AIP (https://aip-research-center.github.io/)) Research Centre and ITIC Pty Ltd (https://www.iticlive.com/) for funding this research.

References

1. Acharya, A., Sinha, D.: Early prediction of students performance using machine learning techniques. Int. J. Comput. Appl. **107**(1), 37–43 (2014)
2. Beheshti, A., Ghodratnama, S., Elahi, M., Farhood, H.: Social Data Analytics. CRC Press (2022)
3. Beheshti, S.-M.-R., Tabebordbar, A., Benatallah, B., Nouri, R.: On automating basic data curation tasks. In: WWW Conference, pp. 165–169 (2017)
4. Cameron, S.E.: Teachers as learners: learning in the lives of teachers (2011)
5. Dyckhoff, A.L., et al.: Design and implementation of a learning analytics toolkit for teachers. J. Educ. Technol. Soc. **15**(3), 58–76 (2012)
6. Falchikov, N., Goldfinch, J.: Student peer assessment in higher education: a meta-analysis comparing peer and teacher marks. Rev. Educ. Res. **70**(3), 287–322 (2000)
7. Gašević, D., Kovanović, V., Joksimović, S.: Piecing the learning analytics puzzle: a consolidated model of a field of research and practice. Learn. Res. Pract. **3**(1), 63–78 (2017)
8. Geigle, C., Zhai, C., Ferguson, D.C.: An exploration of automated grading of complex assignments. In: Proceedings of the Third (2016) ACM Conference on Learning@ Scale, pp. 351–360 (2016)
9. Gielen, S., Peeters, E., Dochy, F., Onghena, P., Struyven, K.: Improving the effectiveness of peer feedback for learning. Learn. Instr. **20**(4), 304–315 (2010)
10. Goel, A.K., Joyner, D.A.: An experiment in teaching cognitive systems online. Technical report, Georgia Institute of Technology (2015)
11. Head, A., Glassman, E., Soares, G., Suzuki, R., Figueredo, L., et al.: Writing reusable code feedback at scale with mixed-initiative program synthesis. In: Fourth ACM Conference on Learning@ Scale, pp. 89–98 (2017)
12. Jain, L.C., Tsihrintzis, G.A., Alepis, E., Virvou, M.: Machine Learning Paradigms. Advances in Learning Analytics, Springer, Cham (2019). https://doi.org/10.1007/978-3-030-13743-4
13. Joyner, D.A.: Scaling expert feedback: two case studies. In: Proceedings of the Fourth (2017) ACM Conference on Learning@ Scale, pp. 71–80 (2017)
14. Karthikeyan, K., Palaniappan, K.: On improving student performance prediction in education systems using enhanced data mining techniques. J. Adv. Res. Comput. Sci. Softw. Eng. **7**, 935–941 (2017)
15. Kavitha, M., Raj, D., et al.: Educational data mining and learning analytics-educational assistance for teaching. arXiv preprint arXiv:1706.03327 (2017)

16. Khatami, A., Nazari, A., Beheshti, A., Nguyen, T.T., Nahavandi, S., Zieba, J.: Convolutional neural network for medical image classification using wavelet features. In: 2020 International Joint Conference on Neural Networks (IJCNN), pp. 1–8. IEEE (2020)
17. Lu, Y., Warren, J., Jermaine, C., Chaudhuri, S., Rixner, S.: Grading the graders: motivating peer graders in a MOOC. In: Proceedings of the 24th International Conference on World Wide Web, pp. 680–690 (2015)
18. Lundstrom, K., Baker, W.: To give is better than to receive: the benefits of peer review to the reviewer's own writing. J. Second. Lang. Writ. **18**, 30–43 (2009)
19. Máñez, I., Vidal-Abarca, E., Kendeou, P., Martínez, T.: How do students process complex formative feedback in question-answering tasks? A think-aloud study. Metacognition Learn. **14**(1), 65–87 (2019). https://doi.org/10.1007/s11409-019-09192-w
20. Mikolov, T., Sutskever, I., Chen, K., Corrado, G.S., Dean, J.: Distributed representations of words and phrases and their compositionality. In: Advances in Neural Information Processing Systems, pp. 3111–3119 (2013)
21. Ngoon, T.J., Fraser, C.A., Weingarten, A.S., Dontcheva, M., Klemmer, S.: Interactive guidance techniques for improving creative feedback. In: CHI Conference on Human Factors in Computing Systems, pp. 1–11 (2018)
22. Rokach, L., Maimon, O.: Clustering methods. In: Maimon, O., Rokach, L. (eds.) Data Mining and Knowledge Discovery Handbook, pp. 321–352. Springer, Heidelberg (2005). https://doi.org/10.1007/0-387-25465-X_15
23. Salzmann, C., Gillet, D., Piguet, Y.: MOOLs for MOOCs: a first edX scalable implementation. In: 2016 13th International Conference on Remote Engineering and Virtual Instrumentation (REV), pp. 246–251. IEEE (2016)
24. Sievertsen, H.H., Burgess, S.: Schools, skills, and learning: the impact of COVID-19 on education (2020). https://voxeu.org/article/impact-covid-19-education
25. Singh, A., Karayev, S., Gutowski, K., Abbeel, P.: Gradescope: a fast, flexible, and fair system for scalable assessment of handwritten work. In: Proceedings of the Fourth (2017) ACM Conference on Learning@ Scale, pp. 81–88 (2017)
26. Stephens-Martinez, K., Ju, A., Schoen, C., DeNero, J., Fox, A.: Identifying student misunderstandings using constructed responses. In: Proceedings of the Third (2016) ACM Conference on Learning@ Scale, pp. 153–156 (2016)
27. Troussas, C., Espinosa, K.J., Virvou, M.: Intelligent advice generator for personalized language learning through social networking sites. In: International Conference on Information, Intelligence, Systems and Applications, pp. 1–5 (2015)
28. Troussas, C., Virvou, M., et al.: Using visualization algorithms for discovering patterns in groups of users for tutoring multiple languages through social networking. JNW **10**(12), 668–674 (2015)
29. Van Zundert, M., Sluijsmans, D., Van Merriënboer, J.: Effective peer assessment processes: research findings and future directions. Learn. Instr. **20**(4), 270–279 (2010)
30. Vogelsang, T., Ruppertz, L.: On the validity of peer grading and a cloud teaching assistant system. In: Proceedings of the Fifth International Conference on Learning Analytics and Knowledge, pp. 41–50 (2015)
31. Wang, S., et al.: Assessment2Vec: learning distributed representations of assessments to reduce marking workload. In: Roll, I., McNamara, D., Sosnovsky, S., Luckin, R., Dimitrova, V. (eds.) AIED 2021. LNCS (LNAI), vol. 12749, pp. 384–389. Springer, Cham (2021). https://doi.org/10.1007/978-3-030-78270-2_68
32. Yaron, D., Karabinos, M., Lange, D., et al.: The ChemCollective—virtual labs for introductory chemistry courses. Science **358**, 584–585 (2010)

A Stumble Detection Method
for Programming with Multi-modal
Information

Hiroki Oka⬤, Ayumi Ohnishi⬤, Tsutomu Terada$^{(\boxtimes)}$⬤,
and Masahiko Tsukamoto⬤

Kobe University, Kobe, Hyogo, Japan
hiroki-oka@stu.kobe-u.ac.jp, {ohnishi,tsutomu}@eedept.kobe-u.ac.jp,
tuka@kobe-u.ac.jp

Abstract. Various stumbles occur when learning programming, which
leads to lower learning efficiency and motivation. If such stumbles could be
detected automatically, teachers could monitor learners' progress and support passive students. Stumbles in learning programming can be classified
into several types, which could be divided into those that are evident from
the source code the learner wrote and those that are expressed in their psychological state. These stumbles could be detected by combining biometric data with code-related metrics. In this study, we propose a method to
detect stumbles in learning programming by combining the learner's heart
rate information with code-related metrics. We compared the accuracy of
models using only code-related metrics, using only heart rate information,
and using a combination of both. The results showed that the code-related
model and the multimodal model had the highest accuracy and the multimodal model can detect the most variety of stumbles.

Keywords: Programming learning · Stumble · Multi-modal ·
Sensing · Machine learning

1 Introduction

The importance of learning programming is increasing as society becomes more
information-oriented. In programming education for beginners, lectures using
lightweight languages such as JavaScript and Python are increasing. In addition,
the use of programming environments with visual output, such as Processing [1],
is increasing.

However, it is challenging to complete a program without making errors and
learning programming is always fraught with stumbles. If stumbles in learning
programming can be detected automatically, it will be easier for teachers to
monitor learners' progress in lectures and to support those who are passive. In
addition, it also leads to the design of autonomous learning support systems for
learning programming.

Several studies estimated programmers' context from programmers' data [2–
4]. However, the patterns of stumbles in learning programming are diverse, and

© The Author(s), under exclusive license to Springer Nature Switzerland AG 2022
P. Delir Haghighi et al. (Eds.): MoMM 2022, LNCS 13634, pp. 169–174, 2022.
https://doi.org/10.1007/978-3-031-20436-4_16

existing detection methods miss several stumbles. Stumbles in learning programming could be detected by combining information on the source code with the learner's psychological state, such as concentration and stress. However, to the author's knowledge, no such study has been conducted.

In this study, we propose a method for detecting stumbles in programming learning by combining metrics about the learner's source code and heart rate information that is an indicator of a person's level of concentration and mental load.

2   Related Work

Several studies recorded programmers' data and estimated the programmer's contexts. Carter et al. recorded the programmers' activities and classified them into five categories (Navigation, Focus, Edit, Debug, and Remove) [2]. From the experimental result, they found that the rate of these activities changed when the developers were having difficulties. Fritz et al. conducted a study for predicting programmers' task difficulty in software development using biometric data such as EDA, EEG, and eye-related data from an eye tracker [3]. They could predict participants' task difficulty with over 70% accuracy and 62% recall. Some studies used a combination of biometric data and other indicators. Müller et al. measured data related to skin, heart, and breathing to predict the quality of the code that developers are writing [4]. They collected biometric data, code-related metrics about code change, and interactions of ten developers over two weeks, and classified their code quality. They found that the biometric-based classifier was more accurate than traditional metrics-based classifiers. As the studies show, combining biometric data with other indicators provides a more detailed picture of the programmer's context. However, to the author's knowledge, no studies aimed at detecting programming learner stumbles based on biometric and code-related data. In this study, we combine biometric data of programming learners with code-related metrics to detect stumbles, considering both the state of the learner and the source code.

3   Proposed Method

3.1   Assumed Environment

In this study, we propose a method to detect stumbles in programming learning using both biometric data and code-related metrics. We assume a situation in which programming learners are working on a class assignment, and aim to automatically detect learners' stumbles and provide learning support.

Definition of Stumble. In this paper, we define the state of the *stumble* as a programming learner's situation that he/she is at a loss and unsure of what to do. Example situations are as follows:

- The learner cannot come up with an algorithm to achieve their goals.
- The learner cannot implement an algorithm as a program.

Table 1. Input features.

Category	Metric
Heart rate	LF/HF
	pNN50
Code-related	Source lines of code
	AST edit distance
	Elapsed seconds from last execution

- The learner cannot resolve errors.
- The source code has no error, however, the execution results are not what the learner expected.

Some of these stumbles can be seen from the source code written by the learner, while others may be reflected in the learner's psychological state. For example, a stumble that the learner cannot solve an error can be detected by observing the presence or absence of errors in the learner's source code and their duration. In the case of a learner's inability to come up with an algorithm, psychological indicators such as the learner's level of concentration could provide insight into the problem.

However, it is difficult to identify and detect stumbles such as the execution result being different from the learner's expectation even though there is no error in the source code from a single indicator. Therefore, we propose a stumble detection method for learning programming by combining code metrics related to changes in source code and heart rate information related to psychological states. If the proposed method can automatically detect learners' stumbles, teachers can easily grasp the learning status of students in programming lectures and effectively support students who are stumbling.

3.2 Stumble Detection Method

The proposed method detects stumbles in learning programming by biometric data, which is an indicator for estimating psychological states, and metrics for the source code changes as features to the classifier. The proposed method uses Random Forest [5] as a classifier. Table 1 shows the specific input features. Each feature is described below.

Heart Rate Information. In this study, the magnitude of the LF/HF value is used as a measure of concentration and mental load to grasp the learning situation. In addition, we used pNN50, a measure of vagal tone intensity, which is the percentage of heartbeats for which the difference between consecutive adjacent RRI exceeds 50 ms.

Code-Related Metrics. In this study, to quantitatively evaluate source code information, we use source lines of code, edit distance of Abstract Syntax Tree (AST) generated by parsing the source code and elapsed seconds from the last program execution.

3.3 Web Editor Implementation for Retrieving Code-Related Metrics

To collect source code from learners, we implemented the web editor. This web editor consists of a code editor pane, a drawing output pane for source code execution, and a console pane. The user can write code in the code editor pane and see the drawing output in the drawing output pane and the console output in the console pane. When the user executes the program, the source code written by the user is sent to the server and recorded in the database. At the same time, the drawing output is saved locally as an image.

4   Evaluation

4.1   Procedure

We conducted an evaluation experiment to verify whether the proposed method can detect stumbles in programming learning. The programming language used in this experiment is JavaScript and we adopted p5.js [6], a library for drawing. While the participants are solving each task, we recorded the aforementioned data. We used WHS-3 [7] for recording heart rate. We used the web editor described in Sect. 3.3 to record the source code.

In this study, we assume a situation in which programming learners are working on a class assignment. In particular, we aim to support students who are stumbling on solving tasks in learning programming using visual output like JavaScript (p5.js) and Processing. We prepared two programming tasks and asked the participants to solve them. Each task is to reproduce an image by program execution. The tasks are to reproduce the image shown in Figs. 1 and 2 by executing the program. Task 1 is designed to be solved using iteration and conditional branching. Task 2 is designed to be solved using iteration, recursion, and functions.

In the experiment, after explaining the basic syntax of JavaScript, the participants solved Task 1, and after a short break, they solved Task 2. The participants were five students majoring in engineering. They are all male and have already taken a basic course on the C language. In labeling, the first author labeled each participant's data by watching their recorded face and screen video. We divided the data into two states: stumble and progress.

4.2   Result

We evaluated the detection accuracy of each model by trial-to-trial cross-validation. When training the models, we used SMOTE [8] to oversample stumble instances to adjust for data bias. Table 2 shows the accuracy of each model.

Fig. 1. Task 1.

Fig. 2. Task 2.

Table 2. Accuracy of each model.

Model	Accuracy
Multimodal	0.60
Code-related	0.60
Biometric	0.53

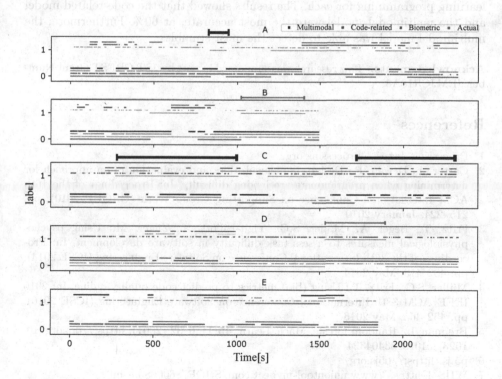

Fig. 3. Prediction results of Task 2 (0: progress, 1: stumble) (Color figure online)

The results show that the biometric model has the lowest accuracy, while the multimodal and code-related models have the same accuracy.

Figure 3 shows the predicted results of each model in Task 2. As the figure shows, the biometric model's predictions frequently shifted back and some labels could not be predicted as a coherent section. Looking at the sequence of predicted data corresponding to each stumble section, the multimodal model covered more stumble sections than other models. This is especially noticeable in the section where the black bar is on top. Stumble sections with red bars were not detected by any of the models. However, the multimodal model could be utilized in a real environment with an application that implements an algorithm such as notifying the user of a sequence of intervals that are determined as a stumble.

5   Conclusion

In this study, we proposed a method for detecting stumbling in learning programming using heart rate information and code-related metrics. We constructed a model with only code-related metrics as input, a model with only heart rate information as input, and a model with both code-related metrics and heart rate information as input, and compared the accuracy of detecting stumbles in learning programming for each. The results showed that the code-related model and the multimodal model were the most accurate, at 60%. Furthermore, the multimodal model was able to detect the most stumbles.

Acknowledgments. This research was supported in part by JST CREST Grant Number JPMJCR18A3.

References

1. Processing. https://processing.org/
2. Carter, J., Dewan, P.: Design, implementation, and evaluation of an approach for determining when programmers are having difficulty. In: Proceedings of the 16th ACM International Conference on Supporting Group Work (GROUP 2010), pp. 215–224, January 2010
3. Fritz, T., Begel, A., Müller, S.C., Yigit-Elliott, S., Züger, M.: Using psycho-physiological measures to assess task difficulty in software development. In: Proceedings of the 36th International Conference on Software Engineering (ICSE 2014), pp. 402–413, May 2014
4. Müller, S.C., Fritz, T.: Using (bio) metrics to predict code quality online. In: 2016 IEEE/ACM 38th International Conference on Software Engineering (ICSE 2016), pp. 452–463, May 2016
5. Breiman, L.: Random forests. Mach. Learn. **45**(1), 5–32 (2001). https://doi.org/10.1023/a:1010933404324
6. p5.js. https://p5js.org/
7. WHS-3. https://www.uniontool-mybeat.com/SHOP/8600085.html
8. Chawla, N.V., Bowyer, K.W., Hall, L.O., Kegelmeyer, W.P.: SMOTE: synthetic minority over-sampling technique. J. Artif. Intell. Res. **16**, 321–357 (2002)

Author Index

Printed in the United States
by Baker & Taylor Publisher Services

Printed in the United States
by Baker & Taylor Publisher Services